Jewish Self-Hate

JEWISH SELF-HATE

Theodor Lessing

Translated and annotated by Peter C. Appelbaum
Introduction by Sander L. Gilman
Afterword by Paul Reitter
Edited by Benton Arnovitz

berghahn
NEW YORK • OXFORD
www.berghahnbooks.com

Published in 2021 by
Berghahn Books
www.berghahnbooks.com

English-language edition
© 2021 Peter C. Appelbaum

Originally published by Jüdischer Verlag in German as
Der Jüdische Selbsthaß, 1930
© 1930 Jüdischer Verlag, G.m.b.H., Berlin

All rights reserved. Except for the quotation of short passages
for the purposes of criticism and review, no part of this book
may be reproduced in any form or by any means, electronic or
mechanical, including photocopying, recording, or any information
storage and retrieval system now known or to be invented,
without written permission of the publisher.

Library of Congress Cataloging-in-Publication Data

Names: Lessing, Theodor, 1872–1933, author. | Appelbaum, Peter C., translator. | Arnovitz, Benton, editor.
Title: Jewish Self-Hate / Theodor Lessing; translated and annotated by Peter C. Appelbaum; introduction by Sander L. Gilman; afterword by Paul Reitter; edited by Benton Arnovitz.
Other titles: Jüdische Selbsthass. English
Description: New York: Berghahn, 2021. | Originally published: Der Jüdische Selbsthass. Berlin: Jüdischer Verlag, 1930. | Includes bibliographical references.
Identifiers: LCCN 2020058112 (print) | LCCN 2020058113 (ebook) | ISBN 9781789209860 (hardback) | ISBN 9781789209921 (paperback) | ISBN 9781789209877 (ebook)
Subjects: LCSH: Jews--Biography. | Jews--Psychology. | Self-hate (Psychology)
Classification: LCC DS113 .L3913 2021 (print) | LCC DS113 (ebook) | DDC 305.892/4--dc23
LC record available at https://lccn.loc.gov/2020058112
LC ebook record available at https://lccn.loc.gov/2020058113

British Library Cataloguing in Publication Data

A catalogue record for this book is available from the British Library

ISBN 978-1-78920-986-0 hardback
ISBN 978-1-78920-992-1 paperback
ISBN 978-1-78920-987-7 ebook

For the self-created soul
That breathed great beauty out into the world,
For the self-destroying spirit
That rises from destruction ever new,
For the self-condemning tribe
That needs no foreigner as judge

Contents

Translator's Preface *Peter C. Appelbaum*	ix
Acknowledgments	xi
Introduction *Sander L. Gilman*	xii

ATRIUM   1

Chapter 1.	Jewish Destiny in the East – History as Meaning – How to Apportion Blame	3
Chapter 2.	Jewish Destiny in the West – The Class Struggle, Antisemitism, and Zionism	11
Chapter 3.	The Psychology and Pathology of Self-Hate – The Logic and Morality of Self-Hate – Prophets and Psalmists	17
Chapter 4.	The Impractical Dreamer – Six Symbolic Figures – Present-Day Examples	25
Chapter 5.	The Suffering of Self-Hate – Its Three Paths – Healing	30

SIX LIFE STORIES   35

Paul Rée	37
Otto Weininger	51
Arthur Trebitsch	65
Max Steiner	91
Walter Calé	104
Maximilian Harden	115

VAULT 141

Afterword 153
Paul Reitter

Translator's Preface
Peter C. Appelbaum

Translating and editing Theodor Lessing's landmark book on Jewish self-hate has been a daunting experience. Parts of it moved me to the depths of my soul. No Jew can comprehend this book and remain unchanged. Lessing's words and constructs are very difficult—not only long sentences with a participle in the middle, but also the propensity to create words and use existing ones in complicated ways. The text necessitated a large number of explanatory notes, augmented by Lessing's own sometimes lengthy and complicated footnotes, which make the text even more difficult.

It should be noted that in cases where Lessing misspells names, his version is provided in the text and the correct spelling in the endnotes. References to Lessing's quotations are given wherever they could be found.

Lessing begins by sketching the lives of European Jews in the early 1800s. Restrictions and discriminatory laws were gradually lifted, especially in Germany, where Moses Mendelssohn ushered in the era of Haskalah (the Enlightenment). Jews responded enthusiastically and began to assimilate rapidly. However, no matter what they did, they were not accepted completely. Some turned to conversion, some to self-hate, persecution of their own kind and self-flagellation, some to communism, others to Zionism. Lessing saw their only solution in the authenticity of "become what you are."

Lessing uses the lives of Paul Rée, Otto Weininger, Arthur Trebitsch, Max Steiner, Walter Calé, and Maximilian Harden to delve into the complex nature of German Jewish self-hate during the latter part of the nineteenth century through the Weimar Republic. During the course of the book the reader is introduced to the philosophies of Nietzsche, Kant, and Hegel; Martin Buber; Plato versus Spinoza; Vedic spirituality; Freud, Adler, and the psychology of the original state; mathematics and relativity; the poetry of Goethe, Stefan George, and Theodor Fontaine; verses by Horace; Darwin's theory of natural selection; and the Wilhelmine and Weimar eras—all of this in the context of the etiology and pathogenesis of Jewish self-hate. The book concludes with an effort to turn Jewish self-hate into a bridge between religions and peoples.

The subject of Jewish self-hate is just as cogent today as it was when the book was published ninety years ago. One need only observe the current divided, quarrelsome, and aggressive American political, journalistic, and progressive academic scene to observe examples of this phenomenon. And yet, the answer is so simple—authenticity, "Become what you are." Sadly, not enough take this message to heart.

Acknowledgments

I thank Benton Arnovitz for having the confidence to give this Herculean task to me, for meticulous copyediting of the entire manuscript, and for guiding it through to publication. Chutzpah is a very Jewish character trait: I tried, and I ended up succeeding beyond my own expectations. Sincere thanks to Sander L. Gilman and Paul Reitter for gracing the book with their respective essays. My most grateful thanks to James Scott for translating the poetry and helping with recondite, complex, and made-up words, and opaque sentences. I thank Marion Berghahn, Chris Chappell, Mykelin Higham, and Elizabeth Martinez for meticulous editorial assistance throughout all phases of book production. All of Lessing's notes are included in italics, along with my own footnotes. Some of the latter derive from public domain sources.

My long-suffering wife, Addie (*eshet chayil mi yimtza*), put up with my endless mumbling in several languages and the spiritual anguish that accompanied my translating and interpreting this seminal book. My daughter, Madeleine, was always ready with a daughter's love. Any errors are mine alone.

This first English-language edition of *Der Jüdischer Selbsthaß* is published with the concurrence and encouragement of Suhrkamp Verlag, since 1958 successors to the imprint of Jüdischer Verlag, closed by the Nazis in 1938.

Peter C. Appelbaum
Land O' Lakes, Florida
October 2020

 # Introduction
Sander L. Gilman

Theodor Lessing's (1872–1933) *Jewish Self-Hatred* (1930) is the classic study of the pitfalls (rather than the complexities) of acculturation. Growing out of his own experience as a middle-class, urban, marginally religious Jew in Imperial and then Weimar Germany, he used this study to reject the social integration of the Jews into Germany society, which had been his own experience, by tracking its most radical cases. This early awareness of the impossibility of acculturation into what he saw as an inherently antisemitic world led him early to become a Zionist (at least a cultural if not a political Zionist) and concomitantly a rabid opponent to the rise of German fascism. A failed academic (because of, in his view, the antisemitic attitudes of both the institutions and the faculty—he was not completely wrong), his writing before and after World War I spanned the widest readership in Germany, from theater criticism to works on the philosophy of history. As one of the most visible Jewish opponents of the Nazis, he had fled immediately after Hitler's appointment as chancellor in January 1933 to Czechoslovakia, where in March of that year he was assassinated by German-speaking Nazis. Certainly his work that most captured the attention of both his contemporaries and our own world is this study of Jewish antisemitism.[1]

Lessing's case studies reflect the idea that assimilation (the radical end of acculturation) is by definition a doomed project, at least for Jews (no matter how defined) in the age of political antisemitism. Lessing's popular book is in point of fact a summary of a massive critical literature, begun in the age of scientific racism with texts such as proto-Zionist physician Leon Pinsker's (1821–1891) *Mahnruf an seine Stammgenossen* (in English translated as *Auto-Emancipation*) (1882). Pinsker was the sort of Eastern Jew that Lessing evokes in his first chapter. (One can note that Lessing's first impulse as a student was to study medicine; institutional factors caused him to shift his interest to philosophy.) Pinsker was born in Polish Russia and educated at the University of Odessa, where he trained to be a physician. His training was "modern," which in the nineteenth century meant German and biologically oriented. Horrified by the series of pogroms against the Jews beginning in 1871 in Odessa, Pinsker wrote in German his plea for a Jewish state, given the inherent nature of Jew-hatred (*Judenhass*) in Europe. As a physician he uses the category of mental illness to explain the collective hatred of the Jews. He sees this as an obsession of the European Christian: "To the living the Jew is a corpse, to the native a foreigner, to the homesteader a vagrant, to the proprietary a beggar, to the poor an exploiter and a millionaire, to the patriot a man without a country, for all a hated rival." He undertakes the first systematic attempt at analyzing "Judeophobia" as that disease of late nineteenth-century Europe that can never be cured:

> Judeophobia, together with other symbols, superstitions and idiosyncrasies, has acquired legitimacy as a phobia among all the peoples of the earth with whom the Jews had intercourse. Judeophobia is a variety of demonopathy with the distinction that it is not peculiar to particular races but is common to the whole of mankind, and that this ghost is not disembodied like other ghosts but partakes of flesh and blood, must endure pain inflicted by the fearful mob who imagines itself endangered. Judeophobia is a psychic aberration. As a psychic aberration it is hereditary, and as a disease transmitted for two thousand years it is incurable.[2]

For Lessing the internalization of such hatred marks the pathology of Jewish modernism after the promises of the Enlightenment inherent in the Jewish tradition that grew out of it, the Haskalah. Pinsker, and somewhat later Theodor Herzl and Max Nordau, saw the separation of the Jew as the only "cure" for those who become infected with the bacteria of antisemitism in the form of self-hatred. (One might note that even the non-Jewish George Eliot in her own proto-Zionist work *Daniel Deronda* [1876] was unable to project such a mental state for acculturated Jews without the use of psychopathological language. Her Jewish characters seem, whether aware of their Jewish ancestry or deny it, to have their mental state shaped by the power of an antisemitic world.)

The general response to cultural antisemitism is a sense that the more acculturated one became, the less able one was to cope with the reality of the world in which one functioned. The novelist Jacob Wassermann (1873–1934) was born in Fürth in 1873, and thus a citizen of the new German state at the age of six. He worked unsuccessfully as a businessman in Vienna and then at the satirical magazine *Simplicissimus* in Munich, followed by a stint as a critic, and then hit his stride as a well-respected and very widely read novelist living in Vienna and Altensee in Austria.[3] A member of the Prussian Academy of the Arts, he was a Jew within the German-speaking world and in no way a Zionist, but he still deeply doubted acculturation as a modern project. In 1909 he defines being Jewish in the Diaspora in terms of neither a religious nor a Zionist project. Rather he distinguishes himself as a creative Jewish writer from the acculturated or assimilated Jew, who incorporates all negative antitheses:

> There is a reason that there are so many literati among the Jews. He is the most atheistic or the most religious; the most socially aware, though in old, dead antiquated form or in the new utopian mode that wishes to destroy the old or he seeks anarchic solitude within himself.... All of this has damned the Jews as a people to the role of the literati.... The Jew as a European, as a cosmopolitan, is merely a literatus; the Jew as an Oriental, not in the ethnographic but in the mythic sense through which the contemporary creative drive is present makes him into a creator.[4]

The assimilated is therefore the culturally inauthentic Jew; the Oriental, the authentic and therefore the only possible true creator of art. The sole possibility is either sublimation (and some level of literary production) or repression (and the resultant self-loathing).

In his autobiography, *My Life as a German and a Jew* (1921), Wassermann like Lessing provides cases studies of the fragile nature of acculturated Jewish identity at the close of the long nineteenth century.

> I have known many Jews who have languished with longing for the fair-haired and blue-eyed individual. They knelt before him, burned incense before him, believed his every word; every blink of his eye was heroic; and when he spoke of his native soil, when he beat his Aryan breast, they broke into a hysterical shriek of triumph.... I was once greatly diverted by a young Viennese Jew, elegant, full of suppressed ambition, rather melancholy, something of an artist, and something of a charlatan. Providence itself had given him fair hair and blue eyes; but lo, he had no confidence in his fair hair and blue eyes: in his heart of hearts he felt that they were spurious.[5]

But for Wassermann this is a form of superego deformation, a pathology of acculturation (or indeed, of assimilation). It is a Jewish disease developed in a modernity that allowed Jews to enter Western culture but undermined their sense of self.

For Wassermann it is "self-shame" that marks the relationship of the Jew to his own sense of self as a human being.

> I was often overcome by discouragement, by a sense of shame at all those tumbling, stumbling selves among whom I too now was numbered, but who from far away had seemed to me superhuman creatures dwelling in an enchanted garden. At times I was moved to wonder whether the narrow spitefulness, the pecuniary squabbling combined with the striving toward universal goals, the provincial dullness and brutal ambition, the mistrust and stubborn misunderstanding where achievement and perfection, ideas and an exchange of impulses were at stake, where thoughts

and images were concerned—whether all this was a peculiarly German disease or a by-product of the metier as such, its somber lining, the same with us as in other lands.[6]

Wassermann notes the inauthenticity of such forms of identification and the concomitant rejection, evident to the outside observer, that destabilizes Jewish identity. It neither enables the Jew to become part of antisemitic culture, nor does it provide a positive Jewish identity for him.

Thus being adapted to being "Jewish" in this manner was seen as a psychological deformation. In his 1907 essay "Die Lösung der Judenfrage" (Solving the Jewish Question), the future Nobel Prize winner Thomas Mann, a non-Jew, saw the "Jewish question" as "purely psychological" because the Jew is "always recognized as a stranger, feeling the pathos of being excluded, he is an extraordinary form of life."[7] Mann's views paralleled the discussion of the deformed Jewish body as a central trope of the debates of the time. The progress of German culture, not Zionism, Mann argued, permitted—indeed, demanded—the spiritual integration of the Jews into Europe, and that resulted in the transformation of the Jewish body. Mann's fantasy of the Jews imagines them primarily as crippled and malformed inhabitants of the ghettos of Eastern Europe. Their movement into European culture in Germany is not mere social acculturation but physical transformation.[8] Mann sees this movement as the replacement of the ghetto Jew, with his "hump back, crooked legs, and red, gesticulating hands," by "young people who have grown up with English sports and all of the advantages without denying their type and with a degree of physical improvement."[9]

We need here to remember that Mann's very first successful attempt at the writing of fiction was his 1896 short story "Little Mr. Friedemann," the tale of the disabled aesthete, "with his pigeon chest, his steeply humped back, and his disproportionately long skinny arms."[10] After a life of self-imposed asceticism because of a youthful rejection, he falls in love with Frau Gerda von Rinnlingen, the homely wife of the military commander of the town in which he lives. She mocks him when he declares his love for her, and his only recourse is to commit suicide. Physical imperfection (even, indeed, the evocation in the late nineteenth century of Friedemann's by then Jewish-sounding name) gestures toward the psychological self-doubt of those with imperfect posture, the physical manifestation of deformed Jewish identity.

The idea of self-hatred as a pathological response to the pressures of acculturation is in point of fact turned quite on its head by the mid-1930s. Just as Sigmund Freud had rejected the notion of any inherent Jewish racial psychopathology (as claimed in all of his medical textbooks from his time as a student in Vienna beginning in 1873, and which are still present in his library) in his claim for the universals of human psychology in the 1890s, so too did his daughter look at self-hatred after Theodor Lessing's study as a human rather than a Jewish response to a specific political setting and as a normal rather than a pathological response to being human.[11] In Anna Freud's *The Ego and Mechanisms of Defense* (1936), the varieties of ego defense mechanisms described by her father (repression, displacement, denial, projection, reaction formation, intellectualization, rationalization, undoing, sublimation) are augmented by a new category very much of the 1930s: identification with the aggressor. Much later she commented that this innovation, which she notes she borrowed from the child psychologist August Aichhorn, was not one "of the recognized defense mechanisms, and I felt modest about this new one. I didn't think it had a claim to be introduced yet."[12] Aichhorn, in his 1925 lectures on juvenile delinquency, stressed the role that the superego had in structuring our relationship to the world.[13] For him, it is "the father who represents to the child the demands of society, forces him to fulfill those demands through the child's identification with him" (220). It is Aichhorn who stresses the normal identification of the child with the same-sex parent. For him the ego retains the form into which it was structured by the demands of the father and by society. Thus we become ourselves through our own identification with the ideal represented by our parents. When this is faulty, delinquency results, and Aichhorn notes that such a pattern leads to a "renunciation of these wishes through the laying bare of unconscious relationships" (5). This is "a matter of reeducation" rather than psychotherapy (5). "Life forces him to conform to reality; education enables him to achieve culture" (7). Aichhorn provides case studies of such re-education through ridding the delinquent of his identification with the aggressive or destructive parent where the child had "identified himself with his father and doing as he did, escaped his own unpleasant situation" (30). Aichhorn postulates that a youth counselor can overcome such identification with the negative aspects of the parent and therefore of the superego through focusing the transference of the youth with the counselor. Thus the destructive forces are reformed and the negative identification modified.

Anna Freud transforms this, seeing that the child identifies with the parent "[by] impersonating the aggressor, assuming his attributes or imitating his aggression, the child transforms himself from the person threatening into the person making the threat."[14] Her focus is not, as was Reich's on the level of the constitution of superego formation, how and why capitalist society shapes the individual through its repressive rule making, but rather on the individual's resistance to all such forces, a resistance that, however, can become the source of mental illness.

The pattern is one that she sees as a part of a normal course of human development, when the child mimics the adult in order to avoid punishment: In "'identification with the aggressor' we recognize a by no means uncommon stage in the normal development of the superego." Nevertheless, it can become pathological.[15]

> It is possible that a number of people remain arrested at the intermediate stage in the development of the superego and never quite complete the internalization of the critical process. Although perceiving their own guilt, they continue to be peculiarly aggressive in their attitude toward other people. In such cases the behavior of the superego toward others is as ruthless as that of the superego toward the patient's own ego in melancholia.[16]

Thus psychopathology can result that is harmful to the ego: "If the child introjects both rebuke and punishment and then regularly projects this same punishment on another, 'then he is arrested at an intermediate stage in the development of the superego.'"[17] The key to what comes to be understood as projective identification is the image of "assimilation":

> The German word is *Angleichung*. The child becomes like the teacher. "Assimilating himself" is a rather clumsy translation. But, you know, the best example I now have of this process is one which I didn't possess at the time. It came later at the Hampstead Nurseries from the little girl who had a small brother who was so afraid of dogs that she said to him, "You be doggie and no dog will bite you." That is a perfect expression of the whole thing.[18]

But it can also be the core of racism, for "vehement indignation at someone else's wrongdoing is the precursor of and substitute for guilty feelings on its own account." Intolerance of other people precedes intolerance toward the self.

Thus by the collapse of the European Jewish project, whether acculturated, assimilated, religious, political, or social, under the inexorable force of Nazi Germany, the idea that self-hatred was not an anomaly of the Jewish experience but a universal force that all human beings used to cope with the vagaries of daily experience had become a central feature of psychology. Indeed, it came to define the approach of social psychology and sociology to the manner by which minorities dealt with their marginal status. It became the core of the court case that ended segregation in American schools, *Brown v. The Board of Education of Topeka* (1954). Together with his wife, Mamie Phipps Clark, the social psychologist Kenneth Clark had begun, in 1939, to work on the etiology of black self-hatred. The Clarks famously substituted dolls for portraits in their version. They used four plastic, diaper-clad dolls, identical except for color. Almost all of the black children, ages three through seven, readily identified the race of the dolls. However, when asked which they preferred, the majority selected the white doll and attributed positive characteristics to it. The qualities ascribed to the dolls were aesthetic. Those choosing the white dolls did so "cause he's pretty" or "cause he's white" and rejecting the black doll "cause he's ugly" or "cause it don't look pretty."[19] But these categories were also read by the children as having moral value: black dolls were "bad" and "mean," while white dolls were "nice" and "good." The Clarks argued that the children were "aware of the fact that to be colored in contemporary American society is a mark of inferior status."[20]

Universal yes, but now also the experience of a wider range of marginalized groups, and not necessarily those who were offered entrance into society but also those self-consciously excluded. The debates about self-hatred became inexorably associated with the political by the 1950s, and Anna Freud's understanding that all human beings used such devices became the guidelines for considering what was "in the best interest of the child." From Jews in Imperial Germany to African Americans in postwar America, the ghost of self-hatred became a trope. But one needed to understand the breadth of this argument as expounded by modern psychoanalysis. For all individuals (and collectives) can identify with the oppressor in complex and difficult ways. Thus African Americans such as the Clarks clearly did not succumb to the process of self-hatred, nor did those in the NAACP who advocated against segregation.[21] Even those in relative positions of power fell into using such a means of ego maintenance. In contemporary Israel, the power relationship between Jews (as defined by the state) and Muslims clearly shifts toward the Jewish majority, especially in Jerusalem. Yet we have the example of Haredi Jewish women wearing full body covering, the Islamic burkas, like their most religious Muslim neighbors.[22] That such Jews see Muslims as the "enemy" is clear, but they also see them as presenting qualities that are worth emulating, even if at the end of the day, they appear to be overidentifying with a greater Islamic culture into which they are integrating. Certainly this is an example of identification with the aggressor, but in a much more complex and contradictory manner, than in Theodor Lessing's account. What we can learn from the trajectory of the discourse of self-hatred is that it may well be a universal and complex phenomenon and is certainly not simply one of acculturated Jewry.

Sander L. Gilman is Distinguished Professor of the Liberal Arts and Sciences as well as Professor of Psychiatry at Emory University. A cultural and literary historian, he is the author or editor of well over ninety books. His *Stand Up Straight! A History of Posture* appeared with Reaktion Press (London) in 2018; his most recent edited volume is *The Oxford Handbook of Music and the Body* (with Youn Kim), published in 2019 with Oxford University Press. He is the author of the basic study of the visual stereotyping of the mentally ill, *Seeing the Insane*, published by John Wiley and Sons in 1982, as well as the standard study *Jewish Self-Hatred*, the title of his Johns Hopkins University Press monograph of 1986. He has been a visiting professor at numerous universities in North America, South Africa, the United Kingdom, Germany, Israel, China, and New Zealand. He was president of the Modern Language Association in 1995. He has been awarded a Doctor of Laws (*honoris causa*) at the University of Toronto in 1997, elected an honorary professor of the Free University in Berlin (2000) and an honorary member of the American Psychoanalytic Association (2007), and made a Fellow of the American Academy of Arts and Sciences (2016).

Notes

1. See Lawrence Baron, "*Theodor Lessing: Between Jewish Self-Hatred* and *Zionism*," *Yearbook of the Leo Baeck Institute* 26 (*1981*): 323–340; Rainer Marwedel, *Theodor Lessing 1872–1933. Eine Biographie* (Frankfurt am Main: Luchterhand Verlag, 1987).
2. Leon Pinsker, *Auto-Emancipation*, trans. D. S. Blondheim (New York: Maccabean Publishing, 1906), 3.
3. See Donna K. Heizer, *Jewish-German Identity in the Orientalist Literature of Else Lasker-Schüler, Friedrich Wolf, and Franz Werfel* (Columbia, SC: Camden House, 1996), 27–29; Hans Otto Horch, "'Verbrannt wird auf alle Fälle...': Juden und Judentum im Werk Jakob Wassermanns," in *Im Zeichen Hiobs: Jüdische Schriftsteller und deutsche Literatur im 20. Jahrhundert*, ed. Gunter E. Grimm, Hans-Peter Bayerdörfer, and Konrad Kwiet (Königstein/Ts.: Athenäum, 1985), 124–146.
4. Jakob Wassermann, *Der Literat oder Mythos und Persönlichkeit* (Leipzig: Insel Verlag, 1909), 78.
5. Jacob Wassermann, *My Life as German and Jew* (London: George Allen & Unwin, 1933), 156.
6. Wassermann, *My Life as German and Jew*, 118–119.
7. In Mann's untitled contribution to Julius Moses, ed., *Die Lösung der Judenfrage: eine Rundfrage* (Berlin, 1907), 242–248. We are citing from the original edition as it presents the text in its original context. Reprinted in Thomas Mann, "Zur jüdischen Frage," in *Gesammelte Werke in 13 Bänden* (Frankfurt am Main, 1974), 7:466–475. All translations are mine.

8. Todd Kontje, *Thomas Mann's World: Empire, Race, and the Jewish Question* (Ann Arbor: University of Michigan Press, 2011), 19–24.
9. Mann, *Die Lösung der Judenfrage*, 244–245.
10. Thomas Mann, *Tonio Kröger and other Stories*, trans. David Luke (New York: Bantam Books, 1970), 5.
11. See my *Freud, Race, and Gender* (Princeton: Princeton University Press, 1993).
12. "Joseph Sandler in conversation with Anna Freud, Discussions in the Hampstead Index on *The Ego and the Mechanisms of Defence*: IV. The Mechanisms of Defence, Part 1," *Bulletin of the Anna Freud Centre* 4 (1981): 151–199, here 155. On the present status of these defense mechanisms, see Nancy McWilliams, "Primary (Primitive) Defensive Processes," *Psychoanalytic Diagnosis* (New York: Guilford Press, 1994), 96–115.
13. August Aichhorn, *Verwahrloste Jugend: Die Psychoanalyse in der Fürsorgeerziehung. Zehn Vorträge zur ersten Einführung.* (Vienna: Internationaler Psychoanalytischer Verlag, 1925); all references are to the translation *Wayward Youth* (New York: Viking Press, 1935).
14. Anna Freud, *Ego and the Mechanisms of Defence*, trans. Cecil Baines (New York: International Universities Press, 1946), 109ff.
15. Freud, *Ego and the Mechanisms of Defence*, 119.
16. Freud, *Ego and the Mechanisms of Defence*, 119.
17. Cited by Lisa Appignanesi and John Forrester, *Freud's Women* (London: Verso, 1993), 294.
18. "Joseph Sandler in Conversation with Anna Freud, Discussions in the Hampstead Index on *The Ego and the Mechanisms of Defence*: X. Identification with the Aggressor," *Bulletin of the Anna Freud Centre* 6 (1983): 247–275, here 250.
19. Kenneth B. Clark and Mamie P. Clark, "Racial Identification and Preference in Negro Children," in *Readings in Social Psychology*, ed. Eleanor E. Maccoby, Theodore M. Newcomb, and Eugene L. Hartley (New York: Holt, 1958), 611.
20. Kenneth B. Clark and Mamie P. Clark, "Emotional Factors in Racial Identification and Preference in Negro Children," *Journal of Negro Education* 19 (1950): 341–350, here 348, 350.
21. William Cross, *Shades of Black: Diversity in African American Identity* (Philadelphia: Temple University Press, 1991), 16–29.
22. "The Ultra Orthodox Jewish Sect Where Women Cover Themselves from Head to Toe," EFE, 9 March 2017, https://www.efe.com/efe/english/life/the-ultra-orthodox-jewish-sect-where-women-cover-themselves-from-head-to-toe/50000263-3202449.

ATRIUM

 CHAPTER 1

JEWISH DESTINY IN THE EAST – HISTORY AS MEANING – HOW TO APPORTION BLAME

1

On the day I begin to write this book on Jewish self-hate, my Jewish brethren in the East are groaning under the weight of bad news. In Jerusalem, a religious war has broken out in the area of the Haram[1] in front of the Western Wall. It began the same way previous wars have begun: overexcited people flinging senseless words into each other's faces until senseless words gave rise to senseless deeds. The problem is that these senseless deeds have released a long-stored-up hatred that has the potential to threaten the great work of the Jewish people in the Land of Israel.[2]

What do I mean by "the great work of the Jewish people"? Before this event, resurrection of our ancient homeland had seemed assured! Even the soberest pragmatists who never had dreamt of a Jewish exodus to Palestine—but thought of themselves as German, French, English, Italian, or something else—had been so won over to the Zionist idea that they founded the so-called Jewish Agency, an action group to solve the thus-far insoluble Jewish problem.[3] But history repeated itself (and will do so again). Villages and farms, newly built with painstaking labor on land reclaimed from malarial swamps; plantations in which every tree incorporated a *chalutz*[4] life; fields fertilized with sweat and tears—all went up in flames.

Artuf burns, Atarot burns, Moza burns.[5] Arab gangs put the Jerusalem suburb of Talpiot to the torch, destroying the poet Agnon's home.[6] The famous Hebron Yeshiva and the Slobodka Lithuanian Talmud schools were attacked. Unarmed yeshiva students, led by the rabbi's son, fled into the prayer room, where, one after the other, they were slaughtered while reciting the *Sh'ma*.[7] And everything happened under the eyes of the British Mandate authority.

How does the world expect Jews to react?

For thirty years and longer, since the start of the Bilu movement in 1882,[8] the noble elite of our people have been working on the solution to the Jewish national question. They are tired of ever-repeating cycles of mass hysteria, which no nobility of thought, culture, or action can ever reconcile. They are tired of the eternal "either, or" (either you give yourself up, or get out of the country). They are tired of the centuries of crackdowns, displacements, regulations—capricious or merciful. They are tired of all the insecurity and uncertainty. And so, the oldest of all peoples have decided to take its destiny into their own hands.

We cannot do right. People say, "You are parasites on others," so we have elected to leave our adopted homes. People say, "You are always middlemen," so we bring our children up to be gardeners and farmers, and people say, "You are degenerate, and have become cowardly sissies," so we go out to battle, proving ourselves to be the best soldiers. Then people say, "Wherever you are, you are really only tolerated." We respond, "We have no greater longing than to emerge from mere toleration."

When we stand up for own rights, they respond, "Have you not yet learned that dogged self-preservation of a special people is nothing more than treachery against universal human, *trans*national values?" We answer that after hundreds of killed and wounded, we have disbanded the Jewish Legion.[9] We have forgone our right to self-defense, placing it under the protection of Europe's collective conscience. What is the answer?

Today, 6 September 1929, the answer appears to be: "It makes no difference what you do: you will be tolerated as long as we can use you. Jews are useful as 'merchants.'[10] However, when we do not need to do business with you anymore, we will simply let you drop." The English-Americans,[11] those supremely power-hungry exploiters of the world, will also just sacrifice the Jews for their colonial-expansionist undertakings. Woe to the powerless. *Nafla kipa al kidra, vay lekidra; nafla kidra al kipa, vay lekidra. Ben kach uven kach, vay lekidra.*[12] If a pot falls upon a stone, woe to the pot; if a stone falls upon a pot, woe to the pot; either way, woe to the pot.

"What," one replies, "should the Jews do?" The question is not to be answered. And because there is no response, this creates an embarrassment of conscience. How can these difficulties be dealt with?

Only in rare cases, by avowing "I am guilty." In by far the majority of cases, however, the response to this dilemma is simply to attribute the guilt for this insufferable situation to the one who involuntarily occasions the condition. This is the law of "meaningfulness of hindsight"—the fundamental law of all history![13]

2

Events of human history, that continuous chain of "accidental" power shifts and acts of caprice, with oceans of blood, bile, and sweat, would be unbearable without being able to read something logical into these seemingly random occurrences. It does not help to establish that all these events are *grounded in causality*; people would much rather prefer *rationality*. When the question is posed, "*Who is responsible?*," the question already carries within it a *moral* judgment.

Even if the destiny of nations were "accidental" and everything could have *come about differently*, people still would, once things happened the way they did, attempt to *interpret* them in a logical and ethical manner.[14]

This attempt to *make sense of* all senseless and useless suffering can (as we already have seen) occur in *two ways*. Either guilt is attributed to "someone else," or one looks for the blame in oneself.

It is one of the deepest and most certain principles of national psychology that the Jewish people are the first—and perhaps the only—nation that has only sought solely *within themselves* the blame for world events.

Jewish doctrine has, since ancient times, responded to the question "Why are we not loved?" with "*Because we are guilty.*" Many great Jewish thinkers have perceived the central core of Jewish teaching in this formula "Because we are guilty" and in the experience of Jewish communal attribution of guilt and communal responsibility.

We cannot go into the meaning of this religious communal guilt (*viddui*) at this stage.[15] But is important for the reader to realize that, as in the *viddui*, the key to the *pathology* of our national consciousness lies in this acknowledgment of guilt, emphasized in the mighty Judeo-Christian ethic.

The tendency to interpret every misfortune that occurs as atonement for sin lies deeply rooted in every Jewish soul. If the reader asks why this is so, I can only point out the terrible fact that throughout almost three thousand years, Jewish history has been one uninterrupted history of hopeless, irredeemable suffering.

There is only one emergency exit—to make sense of this suffering and make it bearable, the Jew must believe that his fate has within it a particular purpose: "God disciplines those he loves."[16] Within this concept of suffering as *punishment* lies the beginning of understanding the concept of Jewish "self-hate."

It is different among happy, victorious peoples. They have no reason for self-flagellating, self-tormenting analysis that endangers a healthy attitude toward life and natural self-esteem. They answer "Why does misfortune happen to us?" with a forceful accusation against those who, in their opinion, *caused* the misfortune.

The Jewish situation is thereby doubly endangered. First, because the Jew replies to the question "Why are we not loved?" with "*Because we are guilty.*" Second, because other nations answer the question "Why are the Jews not loved?" with "He says so himself—*he is guilty.*"

Behind the sociological phenomenon called antisemitism (whereby an entire national type is characterized as *odium generis humani*)[17] lies not only bad will and national egotism, envy, and hate of the competition of peoples. There is also a law at work here: "*making sense of the senseless.*" This historical law rises from an ultimate depth.

The same law sows discord in many individual destinies. How many times are brothers and sisters, lovers and friends permanently estranged from one another simply because no one wants to look into himself and admit that he is to blame? Instead, everyone travels the nearest and most natural path: "Whenever I must introduce suffering into someone else's life, I justify my deeds by the nature of *someone else.*" Only a few examples suffice to illuminate the great significance of this simple fact.

3

All of us must, in order to live, assume some personal "guilt." We must, for example, exterminate a wonderful world of animals, complete, perfect in itself, and originally superior to us. By destroying great beasts of prey such as lions and leopards, we act wickedly. In order to absolve ourselves, we blame the animals for being wicked. When we destroy large snakes, we act cunningly and blame the snakes for their cunning.

If I harbor bad thoughts against another, these must be *justified* precisely by someone else's wickedness.

Anyone who has ever said, "God punish England" or "Germany must be humiliated,"[18] henceforth cherishes an inclination to collect and value highly whatever is expedient to justify his prejudice. Ultimately, we may not hate something bad because of its inherent badness; rather, we *call* bad that which we hate and must hate.

This procedure, whereby "what is hated becomes even more hated," is intensified in the presence of a secret feeling of sympathy, which must at all costs be stifled and deadened. In such cases, love and friendship are transformed into hate and persecution.

When I am disappointed in or disillusioned by someone whom I love or value highly, I usually do not feel the disappearance of my former feelings as my own error. I rather attribute my changed emotions to a *change in the other person*. This usually is a process of self-deception. In reality, it is my own "inner attitude" that has changed, not that of the other person. Whenever a person must bear the weight of conscience and take responsibility for his own deeds, there arise beautiful words and great ideals, in whose name we are able to cast our perceived injustice as our good right.[19]

Let us see how this can be applied as a universal rule to the Jewish question:

The Jewish people have without doubt been victims of injustice. Their perceived continuing unworthy existence would have become a reproach to every healthy nation (including sick nations who still vegetate) had there been no historical formulas that justified as *right* the wrong exercised on the Jewish people. Both Jews and non-Jews *needed* such meaningful formulas. If one wants to exploit us in the future, this must be justified by the insight that we exploited others. If one wishes to push us out and diminish the vitality of our lives, one must invoke everything that justifies restrictive higher education admission quotas[20] and special statutes. There is no historical injustice that cannot retrospectively be proved to have been justified or necessary. Whenever a group of people are condemned to carry a heavy burden, the old refrain is heard: "They nailed our Savior to the cross."

Which researcher into the human soul knows whether centuries-long diminishing of souls does not also transform the nature of the diminished? Is it possible that, in the end, all historical wrongs actually become proven wrongs, that is, *become true*? In order to change humans into dogs, all that is needed is to shout at them long enough, "You dog!"[21]

Notes

1. Haram esh-Sharif (Noble Sanctuary): Temple Mount, site of the Dome of the Rock and Al-Aqsa Mosque.
2. The 1929 Arab riots in Palestine, or the Buraq Uprising, 1929 Massacres, were the culmination of Jewish-Arab tensions over access to the Western Wall in Jerusalem. They largely took the form of Arab attacks on Jews and their property.
3. The Jewish Agency (Sochnut Yehudit) was created in 1908 as an outpost of the Zionist Organization in Ottoman-controlled Palestine, to aid immigration and buy land for Jews to settle, under Theodor Herzl's idea for a solution to the "Jewish question." The Second Aliyah (1904–1914) made the issue more urgent; after the war ended, the Agency's organization was taken over by Chaim Weizmann in Mandatory Palestine.

4. Pioneer.
5. Artuf: agricultural colony established 1888 in the Judean foothills; Atarot: cooperative farm settlement north of Jerusalem; Mo(t)za: neighborhood on the eastern edge of Jerusalem.
6. Shmuel Yosef Agnon (1888–1970), Hebrew poet, novelist, and future Nobel laureate.
7. *Sh'ma Yisrael* ("Hear O Israel, the Lord our God, the Lord is One"). Jewish confession of faith recited in daily prayer and also to be recited just prior to death.
8. Bilu (Beit Ya'akov Lekhu Venelkha), was a movement aimed at the agricultural settlement of the Land of Israel.
9. Name used to refer to Jewish volunteers who joined the British Royal Fusiliers against the Ottomans in the Great War. Preceded by the Zion Mule Corps, which saw service in Gallipoli. Disbanded after the war ended.
10. Ironic, because Germans called the British a "nation of merchants" during the war.
11. "English"-Americans in the original.
12. *Esther Rabbah* 7:10. The original transliterated Hebrew is incorrect.
13. Theodor Lessing, Geschichte als Sinngebung des Sinnlosen *(Paderborn: Salzwasser Verlag, 1921),* 211–252.
14. Lessing, Geschichte als Sinngebung des Sinnlosen *[Munich: Beck 1919],* 50. Gesetz der Logification Post Factum.
15. Confession. List of communal sins (*Ashamnu* and *Al Chet* prayers) read and responded to more than a dozen times on Yom Kippur.
16. Proverbs 3:12.
17. Hatred for the human race.
18. Propaganda from World War I.
19. *In an excellent work,* Der Antisemitismus als Gruppenerscheinung. Versuch einer Soziologie des Judenhasses *(Berlin: Jüdischer Verlag, 1926), the Dutch Zionist Fritz Bernstein has clearly set out the thought that national hatred cannot be explained by historical facts and occurrences, but is rather a primeval psychological fact. Bernstein is amazingly uninfluenced by the prejudices of modern science, especially the everyday phrases of psychoanalysts and individual psychologists. With sound common sense, he shows that the hated does not predate hate, but rather that a need for hate invents and creates the hated facts.*

This social doctrine can be compared to the well-known explanation of emotions by James and Lange. According to them, seemingly well-founded psychological passions are created out of physical need. We do not weep because we are sad, but we are sad because we have to weep. Our hormones do not begin to flow because we are angry, infatuated, or enthusiastic, just the opposite. The necessity for hormonal secretion tends to bring anger, infatuation, and enthusiasm with it.

In a similar way, Bernstein considers the self-clarification and self-advancement by one group of people, and affiliation and rejection of another as unavoidable processes of collective vitality.

"Even the wisest thinker cannot completely prevent the flow of bile. But, to allow bile to flow, indignation and anger must be present. The wise man will not lack rationales by which to control his bile flow. But, in truth, he is subject to the laws of physiology."

This theory might be wrong, because it is based on an incorrect division into physical and mental processes and poses the wrong question about the primacy of one over the other. But it is of great merit to follow such a thought through to its logical conclusion. Bernstein shows the clumsy naïveté of all the usual reasons for racial and national hatred. According to Ratzel (Anthropogeography, 2:563 [Friedrich Ratzel, Anthropogeographie. Erster Theil. Grundzüge der Anwendung der Erdkunde auf die Geschichte *(Stuttgart: J. Engelhorn, 1899)]), every nation should invent a glorious name for itself and a disdainful name for its neighbors.*

20. The *numerus clausus*, whereby Jewish admission to universities was subject to quotas.
21. The *"psychology of self-hate" is linked to the fact that "the spirit of life is that which wounds life." Therefore, behind logic there always is a "self-fissure," behind ethics stands the "will to counter-ego."*

    These thoughts have become fundamental to psychology through the tremendous revolution wrought by the advent of Friedrich Nietzsche.

    Older Jewish literature contains a few approaches to a fundamental theory on self-hate. Interpretations by Moritz Lazarus in Die Ethik des Judentums *[Frankfurt am Main: J. Kauffmann, 1898], 40, 41, are of particular interest. This rhetorician is incapable, but ruthless and keen to take this thought through to its logical conclusion. He does, nevertheless (from a connection with Hajim Steinthal), possess certain decisive ethno-psychological and sociological insights. Significantly, Lazarus places a feeling of indebtedness in the center of Jewish experience. The heart of Jewish ethics is not, according to Lazarus, brotherly love, compassion, or humanity, but rather: "Why do you persecute us?" The answer always comes back: "Because you have sinned."*

    Because the Jew had to establish a cause for his suffering history, he came up against the difficulty that according to Jewish teaching, everything is God's will and comes from God's decree. Judaism recognizes no "devil," no diabolical external force, no "contraposition of God." For the Jew, God is all, and everything lies in and comes from God, including the wicked and the bad. Jewish doctrine does not differ in this regard from, for example, the philosophy of Jakob Böhm or in Goethe's Faust.

    How can the existence of suffering and unjust fate of peoples be rationally justified?

    Only by wrong behavior or perversities of human nature itself.

    "Why do such bad things happen to you? Because God cannot protect you from yourself."

    The meaning of meaningless coincidence and incomprehensible fate was not found by blaming the outside world and the stranger. Rather, the Jew was both prepared and accustomed to take the blame upon himself.

    Even today, it is a deep part of the Jewish nature to ask, whenever something bad happens, "Why am I suffering? What have I done to deserve this?"

    It is exactly this tendency "to take the blame" that has put Jews at a disadvantage in competition with other nations. It is much easier to make a sacrifice of the Jew than of any other nation.

    On the other hand, this self-judgment makes Jews the ultimate nation of ethics.

In its pathological form, this self-judgment can lead to the outer limit of intellectual arrogance. The psychological history of Otto Weininger is a typical development of this "ethical disease."

One could be inclined to see this crass appeal to one's own conscience as a typically Protestant phenomenon. However, we see that self-judgment based upon collective responsibility is in the manner of all Oriental peoples. The Protestant confession of guilt (mea culpa, mea culpa, mea maxima culpa) refers to one's own very personal conscience. By contrast, the Jewish feeling of blame and confession answers the question "Who is to blame?" with "We are all to blame." Said another way: "All of us are guilty of everything, I most of all." This collective admission of guilt declares not only that every Jew is liable for the injustice to every other Jew, but simply that "Israel is responsible for all the world's sins." Knowledge of this collective culpability is still very much alive in Jews all over the world today.

The reader can find other evidence for the guilt of the collective Jewish soul in the five-volume Jüdisches Lexikon (Berlin: Jüdischer Verlag [1927–1930]), under the keywords "arewut kĕlal Jisroel" (responsibility of the entire people of Israel) and "widduj" (viddui: confession of sin). A few important passages are quoted here:

> The admission of every possible moral misconduct, which in reality no single human being could commit, originated from the collective character of Jewish worship and prayer. Rather more than the individual Jew, it is the collective Jewish soul who prays. This is felt to be more comforting because, when everyone admits to collective guilt, the individual is spared the shame of admitting his own sin.
>
> Jewish law recognizes mutual collective religious responsibility, anchored in religious-ethical ideas amounting to a moral legal guarantee of all fellow-Jews. Each individual Jew stands before God as both debtor and guarantor so that "all Jews vouch for one another." This Jewish group liability is transferred to the religious-national realm.
>
> Important halakhic authorities have even wanted to extend this guarantee to Jews who have converted to other faiths. This issue is the origin of the Achdut Movement, which imposes on every Jew the responsibility to remain in communal unity with all other Jews, including those who have strayed from Jewish law.
>
> The Kĕlal-Jisroel thought was anchored in religious awareness. Damned to pariah status for hundreds of years, the Jew had to strengthen himself through the fate of his own people. Until the era of emancipation, the Jew derived a unique strength, and a genuine, concrete union, from his far-flung community scattered far and wide over the surface of the earth.

The reader is referred to my explanation in the second edition of Europa und Asien (1922), 320–323 [Theodor Lessing, Europa und Asien. Untergang der Erde am Geist (Hannover: Wolf Albrecht Adam Verlag, 1922)].

 CHAPTER 2

JEWISH DESTINY IN THE WEST – THE CLASS STRUGGLE, ANTISEMITISM, AND ZIONISM

1

On the day I begin this book on Jewish self-hate, Jews in the West are celebrating a joyous festival; the bicentenary of a man who cast off the fetters of the *galut* and was the first to point the way toward German education, civilization, and language: Moses Mendelssohn, hunchbacked son of a Torah scribe from Dessau, the miracle worker who forged the respected "German citizens of Mosaic faith" out of scattered clusters of "ghetto dreamers."[1]

We must look at his deeds today with a perspective that is different from that of the Age of Enlightenment (Haskalah).

Around 1800, Jews and Parsis,[2] the last remnants of two ancient peoples, scattered all over the world, formed a type of intermediate link between the all-conquering power of Europe and America and the slowly decaying structural world of ancient Africa and Asia.

The ghetto, in the middle of the all-civilizing world of the Christian state, represented a piece of romantic antiquity. Our opposition to the Christian civilizing mission became untenable. It was just as useless as resistance of primitive peoples such as Indians, Negroes, Arabs, Bedouins, Chinese, or Hindus, melted by the sun of European "*culture.*" Jewish resistance to this influence can be understood no differently from resistance of the old Saxons to Charlemagne's "Christianization."[3] Well beyond the time of Luther,[4] Jews always were lumped together with "heathens." You are not a Christian—you are a "heathen barbarian." The development of "modern culture" is inseparable from that of the history of Christianity. Moses Mendelssohn "cleaned up" the Jewish past because (as Heinrich Heine[5] later put it) he wanted his people to have the "entrance ticket" to European culture.

Neither Moses Mendelssohn nor his great friend Gotthold Ephraim Lessing[6] deserves a reprimand for their forlorn and naïve hope that differences in customs and religions soon would become only variants of a single, great humanistic "all-divine religion."

Since then, rabbis in the West have interpreted their religion and have continued its education in their high schools and seminaries in this light. They no longer wish for a Jewish national religion, but rather that Judaism becomes the bearer of a *universal* teaching.

Two types of Jewish converts exist and must be distinguished one from the other. First, those who convert during times of war, changing over from the threatened to the victorious, less threatened camp. Second, thoroughly upright men who enthusiastically and joyfully throw themselves into their brothers' arms and hearts, overcoming all barriers.

From the first decades of the 1800s, Jewish conversion was regarded as an asset to all the nations of Europe. Enmity was solely *religious*, not national. This was, of course, before the era of "racial antisemitism." Jewish converts often were raised to European nobility, and there now are few noble houses who—albeit sometimes unconsciously—do not contain some Jewish blood.[7] Often, "seeing to have been converted" was synonymous with support by community, state, or noble house. But one would have had to think of people as better than mere human beings if one wished to blame Jews for mass conversion to Catholicism or Protestantism during the Age of Enlightenment. They really believed in love, at the very least in "tolerance." They heard the glad tidings of liberty, equality, fraternity, and it seemed to them that these revolutionary proclamations were honestly meant. Ghettos were eliminated. Laws against Jews disappeared. *Kammerknechtschaft*,[8] restrictions on freedom of movement, as well as poll, escort, and body taxes[9] and a hundred other burdens gradually disappeared between 1800 and 1850. Talmudic law became a matter for scholars. Jews, as equal citizens, were subject to civil law. Their religion became one of many denominations.

Mendelssohn's grandchildren ceased to be Jews. They logically did what all Western Jews would have done had a new power not offered them a counterweight to the process of dissolution and assimilation— the *class struggle*.

2

The class struggle, which began at the dawn of the industrial age, proved to be a war much more important than that against machines, technology, commerce, and industry, which have subjugated the whole earth. What do old religious arguments mean today? National differences have become much less important than differences in economic classes and their problems.

Karl Marx, theoretician of the class struggle,[10] saw nothing more in the tribe from which he stemmed than the "rootless appendage of the Capitalist class and its money-based economy." So-called Jewish emancipation meant, for Marx, their embourgeoisement, which was in its turn the same as "surrender to Capitalist society, which eventually would be replaced by the New Socialist Order." Marx did not recognize the national struggle of the Jewish people. This could be found only in the East, where Jews are predominantly artisans and workers. Most historians who depict Jews as a nation of Shylocks do not even know that charging of interest and usury is forbidden by Jewish law.[11] This only changed during the thirteenth century, when the feudal age forced Jews into coinage and finance.

In the West, Karl Marx saw nothing but party and interest struggles. A Communist such as Moses Hess, who was a Jew and Zionist at the same time, stood alone in the party of the proletariat and the struggle against the bourgeois world.[12]

The world of bourgeois *success* greeted the existence of the Jews and the Jewish question with a thousand expressions of joy! It was, after all, only right that opponents of the *bourgeoisie* simply attached the Jews to this sinful Capitalist world. A sinful world requires a scapegoat.[13] All adversities of bourgeois colonization and world-enslaving commerce—even that exploited against the Jews themselves—are "explained" by the history or very existence of the Jews.

Was it not a simple thing, to connect the presence of much-vilified "capitalism" with the history and nature of the Jews?

What would human life be worth without self-love and self-blessing? Goethe[14] says that "theology is the egocentric self-deification of man." A new theology has developed; it (in contrast to the theology of the Middle Ages) has turned Christianity (and the sins of Christianity) into the work of the Jews. Paul was guilty! The "Christianity of Christ," the so-called primitive Christianity, which had been un-Jewish, arose (in some or other mystical way) out of the soul of Aryan peoples. But Paul the Hebrew arrived, and with him earthly annihilation and soul destruction, as a result of which *"original, real* Christianity" became polluted and "Jewified."

It has only now begun to dawn on the civilized world that it isn't the Jews who have driven humanity into the world of the spirit. Rather, the path that the civilized world *must* take to the spirit has transformed both heathenism and Judaism.

3

As bitter as it is to admit, however, it must be said that this setback for the Jewish people at the same time saved it. Assimilation in Western

Europe otherwise would have proceeded smoothly, and in a few generations have been complete, in the absence of a counterposing wave of *hate*.

The "progressive Jew" sitting at tables all over Europe suddenly was confronted with a thick wall of hate, which brought with it a sense of self-reflection. Zionism arose: the germ of national renewal. For early Zionist leaders such as Pinsker and Nordau, and even the glorious Herzl,[15] Zionism was just a sober defense mechanism stemming from defiance, pride, a desire to help, compassion, or other reactive feelings. However, such a negative Zionism could not last long. The following generation were already Zionists simply because they felt Jewish, not because they felt hurt as Jews.

Power is lazy. Capital is cowardly. Those who have become sated become indifferent.

Where German Jewish associations[16] remained on the convenient middle path, and where mundane liberalism, democracy, and progress didn't get ahead of themselves, the Jewish tendency toward *koved* (high-profile bourgeois respectability)[17] came to the fore. Jews aspired to great names and great titles: leading personalities in the arts, science, and commerce.

Our unmatched heroic deeds are counterbalanced by the fact that we have always been rootless nomads in Europe. However, on this Mendelssohn bicentenary, when Hebrew language and writing, rite, dress, popular custom, celebration, and myth of destruction have begun to pass into oblivion, we have been allowed a brief period of *fantasy*. Although fantasy, this daydream has nevertheless appeared to remain in the sphere of the possible, when we look at the fate of other nations, no less threatened by "Christian culture." One example suffices: the "non-cooperation" movement unleashed in India since 1900, in response to Britain's violation of their country.[18]

What would have happened had the Jews unleashed their own "non-cooperation movement"? What if in 1750—when the yellow patch, oppression, anti-Jewish laws, and *Kammerknechtschaft* gradually began to be lifted, with waivers of oppression, and implementation of full bourgeois emancipation—they would have responded: "For the past two thousand years, we have lived for the coming of the Messiah, who has been promised to lead us back home. Now your benevolence and friendship offer us beautiful Europe and great America as fatherlands. But, as payment, we would have to break with our own historical traditions, in order to adapt and grow into the Great Christian West. We cannot do this! We have never demanded of you that you convert to our religion. We have never sent missionaries among the nations or been addicted to conquest. We want to bear our sidelocks and yellow patch undisturbed. We want to preserve our Hebrew language and names. We refuse to participate in your holidays and memorials, each of which can only remind us of our past martyrs. You are welcome to your images and gods, but you should in turn leave us to ours. We are, and must remain, different. It is not we, but you yourselves, who have announced it so to the world: God has become man. We do not follow the creed of the Holy Trinity. Our God has neither form nor name, beyond man and the abominations of world history. You are free to despise us, but we in turn refuse to accept your benefits: your offices and schools, your ways and means. We do not want to participate in your arts and sciences. We voluntarily carry forward *galut* and ghetto, awaiting our Messiah to appear out of Bethlehem."

Would such a reply have been possible?

It would have been possible if a word from Rambam, a verse from Halevy, a letter from Rashi still represented the Jewish world, when the nation was led by their sages during their exile.[19]

Jews have contributed greatly to European culture, and Europe has, in turn, benefited from the Jews. But the price that Jews have paid to become European citizens is either ignored or spoken of in hushed tones: betrayal of their hopes, and sacrifice of their timeless dreams. Today, Jews are not guided by sages, but by lawyers and bankers.

Modern, liberal, progressive, highly cultured Jews are very proud of the fact that during the past century, Jews have become state chancellors, ministers, generals, high officers, great researchers, professors, authorities, arbiters of good aesthetic taste, authors, poets, and who knows what else.[20] They would have done much better to say, "We are ashamed of the many counterfeiters of our national treasure, those who possibly represented only the phosphorescent glow of our disintegrating national corpus. They were perhaps only the evanescent flames of a European day of light in which our nobility has burned up."

Disgrace to all sons who prefer to "dedicate themselves to the literature" of the world of luxury of great European cities, or to adopt "academic careers" instead of carrying stones to the highway to Jerusalem.

Notes

1. *Galut* (exile): diaspora. Moses Mendelssohn (1729–1786), German Jewish philosopher to whose ideas the Haskalah, the "Jewish Enlightenment" of the eighteenth and nineteenth centuries, is indebted. In the German Jewish context, "Jewish" was usually replaced by "Mosaic."

2. Parsis or Parsees ("Persian" in Farsi) are a Zoroastrian community who migrated to the Indian subcontinent from Persia during the Muslim conquest of Persia of 636–651 CE.
3. At the Massacre of Verden in 782 CE, Charlemagne had over four thousand Saxons put to death as part of his efforts to Christianize that people.
4. Martin Luther (1483–1546), professor of theology, priest, monk, and a seminal figure in the Protestant Reformation.
5. Heinrich Heine (1797–1856), German poet, writer, literary critic.
6. Gotthold Ephraim Lessing (1729–1781), German writer, philosopher, playwright, and dramatist. The chief protagonist of his play *Nathan der Weise* (Nathan the Wise), the greatest plea for religious tolerance ever to come out of Western Europe, was modeled on Moses Mendelssohn.
7. During the sixty-year reign of Franz Joseph I, conversion was not necessary to be raised to the nobility. Lessing is talking of Germany.
8. Judicial status of Jews, begun in the twelfth century, as "property" of the Holy Roman emperor.
9. *Opferpfennig, Geleitzoll, Leibzoll.*
10. Karl Marx (1818–1883), German philosopher, economist, political theorist, and social revolutionary.
11. Deuteronomy 23:19.
12. Moses Hess (1812–1875), French Jewish founder of Labor Zionism. His Socialist theories incorporated racial conflict and diverged substantially from Marx and Engels.
13. Leviticus 16:8.
14. Johann Wolfgang von Goethe (1749–1832), leading German writer, poet, statesman, and author of *Faust*.
15. Leon Pinsker (1821–1891), physician who helped to create and lead the Hovevei Zion (Lovers of Zion) movement; Max Nordau (1849–1923), Zionist leader, physician, author, social critic, and cofounder of the World Zionist Organization together with Theodor Herzl; Theodor Herzl (1860–1904), journalist, playwright, political activist, writer, and father of modern political Zionism.
16. Associations of Jewish citizens of Mosaic denomination (original text).
17. Honor (Hebrew, Ashkenazi pronunciation).
18. Indian national independence movement, led by Gandhi, Nehru, Patel, and Jinna.
19. Rambam (Rabbi Moshe ben Maimon, Maimonides) (1135–1204), Sephardic Jewish philosopher who became a key Torah scholar of the Middle Ages; Yehuda Halevy (ca. 1075–1141), Spanish Jewish physician, poet, and philosopher; Rashi (acronym for Rabbi Shlomo Yitzhaki) (1040–1105), French rabbi who produced extensive commentaries on the Talmud and Old Testament.
20. The first four categories were not possible for German Jews in Prussia.

 CHAPTER 3

The Psychology and Pathology of Self-Hate – The Logic and Morality of Self-Hate – Prophets and Psalmists

1

This book deals with the theme of "self-hate." This is not just a Jewish theme, but one for the entire human race. It can best be clarified by study of the psychopathology of the Jewish people.

Anyone who wants to deal honestly and thoroughly with this subject must start at the beginning, when human spiritual consciousness first appeared to the questioning eye and spirit, from the void of the *pre*-human condition.

We must plumb the primordial source, where *separation between Ich and Du* shines forth for the first time from an all-encompassing unity that knows neither Ich nor Du.[1] On one side we find an intuitive subject, on the other the suppressible world of "objective realities." This is by no means an "abnormal" phenomenon (unless one considers the very existence of the mind to be a disease). It represents the miracle of the mind itself, whereby life, in other words human creation, can turn against itself—constantly, maliciously, sometimes even counterintuitively.

The flowers, the trees, the springs, the flooding water, burst forth under the spell of the rhythm of that which is unquestioned-but-sure.

Nature takes eternal breath, unconcerned and blissful. Only in the instinctual, primitive animal world (especially domesticated animals) do we find a few intimations of self-hate.

A huge force of powerful developmentally inspired passions (lust for power, vindictiveness, compassion, remorse) contain undercurrents of this secret self-destructive urge. This drive is powered by a hidden "spiritual pain," a strange instinct for all restricted life to destroy that which hems it in. One can find examples of this "self-torment" in the animal world (especially when they are restricted, forced to live with humans, and diseased). A study of these primitive conditions is necessary to understand the rupture that threatens the oldest of all peoples with this first human example of a life-destroying disease.

How do we simplify the concept of self-hate?

Learned psychology books proclaim two concepts: *philautoi* (self-love) and *misautoi* (self-deprecation). All human activity is the naïve, immediate expression of our *natural* lives. On the other hand, our works and deeds originate from our need for compromise, completion, and healing. They do not reveal what we *are*, but what we would *like to be*. We are confronted with images of goals, longings, and other ideals, but we are not happy or satisfied until these are realized. There were eras during which people loved to play with such cheap comparisons. They spoke of the contrast between "naïve" and "sentimental," "direct" and "indirect."

Heinrich Heine[2] mocked: "My German friends assert that I am not a naïve genius like them, but rather have the well-known Jewish talent for pretending. Because I intend, for the rest of my life, to continue pretending, I hope that this will have the same outcome as my friends' naïveté."

Goethe's lament that "everyone hates each other, and no one does something good for himself or the other" reflects the same feeling.[3] Goethe characterized this with the Greek word *heautontimorumenos* (tendency toward self-tormenting).[4] He maintained that the suffering of modern man is based on the fact that "he thinks badly of himself." This is a *disease*, which will spread in the future.

Many popular sayings, idioms, and figures of speech testify to the prevalence of this disease among Jews. No other people has a similar treasure trove of self-critical, self-deprecating wisdom. One still hears examples such as "The Jew cannot celebrate a festival[5] properly" (he must always make his life miserable) or "Where the goy[6] laughs a Jew cries." This oldest of all peoples has a rich, ancient heritage of deep insights into the connection between suffering and spirit, knowledge and need. The tradition of Jewish suffering goes together with Jewish shrewdness. "God becomes powerful only in the weak," "all knowledge is suffering,"[7] "a hump makes a man funny,"[8] "distress teaches a man to pray." Derivation of human values from a *negative* goes with such perceptions, and self-hate is the reflection of this *negative* perception.

I cite a well-known story: An *Ostjude*[9] with sidelocks and kaftan makes himself comfortable in a railway compartment by placing his feet on the upholstery of the opposite seat. A fashionably dressed stranger enters, whereupon the Jew withdraws his dirty shoes, apologizing to the man. This starts up a conversation: "Are you going home for Pesach?" The *Ostjude*, recognizing a coreligionist in the stranger, puts his feet back on the upholstery, with the reassured exclamation in Yiddish: "Just so."

This secret or open self-contempt fails to recognize the great and good, just because it has a Jewish origin. It is as if old doubts still were in bloom: "What great thing can come out of Nazareth? How can prophets arise in Galilee?"

The concept of "Jewish antisemitism" appears antithetical in and of itself, but in reality this is not so. For example, if a Jew is called a *rosche* (Jew-hater),[10] someone immediately responds, "That is a really Jewish characteristic."

The origins (fertile or poisoned) of this tendency toward self-misjudgment require further study. The humiliated self-consciousness of a long-*enslaved* people sees their commander or despiser as their born *master*. By contrast, someone born from his own circle of suffering comes up against the unspoken prejudice "If he were the right one, he wouldn't be sitting at our table," or "How can this man be of value? After all, he is the same as *we*."

2

We have to dig deep, to penetrate the heart and soul of Jewish self-hate. The following question must be posed: Under which conditions or processes is a man able to split the balanced unity of life? Under which conditions or processes is a man "seamless"?

Then it should be no unimportant discovery that conflict can come about only in a *waking* state, where preconscious and conscious life exist, can be observed, and incur reflection. All objectivized experiences require this prior act of "self-alienation." Without such a split, first into "experience," and then "reflection *on* experience," phenomena such as judgment, attention, humor, understanding, critical order, analysis, and freedom of choice, self-determination would be impossible. Everything that is "mine" *requires* duality.

By contrast, "two" and "duality" do not play a role in the purely religious experience. They also do not play a role in purely receptive processes, which we customarily call "aesthetic" experiences. (It is to be hoped that the latter incorrect, misleading word will soon disappear.)

We must differentiate between two groups of experiences. First, those that lie beyond the concept of "self-estrangement" (i.e., the subject-object relationship), and second, those founded in self-duplication of the subject-object relationship. The first group comprises religious-aesthetic, the second logical-ethical, experiences. Only the latter are, in the narrowest sense, "human" experiences.

Why is the religious-aesthetic the opposite of the logical-ethical, that is, truly *human* life?

There is no one side or the other in both types of experiences. No Ich and no Du, no subject and no object!

"To have a religious experience" means to be "*bound* into the absolute." In other words, not to *face* a cosmos. This means: to progress beyond the *only* human and *only* conscious, beyond the "spiritual" and "ethical," and become a part of the immeasurable fullness of the Divine Being.[11]

We may understand those experiences that impart "the life of things"—knowledge of things, I, being, and existence[12] to our *own* life—through abilities to intuit and empathize, which remain beyond the subjective-objective conscious relationship. Said another way: religious and aesthetic experience (no matter how much the two differ) both comprise *immediate* existence. In contrast to this immediacy, *knowledge* of the living, in a spirit-creative but life-destructive manner, *confronts* the life-element. The possibility of polarizing *hate* only arises where the spirit begins to detach from the soul.

We already have observed that this indirect, reflective attitude of life to life has two distinct sides. Our "I" can overpower the life element in two ways: knowing and wanting.

Knowledge of life is not life itself; however, it does require patient and thorough pursuit of the "traces of life." The "logical I" clings to the soul like a blood-sucking parasite, sapping all the juices of the unconscious, transforming them in thought and form into the "conscious world of the alert mind."

The "willing I" is different! Will differs from knowledge in the same way as value-preserving judgment "it shall be" differs from the judgment "it is so." It judges and regulates! It forces the living to model itself according to desire and image. Knowledge destroys the life-element, but will limits and humanizes it.

Both logic and ethics testify to ability of life to turn against life. The logical "I," turning against the "bearing soul" results in "knowledge of ourselves." This realization can perhaps be painful and self-denying but is not a hostile intrusion into our innate being.[13]

But woe betide when ethical will turns against our innate nature. Because then begins suffering of the ego, self-mutilation, merciless self-denial. Then pride of spirit triumphs over netherworlds of the soul.

Self-hate goes together with a waking, attentive mind tyrannizing the preconscious life that sustains it. Second, and in a narrower sense, "will" and "he who wills it" triumph over logic and logical judgment.

Study of the psychology of the Jewish soul confirms both processes. Jewish spiritual development reveals a fateful exaggeration of the spiritually conscious over the aesthetic-religious. Within the spiritually conscious life, ethical intension predominates over logical perception. Why is this so?

The explanation lies in the general destiny of all old, embattled, needy creatures, cut off from life's element. Jewish psychology is an illuminating example of the psychology of a suffering minority.

A minority always must try its best to behave circumspectly. It lives suspiciously, watchfully, ever scrutinized by its critical consciousness. Every threatened group must pay special attention to self-preservation, with the inherent risk of losing its immediacy and becoming trapped in super-vigilance. This is associated with a tendency toward irony—something lurking, a bystander, a quiet self-doubt. The real danger for the Jewish people does not lie in this alert vigilance, but rather in the taut energy of the will, which Goethe called "Jewish nature. Energy, the cause of everything! Immediate goals! Even the most insignificant Jew acts with resolute effort, with earthly, temporal immediacy. Even Yiddish and Hebrew contain something histrionic . . ."[14]

3

The Jewish people cannot remain prayerfully in the presence of trees and clouds, nor calmly indulge in the unique and particular. They were always obligated to bold generalizations, which became fainter with time. Jews had to mumble, carp, and trade, in order to make a living. But "values" mean that directly given life is destroyed by and in favor of an abandoned *higher* world. Every "ideal construction" murders life. If we measure experience only by the very least example, what can remain?

In ancient Israel, there was a balance between joy in what was given and construction of the yet-to-come. Israel was a nation of psalmists and prophets. In the new Israel, psalmists have become fewer, but prophets have multiplied. Instead of minstrel songs of life, one hears songs of hope and anger. One may be driven to believe that Jews have become so long transformed into a people of spiritual-ethical *will* that they have lost the feeling for faith, poetry, emotional security, salvation, eternity, and tranquility! Instead of beautiful life's darlings, they have become fiery zealots and furious seekers after justice.[15]

The fighter and sufferer becomes both actor and perpetrator, trader and merchant, always regarded more highly than seers and dreamers. The Jew has always been placed into a position of struggle. He cannot demand gratitude like a blossoming flower or a child, just because of his flowery existence. He must create *"values,"* to justify his existence to himself and to others. The result is that, driven out and falling out of himself, his sense of self-worth disappears. As a result, a gruesome caricature appears, like a merchant selling spoiled goods, calling out to his customers, "Believe me, my *merchandise* is good, only *I* stink."

Notes

1. This refers to the seminal book by the Austrian Jewish philosopher Martin Buber (1878–1965) *Ich und Du* (Leipzig: Inselverlag, 1923), first published in English after Lessing's murder: *I and Thou*, translated by Ronald Gregor Smith (Edinburgh: T.&T. Clark, 1937).
2. Heinrich Heine (1797–1856), German poet, writer, literary critic.
3. Johann Wolfgang von Goethe (1749–1832), leading German writer, poet, statesman, and author of *Faust*.
4. *Heauton Timorumenos* (Ἑαυτὸν τιμωρούμενος, Greek for *The Self-Tormentor*) is a play by Publius Terentiue Afer (185–159 BCE), a playwright in Republican Rome.
5. The text states *Jontof* (Ashkenazi pronunciation of *yom tov*, Yiddish *yontif*—festival).
6. Word for gentile, sometimes used derogatorily.
7. Much knowledge is grief to the soul (Ecclesiastes 1:18).
8. Moses Mendelssohn was a hunchback.
9. Eastern Jew.
10. Ashkenazi pronunciation of *rasha* (wicked man).
11. *Sein* as opposed to *Dasein*. The difference between these two words, as interpreted by Hegel, Nietzsche, and Heidegger, is beyond the scope of this translation. They have no direct English equivalent.

    Lessing's comment: *The fact that I separate all religious life and experience from everything logical, ethical, and therefore spiritual, will provoke understandable objection among Jews.*

    One must go very far back in Jewish history, refind and re-honor the much vilified and deliberately eradicated heathen *elements of Old Testament myth. In my opinion, only by doing so can the people of the book also be perceived as the people of the earth, to refind truly religious Judaism.*

    I have alluded to the heathen components in the Old Testament in my book Europa und Asien. Untergang der Erde am Geist, *2nd and 3rd editions.*

    I would like to mention a current German thinker, Heinrich Berl. No one else has better recognized the Bible as a natural myth or identified the true heart of Ju-

daism behind all the rabbinism, Talmudism, and hairsplitting. In his small but significant book Das Judentum in der Musik [Stuttgart: Deutsche Verlags-Anstalt, 1926], he has shown himself to be the most affectionate connoisseur of everything Jewish, among all modern-day non-Jewish scholars.

I would not have thought it possible to conceive religion not as the "blissfulness of eternal life," but as the cult of eternal death, and enthusiastically describe God as "the great nothing," or the "way to God" as "the progressive decadence of life annihilation." I cite a modern Christian theologian.

Konrad Fiedler in Der Anbruch des Nihilismus, 214 [Kuno Fiedler, Der Anbruch des Nihilismus. Aphoristische Gedanken über das Verhältnis von Religion und Bürgerlichkeit (Balingen: Verlag der Weltwende, 1923)], describes the relationship between the Old and New Testaments as follows:

> God and the devil are one. Has one not noticed that the God of the Old Testament is the devil of the New Testament, or that the devil of the Old Testament is the God of the New Testament? Yahwe is the Creator of the World (the demiurge of the gnostics) who commanded: "Be fruitful and multiply" (Genesis 1:28). From him comes all the bounty of life: food, drink clothes, shoes, house and farm, fields, cattle, money, goods, a pious spouse, children, good and true overlords, a good regiment, good weather, peace, health, breeding, honor, good friends and neighbors, and the like. By contrast, satan is the great ravager, who destroys everything that God has given. We recognize it well in the story of Job. (Nota bene: This is all nonsense. The Old Testament knows absolutely no evil outside of God: see page 228.) Against this, let us consider the temptation of Christ. What a difference! Here we really find satan, "prince of the world," who has at his disposal all the riches of the earth, while God in Jesus negates and rejects them. This changed relationship becomes even clearer with Paul in his Letters to the Romans and Corinthians (see Corinthians 4:4), and is clearest of all in John, who says for all the world to hear: "For everyone who has been born of God overcomes the world. And this is the victory that has overcome the world — our faith" (1 John 5: 4). How do we explain this victory? Very clearly: the New Testament provides religion, and the Old Testament — perhaps excluding the Prophets — provides bourgeoisie, the opposite of religion. Does that make sense?

Yes, it truly does! You are "the world," and the naïve realism of your clumsy and self-righteous mind *is so confused with the element of life and the living that you cannot differentiate between truth and conscious reality, or reality and* élan vital. *Christian theology knows as little as does Judaism what religion really is. Reverence for plants, worship of animals, service of sun, stars, sex, Dionysus, Eleusinian mysteries, the intoxication of Sukkot — these all used to be* religion. *In the haughtiness of your life-corroding spirit, do you not intuit any of this? You confuse the European-America and its cult of "God" (the general and sovereign ego), you confuse Christianity, its "world history," its "developmental process."* You confuse ethos and logos with religion just as presumptuously as Schopenhauer once confused Nirvana of the Vedas and Upanishads with the completely different Nirvana of Buddha, as he mixed the most obnoxious Brahmanism with Buddhism and Christianity, neither knowing nor intuiting Judaism.

12. Ding, Ich, Dasein, Existenz.
13. Sein.

14. Johann Wolfgang von Goethe, *Maximen und Reflexionen. Aphorismen und Aufzeichnungen. Nach den Handschriften des Goethe- und Schiller-Archivs*, ed. Max Hecker (Weimar: Verlag der Goethe-Gesellschaft, 1907), 275; *Judensprache* (original).
15. My emphasis on prophecy as a spiritual-ethical, not religious, phenomenon owes a great deal to the excellent works of Martin Buber. His theology is truly prophetic. In his foreword to Chassidische Bücher, Buber cites the faith of the Baal Shem Tov against that of Spinoza, by ascribing to Israel the mission of "making God addressable," "addressing God," "to proclaim the world as a word, and the life of every creature as a dialogue." Spinoza takes it upon himself to "take from God his ability to be addressed."

    Martin Buber is even more decisive in his book Ich und Du, describing the religious experience as an "encounter event," a dialogue, a speech and a reply, a drama with tensions and relations between the temporal soul and primeval reason for life.

    Buber clearly shows that this theology is secretly a single idiomorphism. "Religion" requires no theology, least of all an "existence of God." Everything always and forever revolves around the "I." And the "Thou" becomes the "I" once again. Buber's "God" is a spiritual being who becomes (like every dialogue and drama) intimated and borne by human volition. The great religious genius of our day Jiddu Krishnamurti, who lives far from all churches and religions, in a center where all things become equally inconsequential, answers every question with the proof of how false the question is. Music is no dialectic, lyric no dialogue.

    The supreme commandment, to make no likeness or graven image, implies in itself the prohibition of the Word, which is always iniquitous and seems to me to be the most sacred expression of the soul, which strives to do what it is and has, and not get lost by detaching itself.

    It is not the philosopher's task to resort to theology—even the use of its concepts is strictly forbidden.

 CHAPTER 4

THE IMPRACTICAL DREAMER – SIX SYMBOLIC FIGURES – PRESENT-DAY EXAMPLES

1

We step into a heart-rending world! There is no talk of a happy people who go down in history, finding an echo in many hearts. We find only fruitless labor and hopeless torment of soon-to-be-forgotten individuals who have, as it were, lived high on airy wires, floating between peoples and striking airy roots only in the spirit world.[1]

In each of these individual fates we are confronted with the tragic countenance of Western European Jews. We see a face that is often faceless and washed out, looking out at us from the encyclopedias of time, out of plays and belles-lettres. It stands on the barricades. It fights for the suffering. It speaks German in Germany and American in America, and the finest Chinese in China. It is the face of an Ahasuerus,[2] who can achieve everything, paw through everything, understand everything, and still live in fear, neglecting the important and overlooking the great.

All regions on earth have spat these people out into the collective reservoir of "international culture." They hustle down racecourses, know only work, masters of every art and achievement! They use and exploit the millennia-long genetically preprocessed wisdom of their fathers, delighting in titles and resources, until a foreign country swallows them up and a lying tombstone bearing a lying inscription stands on their hill. There is no cemetery of any people of any faith that does not include Jews.

2

I must limit myself to six symbolic figures from the endless number of Jewish souls who represent not only their own, but "human destiny" as a whole. All twentieth-century German Jewish intellectuals, writers, and thinkers demonstrate—each in his own way—the tragic drama of a destiny that flees from the center, turning in on itself.

My depictions are full of *love*. The reader misunderstands this book if in my description of Jewish self-hatred he searches for an *aversion* to "apostates" or a desire to retain or restore the Jewish soul. The dissolution described here becomes the crossroads of hundreds of thousands of Jews. No one can be spared the choice, and each must decide for himself again and again.

If it is possible to "love someone who hates you," it would be easier for us to love those who cannot love themselves. From what do Jewish self-haters suffer if not an unhappy *love for the enemy*? All of the people whom I describe were colorful, open-minded souls, men of both transition and doom.[3]

In his youth, the author also underwent a period of exclusive devotion to "German culture," with corresponding resistance to "Judaism." Where would a truth-seeking, high-minded young man, born in twilight and forced to choose between two peoples, not struggle with the same question? All people of Jewish blood have at least some *tendency* to "Jewish self-hate." A few outstanding examples follow.

3

The most powerful example of the self-hating creative Jew is the great *Rudolf Borchardt*.[4] A tragically weathered figure, uptight and childlike at the same time. A man with undoubted natural genius, in service of a singular anomaly. A Jew who not only serves the German people (no contradiction here!), but also, with his own unique personality, incorporates the physical *reality*, the body and soul, of the best and purest in Germany! It would be as difficult to replace him as artistically to outdo a beautiful natural form with artificial material.

Just as a synthetic perfume, even if filtered from street dust, can be far more fragrant than natural floral perfume, or the play of colors produced in a jar can far surpass the colors of nature, so too the work of our cognitive discipline can substitute for the original a second, apparently more perfect, nature. If we see through the sublimity of our spiritual-ethical substitute worlds, in which destiny does not dictate, "Become what you are," but the all-accomplishing spirit prescribes, "I am what I make of myself," we stand shaken with pride and horror at the monstrous deeds of human vanity. A little lie thus lurks even in great works of art. Borchardt is not burdened by lack of self-worth, mental or moral power. Just the opposite: his problem lies in the fact that he has irrefutably solidified the spiritual cosmos of the will, deceiving destiny's tragedy, by his dignity and strong moral character. However, by doing so, he has unprincipledly beggared and misused the natural foundation, like someone who removes construction material from the site on which his house is to be built. By doing so, he has proclaimed much more than self-reliant nature could have done on its own.[5]

The complex nature of Jewish self-hate is illustrated also in the best works of *Hugo von Hofmannsthal, Franz Werfel,* and *Jakob Wassermann.*[6] Wassermann's honest and heartfelt revelation of the Jewish dilemma *Mein Weg als Deutscher und als Jude* [My journey as a German and a Jew] can only be compared to the tormenting games of forfeit that our grandmothers played one hundred years ago, the so-called *jeu de bateau.* Two good people are named, and the player must imagine that he can save only one on a sinking ship. He has to answer the question of conscience of whom to choose: friend or brother, mother or wife?[7]

Berthold Auerbach, now-forgotten author of Black Forest village tales, wrote a letter just before he died, when the first wave of Stöcker- and Hammerstein-inspired racial antisemitism began to appear in Germany.[8] The letter states that he is, and has throughout his entire life been, German to his very core. He has been the voice of the German countryside. But now he hears the refrain "Get out of town, Jew; you do not belong here." This is the natural, poignant pain of being ignored and spurned by a beloved mother. But even more, it is that of having a mother who despises her finest son, thereby *begrudging him a son's duties.* It would be good to sense that the mother has realized what she has outraged and thrown away. But I cannot say that I have ever been sure this will come to pass, certainly not now.

I must also mention an avenger and judge who has made it his life's aim to struggle and fight against what is currently occurring—the unreserved moral zealot Karl Kraus, that most brilliant example of Jewish self-hate.[9] Kraus is and remains a powerful man of letters, irrespective of what he does or where he is. His writings are infused with passionate hate against literature itself. He writes for newspapers, to fight journalism. He puts himself in the middle of the time, to relate how much he despises it. He is master creator of the word itself. But he hates the desecration of the word and consumes millions of words to praise the chaste blessing of sacred silence. In no other figure can we better see the intractable tragedy of ingenuous self-hate of moral man in present-day Germany. Because here a beautiful and pure natural power has been wasted in an ultimately fruitless effort from which, after only a few generations, nothing will remain but a pile of useless printed paper.

It is not that he has cleansed the Augean stables,[10] but rather that, as a rebuke to Hercules, he has put all this stinking filth on display in the public Erechtheion.[11] He has lit his torch to reveal this excrement to the petty and small, wherever they may be. We could have honored ourselves much better by passing through to greatness instead of pettiness. Kraus is today's *soberest* Jew-hater. He reveals like no other the innermost mystery of hate.

German's foremost antisemites—Lagarde or Treitschke, Dühring or Chamberlain—have all become haters from ecumenical will to power.[12] They wanted to deprive Jews of earthly spiritual leadership because they coveted it for themselves. This was no small, superficial will! But even in so noble and spiritual an outward form, the most moral-seeming nature is nothing but a variant of human *ambition* and *envy*. All types of excommunications and harsh judgments have in them an urge for *validity*. The goal-oriented, ideal-obsessed mentality ascribed to Jews by these great thinkers—belongs to *them themselves*.

A Timonian disdain for the world has never developed without vanity,[13] nor ranting misanthropy without self-hate. If we could gain insight into the ultimate depth of implacable and puritanical moralistic zeal, we would notice with a shudder that all great condemners of the human condition have in them the wolfish addiction with the insatiable "*ego*" that—even in a Dante, Robespierre, and Savanarola—gnawed at the soul and pure immediacy of nature.[14]

Notes

1. Both here and in the chapter title, the word *Luftmensch* is used.
2. Name of the king in the book of Esther. Lessing is referring to the eternal wandering Jew.
3. *Übergang* and *Untergang*.
4. Rudolf Borchardt (1877–1945), German poet and essayist who would be blacklisted by the Nazis. By the time this book was written, unofficial Nazi discrimination must already have begun.
5. See Theodor Lessing, Europa und Asien. Untergang der Erde am Geist, 5th ed. (Berlin: Verlag der Wochenschrift der Aktion, 1918), chapter 20, "das Schaffen und die Schaffenden."
6. Hugo von Hoffmansthal (1874–1929), Austrian novelist, librettist, poet, dramatist, narrator, and essayist; Franz Werfel (1890–1945), Austrian-Bohemian playwright and novelist; Jakob Wassermann (1873–1934), German writer and novelist. All three were of Jewish extraction.
7. A German philosopher, Eduard von Hartmann, in his book on "the Jewish question in the German Reich" deals seriously with the jeu de bateau (boat game) question. He regards it as a desirable criterion by which to decide if a Jew has

stopped being a Jew and become completely German. Ask the Jew a question: "If you can save someone's life, and must choose between a German and a Jew, whom would you save?" The question is completely pointless, because who would prefer a beloved stranger over a beloved countryman? We must object to this great philosopher. At its root, every kind of ethic is, and must *always be, an "ethic of my own kind." Someone who does not first do his duty in the narrow circles closest to him could not be of benefit to his wider circle, and not be an ethical human being. How would a German answer the question "You can save either a Martian or your wife. Whom would you choose?"*

8. Berthold Auerbach (1812–1882), German Jewish poet and author; Adolf Stöcker (1835–1909), court chaplain to Kaiser Wilhelm I and leading antisemite, largely responsible, together with the historian Heinrich von Treitschke, for development of German racial antisemitism in the late 1870s; Wilhelm von Hammerstein (1838–1904), Prussian politician of the German Conservative Party and editor-in-chief of the *Kreuzzeitung*.
9. Karl Kraus (1874–1936), Austrian satirist and essayist.
10. Fifth labor of Hercules.
11. Ancient Greek temple on the side of the Acropolis in Athens, dedicated to Athena and Poseidon.
12. Paul Anton de Lagarde (1827–1891), German biblical scholar and orientalist and vocal antisemite; Heinrich von Treitschke (1834–1896), German antisemitic historian and political thinker; Eugen Karl Dühring (1833–1921), German antisemitic philosopher and economist who opposed Marxism; Houston Stewart Chamberlain (1855–1927), British-born Germanophile political philosopher whose advocacy of racial and cultural superiority of the so-called Aryan element in European culture influenced pan-German and German nationalist thought, particularly Adolf Hitler's National Socialist movement.
13. Timon of Phlius (ca. 320–230 BCE), Greek philosopher and writer of satirical poems.
14. Dante Alighieri (1265–1321), Italian poet and author of *The Divine Comedy*; Maximilien de Robespierre (1758–1794), French lawyer and politician, key figure of the French Revolution, and instigator of the reign of terror; Girolamo Savonarola (1452–1498), Dominican friar and preacher in Renaissance Florence noted for his extreme asceticism.

 CHAPTER 5

THE SUFFERING OF SELF-HATE – ITS THREE PATHS – HEALING

1

But now I position myself protectively before the most misbegotten and poorest ghetto offspring and pose several questions to the non-Jewish world. Do you know what it means to curse the ground on which you must grow, and drink poison from its roots? Do you know what it means to be badly born to a popularly ascribed birthright of calculation and shallow self-interest—to be badly born, whether pampered or neglected, mollycoddled or battered? And then to nurture a lifetime of senseless hate—against father, mother, teacher, educators, all those who have begotten and shaped us in their own unflattering image, without us even wanting to come into such a world?

We observe everywhere and in all peoples the same spectacle of anthill mentality and mongrelization, of mindless, assembly-line human reproduction, of which the majority is either misbegotten or ill-bred.[1]

In all peoples, however, when destinies go wrong and when perfection and successes are rare, a nation is like a great stream that can accumulate all the dark tributaries, transforming everything back into clear, clean-flowing ripples.

Even the most wretched person draws breath like a leaf in a living forest, born by that from which he stems. A venerated history gathers him up, and a permitted culture consumes him in the chorus of the great collective.

By contrast, the Jew stands *outside*. His nationality has been, for centuries, a small, quiet lake, always in danger of being silted up. He has had no one but his dead, and he has unlearned their language. No nation carried him, no history absolved him, nothing fashioned him,[2] and his hero was the eternal patient sufferer.

We all gladly pronounce the beautiful saying "Happy is he who remembers his ancestors with joy."[3] But what can a child do when he must turn from his ancestors with shame because they have irresponsibly wasted and squandered their sexual energies, by casting their progeny into the world as if by *accident*? Such a child, hemmed by wickedness and inadequacy on all sides, uses up his poor strength in a hateful tug against intractable chains.

We are taught the blessings of "community." We should much rather learn about solitude. Everyone seeks community, few seek solitude. It is possible for a man to *detest* the community in which he is born and educated, in which he remains all his life, but be completely incapable of ever separating his private destiny from that of the community.

There are countless Jews who continuously grumble about *kehilla* and *mishpoche*,[4] but still live by the dire maxim "Bind my hands and bind my feet, but, at all costs, dispose of my remains in the family."[5] How can this be explained?

What does the uprooted person expect on the other side of the fence? He would have to be secretly and humiliatingly aware: "I do not really belong here. They are not better and do not achieve more than I do. But they have one thing that I lack: *they like themselves*."

How can it be that people other than Jews like themselves, but Jews do not? If he would have to live with this dislike among his fellow sufferers, the Jew would collapse. But he bears his tragic destiny alone. However sooner or later (sometimes appallingly early) increased self-recognition brings the cruel hour when the plant's exasperating struggle against its soil leads to destructive self-analysis.

Can a miracle occur? Can a swamp bring forth roses? Can a laurel bloom in the desert?

The Jew must preserve his botched life, from now until the end of time, according to the immutable laws of nature.

But what if he cannot bear the status quo? How would you bear it, seeing see all your weaknesses increased a thousandfold in the reflection of your environment? You cannot destroy the image by breaking the mirror into pieces. In reality, you are damning your own soul.

2

I see three recourses for such a burdened soul.

First, the misbegotten person can become a world judge. He can become inquisitor, zealot, stern ethics disciplinarian, preacher of repentance. There is a certain ethical power that can come only from tainted blood. This type of moralization tortures the nearest (who are at the same time the furthest) with solemn demands that cannot be fulfilled, not even by this prophet. Such a man escapes out of his own spirit and also from an unloved world. This continues as long as he lives *in the spirit*, but woe betide him when he falls to earth. Because he is no Antaeus, who derives twice the strength for flight from contact with his mother.[6] He is a moving ball, destiny's plaything. Each time he touches the ground his momentum weakens, until he finally remains on the despised spot—a despairing skeptic, consumed by the spirit! And then he discovers the unpalatable truth: "I am an unbalanced person searching for balance. A priest, who makes virtue out of need. A liar, who stuffs his holes with ideas. An unpleasant person, who turns his self-dislike against others. A cheat, who lives in the air because there is no place on earth where he is not disgusted with humanity."

This way ends in death of the soul.

The second way is greater and nobler than that of judges and prophets—where you turn all barbs against yourself. You acquit all others. You become your own judge and executioner. You faithfully devote yourself to foreigners instead of to yourself, your friend, your beloved . . . Woe betide you!

You have made your heart a footstool to be trodden upon. The more you give, the more surely you are used up, unseen and without thanks.

You turn your weapons against yourself. You show your friend how vulnerable you are. Unhappy person! One day you will be murdered with the same weapons that you have given him. You speak badly of yourself: a day surely will come when your beloved will be able to use that against you. Become an oppressor and people will honor you. Become violent and they will love you. Become a lamb and wolves will devour you.

Offer yourself as a victim—well and good! They will kiss your hands and then celebrate the slaughter. Those you love most deeply will slaughter you and never will recognize or repent of their deed—no matter how despicable or villainous it may be. They always will find grounds to consecrate their actions. No one loves or pities someone who does not love himself enough.

The second way ends worse than death of the soul. The third way remains:

The great conversion: "mimicry." You become "one of all the others" and look really fabulous. Perhaps a little too German to be really German. Perhaps a little too Russian to be really Russian. And because Christianity is still such a novelty, you practice it a little too diligently. But at least: now you are secure. Really?

Your body is safe. You are dead—you have died with your conflict. You have committed suicide in order to attain happiness and fame. But millions of dead weep in your soul, and the dead are more powerful than all your happiness and fame combined.

So is everything in vain? What is the answer?

3

Let us look more deeply for the cruel truth! Our wounds can either not heal at all or heal only in the light. If you are misbegotten, ill-bred, or insecure, you still are burdened with your own guilt or that of your fathers or of strangers. Do not try to settle, gloss over, or gild anything.

Be what you are and accomplish what is in you the best way you can. But never forget that tomorrow you and this entire earthly world will decay and change.

Fight incessantly. But do not forget that *every* life, even the most defective and criminal, needs love.

No being can do more than fulfill himself, as much as soil, weather, and climate permit.

We all take our existence[7] far too seriously.

Who *are* you? Are you the son of Nathan the shifty Jew merchant, who accidentally inseminated sluggish Sarah because she brought him a large dowry? No! Your father was Judah the Maccabee,[8] Queen Esther was your mother. The chain continues from you, although some links might be defective, to Saul, David, and Moses. They are in all things present and past and can be again in the future.

Do you carry a burdened heritage? Good! Unburden your heritage. Your children will forgive you for being your parent's child. Do not cheat your destiny but love it, and follow it until death. Take heart! Through all the hells of your human "I,"[9] you always will return to the heaven of your eternal self,[10] to your eternal people.

Notes

1. A reflection of Fritz Lang's *Metropolis* (1927).
2. This applied to secular education. Jews had a rich and enduring education in Torah and Talmud.
3. Johann Wolfgang von Goethe (1749–1832), *Wohl dem, der seiner Väter gern gedenkt*, Iphigenie 1, 3.
4. Community and family (Ashkenazi Hebrew pronunciation) (Leipzig: F. A. Brockhaus, 1819).
5. Probably reference to ancient Jewish burial custom of binding the hands and feet of the corpse.

6. Antaeus was the son of the gods Poseidon and Gaea, one of the Gigantes, in Greek mythology. He drew strength from his mother, Earth, and was invincible while he was in contact with her.
7. *Dasein*.
8. Jewish priest who led a revolt against the Seleucid Empire, 167–160 BCE.
9. *Ich*.
10. *Selbst*.

SIX LIFE STORIES

Paul Rée

Paul Rée, young, independent, and from a wealthy family, was a lover of arts and sciences. He arrived in clever, stately Basel in February 1874.[1] The honorable, orderly city must have appeared to him as if it were created for the unemotional intoxication of a free spirit. He bathed in the Rhine, took his customary daylong walks on the sunny river banks, and enjoyed company of worthy professors. There he found a friend, without whose universal impact we today hardly would have known of Rée's existence.

Depiction of the life and work of Paul Rée is a bold undertaking. Apart from a 211-paragraph booklet, published posthumously by a reverent hand under the title "philosophy," nothing of him remains for posterity. We know the outlines of his life, and many still alive remember how he looked, walked, and spoke. But he destroyed all his own letters, books, and diaries. He wanted to go through life with closed visor, which he died without having opened. He was a shy, reticent type, and his social development seems to have become gradually frozen in place.[2]

Those who saw him describe him as a beautiful, perfect being. He was tall, dark-skinned, clear-browed, with deep, thinking eyes. He was a masculine man, harmonic and balanced.

One of his acquaintances, the sociologist Ferdinand Tönnies,[3] described Paul Rée as follows:

> I knew and valued Rée as an unusually subtle, clever man. The quiet security of his tread, his calm, soft way of speaking, were impressive, and the better one knew him the more good-natured and gracious he appeared. He often turned his ironical humor against himself and others. He knew how to clothe petty malice in an engaging manner. Although at heart a modest man, he had great confidence in the rightness of his cause, because he considered himself one of the very small number of unbiased thinkers. He mulled tirelessly for months and years over certain specific, crucial problems. His wish was to stand outside life, the better to observe it. He was haunted by the wretchedness of man and invalidity of the belief that keeps him captive, ever and again making new captives of the apparently free. One is tempted to call Rée's early and later aphorisms

misanthropy, but they reflect much more pride of perception. Rée loved conversation but became perplexed easily and let his deep, animated eyes move back and forth as if doubting, helping himself out of embarrassment with a jesting phrase: "The art of conversation is difficult. When one speaks, others become bored. The same is true when one listens to oneself." On the streets of a Catholic city such as Innsbruck, where we spent some time together, he was taken for a priest. Children crowded around to kiss his hand. His large, beardless, serious countenance, long black coat, measured tread, deep inner isolation, gloomy view of life, and rigidity of male individuality were all priest-like characteristics. In many ways he reminded me of Schopenhauer.[4]

Paul Rée was born on 21 November 1849, the second son of a rich landowner in the country estate Bartelshagen in Pomerania. His father's family came from Hamburg, his mother Jenny Jonas from Schwerin. After initial lessons from private teachers the family moved to Schwerin where—with a few breaks in Berlin and a private school in Ludwigslust—Rée attended the Fridericianum Grammar School in Schwerin, where he passed his school-leaving examination on Michaelmas Day in 1868, and then traveled to Leipzig at his father's request, to study law. In 1870 he performed his military duty as one-year volunteer. When war broke out, Rée was one of the first in the field and was wounded at Gravelotte.[5] After returning from war, he took up his studies again but soon turned to philosophy under the influence of Schopenhauer. He turned to the still unusual concept that universities call "psychology": in other words the philosophy founded in England by Bacon and Mill, which attempts to ascribe every phenomenon to a spiritual condition, said more accurately to laws and codes of conduct, of a world-foundational *consciousness*.[6] For this philosophic thought, categories of logic and axioms of mathematics are derived from a science of biological substrata. Behind every truth lies a need for life—something "human, all too human."

The worldly young scholar, whose first work was an anonymously written small volume called *Psychologische Betrachtungen* [Psychological observations], was favorably received by the conservative world of Basel professors. Three luminous spirits sat bent over their books in three neighboring houses. Johann Jakob Bachofen, Jakob Burckhardt, and Friedrich Nietzsche brooded simultaneously over the same riddle of metaphysical primal division. They used similar terms to describe their mythological formulas but did not know each other.[7]

The young Rée felt himself to be a mediator and facilitator and liked to call himself a botanist. He was a continuous visitor, a restless wanderer of landscapes and mountains, cities, people, libraries, museums, and churches. He listened and observed silently (like Nietzsche, he was a man of quiet, refined spirit), finding things slightly comical, slightly tragic, slightly contemptible. His was the life of a noble stranger who travels through life with loving eyes, happily accepting and disseminating, but never putting down roots or belonging.

"I have a new system," he said. "I observe all life's content, mainly human customs and ideals, their secret motivations and backgrounds. At the end of the day, our poor humanity lies at the basis of all spiritual realms. If a proposition is true, a good deed occurs, or an image appears beautiful, the unconscious processes in which the true, good, and beautiful are rooted do not have to be—in and of themselves—true, good, or beautiful."

Paul Rée was a proponent of the philosophy that Nietzsche later called the philosophy of the morning or the gay science (the joyful wisdom), which he depicted in his books *The Wanderer and His Shadow*, *Beyond Good and Evil*, and *Human, All Too Human*. The thirty-year-old Nietzsche, who was five years younger than Rée, became his pupil.

The first meeting between the two philosophers caused happy, mutual astonishment. Nietzsche wrote to a friend: "We discovered that we were true kinsmen—the mutual enjoyment of our conversations was limitless." Rée was working on his book on the origin of moral perceptions, while Nietzsche was a hopeless romantic, a "respectful, obedient dog," under the spell of Schopenhauer and Richard Wagner.[8] Nietzsche learned the art of the diamond-sharp, hair-splitting psychological scalpel from Rée, and in time the pupil surpassed the teacher. Rée perceived in the fledgling scholar of Greek language and literature the buoyant imagination, the creative ardor, that he himself lacked. This had a sobering effect on his otherwise sharp perception and made him feel poor and guilty during quiet hours of reflection. But, because both had virtuous and austere natures, they talked around each other for months. And when they finally began to complement one another, a tragic lightning bolt brought an end to their association in a flash.

Theirs was a fateful star-crossed friendship.[9] Had it been possible to bridge the gap, who knows whether one would have descended into the night of madness and the other have committed suicide.[10]

During the short year that their friendship lasted[11] each believed that their dream of friendship had been fulfilled in someone who was both leader and example. Each loved the other more than himself. Nietzsche called this period the "period of my Rée-alism," and Rée was prepared to become Nietzsche's disciple and apostle. Nietzsche was the gentler of the two but made of cooler, Nordic stuff. Rée, warm and tender, had the more primitive, ardent nature. One had a more feminine, sensitive, but cold and me-oriented nature, the other was motherly, devoted, all too "altruistic." Rée was more excitable, Nietzsche was sensitive and logical. Both were austere and withdrawn.

To a casual observer, Nietzsche seemed both taker and receiver. He called the masculine Rée his leader. But it sounded like mockery because Rée felt (even though later he didn't wish to) that his more feminine friend would be stronger and more durable. He knew in advance what would occur: "the seed will grow gloriously, the sower soon will be forgotten."

Two disparate yet related natures wanted to harmonize, but an evil demon stood between them, towering over the dam that eventually shattered their relationship.

An unspoken secret hovered over Rée, a trap that could not be released by contempt for the world or smiling humor.

He was a Jew, although it is doubtful whether Nietzsche was aware of this. Rée belonged to the wondrous kind of young Jews (very common in those pre-Zionist years) completely dissociated from their rites and heritage, guarding the consciousness of their Jewish origin like a secret affliction, a mark of Cain or disfiguring birthmark. On the other hand, they were too refined to endure the taint of their birth without effects on their psyche.

The well-bred young researcher shied away from any articulation of his Jewishness. He became perturbed when conversation turned to his open wound and broke his thick shield of silence only once, when he spoke to his beloved[12] of his origins. The outbreak of lament over his faulty birth was so harrowing and incomprehensible that, more than a generation after its revelation, she said that she had looked into an abyss, the like of which she never saw again.

This secret "self-torment" was the root cause of Paul Rée's seminal role in development of European "psychology," while under Nietzsche's powerful influence. Before we consider Rée's personal suffering, and pursue it to its awful demise, we must clarify the relationship between modern psychoanalysis and Jewish self-hate.

It is not my intention to assert that modern-day psychoanalysis is due solely to Jewish intelligence. However, it is clear that the concept of so-called psychoanalytic methodology inspired by Paul Rée via Nietzsche's formulas, which has become part of our culture, has much in common with certain Jewish talents. Leaders of the schools of Sigmund Freud, Alfred Adler, and other psychoanalysts, whose methods have recently become all the rage, were not aware of their reliance on Nietzsche, nor on the schools of Herbart and later Theodor Lipps, who long before had grasped the entire conceptual framework of psychoanalysis.[13] Modern psychoanalysis originated in certain circles of educated Western European Jewry. This connection cannot be coincidental; all we can do at this stage is to shed light on it.[14]

The tree blossoms! The flower exudes fragrance. The bird sings. Men love, write poetry, fantasize, pray. If we were to ask Nature *why* all this happens, it always would reply, "It is the result of overabundance of beautiful, strong rich life that constantly fulfills, devotes, perpetuates."

The interpretive mind answers differently, inasmuch as the willing or thinking, evaluating, or judging mind always is linear and *intentionally driven*. Such a goal- and purpose-oriented life can answer the question "why?" only with "causality," correlating with contradiction, congestion, distress, and a *state of emergency* to be thwarted.

"Explained" is for us a real phenomenon only when we have understood its need. However, those who work scientifically and practically rarely consider that association of phenomena with emergency is part of the natural cycle. Philosophizing dilettantes naïvely believe to have found something new to expound when they "ascribe" phenomena such as beauty, love, dreams, religion, ardor, ecstasy, genius, fantasy, images, and every conceivable living thing to some type of emergency or congestive disorder that needs to be put right.

The tree blossoms . . . "To prevent dying from dehydration and take in nourishment."

The flower exudes fragrance . . . "To lure insects and cause pollination."

The bird sings . . . "To respond to a state of estrus and attract a mate."

The human soul prays, loves, believes, dreams, educates . . . "Out of some type of trivial, comprehensible type of 'repression,' 'compensation,' 'overcompensation,' 'sublimation,' 'need for balance,' or 'emergency response.'"

Wherever life's real wonder and experience *are lacking*, emergency teleological research becomes the treacherous symptom of a people filled with self-doubt and biologically dying out. (Of course, "living of life" is not the same as the "life experience" expounded by busy lawyers and neurologists.)

When a nation blossoms, nature fills itself creatively, and does not turn against itself in spirit, a miracle occurs—the *natural*. We must remember, however, that behind all psychoanalysis lies the difficult-to-dig-up root of moralistic "self-contempt."

Dreams, faith, Eros, music, beauty, ecstasy, and genius are not questionable, derivable, or problematic. They comprise everything *beautiful*. As the Hindus say, they are the *anandamaya atman* ("blissful contentment—after overcoming all worldly desires—of the individual's soul").[15] They do not belong, like ethics or logic, to the array of *values*. Beauty is the expression of life well lived: weight-removed, weightless, blissful, joyful in itself.

However, when bonds of nature loosen and substance weakens, the feeling of life itself is oppressed, the wonders of life become derivable and require explanation. Eros, faith, genius now do not appear natural, fulfilling, and *free*, but an emergency exit of a threatened or threatening situation, a target, trade, and success phenomenon. Unphilosophical minds overpower those of philosophers: family doctors, pedagogues, pragmatists, pastors, all *causally genetically* attuned and busy at work, improving, achieving, and "solving" all the world's problems. Americanisms such as "individual psychology," whose entire wisdom and interest lie in "how can I *succeed*?"—appear. Only barren, unfruitful souls remain silent, allowing this "new" interpretation to honor the undeniable usefulness and applicability of an easily learned lesson, to prove truth and validity of all emergency cognition.[16]

A "psychoanalysis of psychoanalysis" yields a curious fact: that analytic psychology is *possible* is *itself* a "psychological problem." Whenever the vitality of a race is exhausted, religion changes into ethics, and mythical creativity into theology. Cosmic Eros changes into "libido," and utter desolation of the soul into freethinking theorems. "Myth," "Eros," and all extra-human and reawakened realities can thereby be "ascribed" to a single human imperative, necessary for action.

The essence of psychology is therefore to make life's "sore spots" into positive probation of life and find in every sore spot a bridge or compensation. Psychology reveals humanity as either vulnerable or with self-inflicted wounds. It sheds light on the pathognomonics of a weakened people who have gone astray.

We may ask: Why has such psychology become the prevailing fashion of *our age*? How can such great enthusiasm become a symptom of declining creative power? The answer provides an in-depth insight into the psychology of Jewish self-hate.

There is no feeling of superiority that reassures even the soberest, and no security that strengthens us more than the knowledge "*How it is done!*"

Knowledge of which manure makes the best roses and best strengthens their growth, and how we can use this for the best rosiculture, consoles us a little for the knowledge that we are far less beautiful than roses. And yet, we must fulfill ourselves. Contemporaries, aware of this to the point of absurdity, sit in wonder before such magical games with the superiority of the initiated. They cannot perform the play themselves, but still smile at each other and applaud each simplicity-perplexing miracle. "Sleight of hand! We were *behind* the scenes." "We know all the tricks!" "We connoisseurs even know a Greco-Latin expression for this miracle. Yes, we know how this is done: we do not wonder at it, and are *not* surprised!" This is how the deconstructors of the miraculous praise themselves. But what they do *not* know is the following:

All wise men have become immensely stupid. They regard a yellow spot in their eye as the reason they can see things clearly, and explain life's flow as remnants the flood tide left behind in dried-up souls. When water is boiled away it leaves behind hard limestone deposits, which they (and only they) examine microscopically, declaring them to be "life-deposits," the precipitating factor and main driving force for all great events. For them the force isn't this little, miserable bit of "sexuality," last remnant from the religious, metaphysical primal womb. No, just the opposite: religion and metaphysics are the "sublimation" not of the soul, but of lime scale.[17] Everyone knows and confirm this.

Let us proceed with the life of Paul Rée, which we have already described as a process of gradual freezing—the same fate that threatens Western European Jewry

We must examine the conclusion of an "analytic-genetic" psychology that recognizes its background but does not dream or believe in a world of magic and gods anymore, Rather, it sees the great "lingering illness" of life-creating bliss as compensated by the tremendous *progress* of the cleverest race on earth, creating a spiritual surrogate-world in place of biblical miracles—desolating science, narrowing and sapping the will. *Every step toward human earthly domination and technology also causes miracles to disappear.*

The flame of a glorious people flickers out. For them, the unremitting accompanying refrain "I am a Jew" is not a blissful happy destiny, but rather the driving goad of a life-diminishing obsession.

We see the above reflected in the life of Paul Rée. We know very little of the personal course of Rée's gradual personality glaciation because the patient tried to deal with it by walling off his feelings in the way that any organism attempts to remove a foreign body. He encapsulated and hardened them, leaving them as a dead island in a healthy substrate.

After Rée and Nietzsche visited the Bayreuth Festival together in 1876,[18] Nietzsche (who had been ill since 1871) became aware of growing eye weakness. Physicians in Basel recommended a yearlong vacation and spending time in the south, so they decided to spend winter 1876 together in Sorrento. A younger pupil of Nietzsche suffering from consumption joined them. Malvida von Meysenbug, their motherly friend,[19] took over their care in the Villa Rubinacci. Frau Cosima and Richard Wagner—at the time occupied with *Parsifal*—also looked them up in Tasso's birthplace.[20]

To compensate for Nietzsche's weak eyes, a well-recommended young girl—daughter of a Russian general—was brought along for transcription and dictation. This young Lou Salomé[21] was tasked to make copies for Nietzsche. However, she unwittingly became the wedge that prematurely drove their beautiful relationship apart.

They strolled through Naples's old streets, took trips to Capri, and viewed the beautiful lads and girls of Sorrento dancing the tarantella on lovely summer evenings. But something foreign intruded into their intended work together. Both wooed the same young girl; each wanted to introduce her to their own individual ideas and lifestyles. However, it was not clear that at that stage, they actually had become rivals in love.

Rée loved and the love was returned. However, at the terrible hour when Nietzsche told him that he wanted to make the young girl his wife, Rée immediately knew what sacrifice he would have to make, without anybody knowing. He turned into Nietzsche's advocate and (although this caused him much self-torment) wooed her for him.

He said to the seventeen-year-old young woman, "To be Nietzsche's consort is better than to be the consort of a king." But she answered, "He is the most honorable, but I cannot love him as a man."

Were Rée a coarser man, his way would have been open, but for him it was locked shut. Had he given in to his own feelings—which touched his heart in a thousand ways—he would have considered himself a traitor to his friendship, by turning his friend's defeat into his own personal triumph. When such knotty problems confuse friends on a lonely island, they can be solved only through separation and flight.

Because Rée proudly overcame himself and withdrew, Nietzsche became more unapproachable and colder. But there still were free, cheery hours during which the two philosophers vaulted over all human suffering and passion, into the world of the spirit that they had built together.

It was not a question of masculine jealousy in the common sense that came between them. Nietzsche's work and nature were characterized by vulnerable pride that easily gave way to frosty arrogance. Every harmless gathering, every lapse into silence, every prejudice in his presence, every merry laugh that did not include this sick, suffering man, was easily misinterpreted as a slight on his dignity. This was, after all, the one and only time that he thought of courtship, when as a man he was attracted to a woman, and he was wounded at his most sensitive spot.

When a man is not secure in his masculinity, he begins to withdraw into a male-dominated society: where we are "human, all too human," we become inhuman. Rée understood this but still felt inferior to Nietzsche's more austere and chaste approach. Had they been able to confide in one another, this ridiculous game would not have degenerated into tragedy, but would have dissolved into liberating laughter. But they hardened their hearts and became caught up in a vortex of sensitivities, so that in the gray hours one suspected, the other triumphed laughingly or went into an insulted huff because his devotedness and friendship were so underestimated.

Rée was the first to see that their friendship was irreparably damaged. He broke free and traveled off without any explanation, thereby saving their mutual relationship, which had from then on to become formal and businesslike. They still exchanged friendly letters but their young dreams faded; each found himself alone once more, and the letter exchange gradually stopped.

During the Italian winter of 1875–1876, they had many discussions about the natural sciences. Both dreamed of an earthbound biological ethic that would nourish a well-bred, well-born new kind of Übermensch.[22] Today [1930] a generation later, it is easy to overlook what Friedrich Nietzsche's *Thus Spoke Zarathustra* owed to his encounter with Paul Rée. Apart from many expressions and figures of speech, the decisive proof comes from the unromantic turning aside to the instinctual powers behind the mind and the spiritual otherworldliness of man. The entire present-day science of psychology and psychoanalysis is based upon the discussions between Rée and Nietzsche. Not a single idea has been added to them.[23]

The decisive issue to arise out of these conversations was not Nietzsche's turn toward psychology, but rather his courage to dictate new future values.

I doubt whether Nietzsche would have progressed to his newly designed re-evaluation of all values had he not met Rée. The essence of Rée's teaching, which saved him from descent into the infertile field of "soul chemistry," was his conviction of the positing nature of all evaluations and doubt regarding the existence of natural law and notion of any *inherent* ethic.

This was the germ that passed on to Nietzsche. He held onto that little piece of rope and climbed onto the glacier that Rée saw but could not surmount

In their best days, they dreamed of traveling together. They wanted to become students and start from the beginning again, studying natural sciences for ten years in Munich or Berlin. But Nietzsche's deteriorating health put an end to such plans and drove him into lonely exile. Rée, the apparently happier one, realized his study plans.

Soon after his separation from Nietzsche around 1880, Rée attempted to study philosophy in Berlin or Jena. The insights he gained in these busy philosophical workshops disgusted him completely. He dabbled in natural sciences in several small universities and, between 1875 and 1885, produced a few works. He published nothing else, but rather tried to buy up and destroy all copies of his books. While Nietzsche's overpowering works appeared in print during 1880 and 1890, Rée studied ceaselessly, and the more he learned the more silent he became. In his thirty-seventh year he decided to change from natural sciences to medicine and, in 1890, passed all three medical examinations in Berlin. That same year his elder brother, whom he loved, took over running the large landed castle estate of Stibbe in West Prussia. Rée decided to go to Stibbe and work there as a physician. During ten years as physician in the solitude of the West Prussian countryside, Rée became honored by the local farmers as a saintly figure. He led a modest, monkish life, restless but always obliging. He remained within the boundaries of his estate, burning the midnight oil night after night. Stibbe was sold in 1900, and the brothers left for Berlin. Rée couldn't decide to abandon his beloved solitude and chose to settle in the Engadine, a Swiss valley that he loved very much. He chose the town of Celerina, a mountain village near Saint Moritz. At the same time, August 1900, Nietzsche's night of madness ended in his death.

Rée lived strictly and harshly in Zarathustra's lonely mountain world. He devoted himself to the local farmers, who idolized him, but he must have felt like a foreigner from another planet. He had no more need to surround himself with people of his social class and no more desire or ambition to work or participate in the cultural sector. He wanted nothing to do with his earlier writings and prefaced the few short manuscripts in his estate with a single sentence: "My early writings are immature juvenile works."

When a man chooses solitude, he retains the geniuses of his people, its books, language, images, sculptural and musical creations, its singers' songs, the great men and women of its history, and its beloved dead.

In contrast, the Jew has only geniuses whom his soul does not really know. Even if his forefathers came, would he understand them? An isolated soul flees to the false pride of his record and into the competition of social will to legitimacy. If the flight succeeds, society devours him; if it does not, he devours himself.

Paul Rée self-destructed.

Only a happy society can provide home and hearth to a great man, because it loves and trusts him and is happy to carry him aloft as a beautiful expression of its collective soul.

Where there is no nation, but rather an anarchical society of dissociated individuals with secondhand memory and common social goals, a great and deep thinker never is received with joy. They are envied, because each wants to outdo the other in everything of value. Unfree people do not love each other. They may be associated with an act or misdeed but are incapable of love.

In the solitude of the Engadine Mountains, the image of his dear friend often rose up before him. That man had also trodden these paths. Here was the southern sea that enticed Nietzsche into the nameless, the horizon that gave him form and limits, the mistral that sang to him of freedom. He too was lonely here and went into decline. But it was a different loneliness and a different decline: he was reborn in national history, legends about his personality grew, and myths wove into his very being. Was he human, all too human?

Chosen by his people and his age, he became deified. It made no difference whether he was mortal or ill, angry or cold, or remained as he was. The mortality of a legendary individual is not verifiable.

Can this happen with a Jew? It happened once before with Jesus and again (more dimly) with Spinoza. He can represent the spirit, an all-human, impersonal, cold apotheosis. He can become a Trotsky but never a Lenin, not the blood and soil of the homeland.[24]

Every time a genius rises up from the German people—Goethe or Schopenhauer, Hebbel or Wagner, Hölderlin or Stefan George—he has his bodyguard of important Jews who, Homer-like, have sung his praises and, transfigured him.[25] Jews always were the first to recognize, love, and elevate such figures, but no matter how noble, they can never be authentic *Volk* heroes.[26] That is the reason for their shrill tone, harsh colorfulness, exaggerated humor, and youthless eyes.

A Jews knows that he can become torchbearer and serve as advocate and guide. He can become the chancellor,[27] broker, manager of the German state, can be heard wherever there is a need to find words to explain intercultural difficulties, the suffering of the many, or cries for help by outcasts and aggrieved. But no matter how German they may be, they never can become the idol, a simple lover or beloved, of the German people. Because Jews did not grow out of the German bosom or heart, their fate is to serve, illuminate, purify, guard, and surrender to the foreign. My brother the enemy always will be the one to gain glory.

Paul Rée tried to be a friend of the great—this was his path and his destiny, he could do no other. But his love was rejected and he was needlessly frozen out. Understandably, the lonely man became embittered.

His refined self-discipline prevented his outbreaks of bitterness from becoming public. He never demeaned himself by shaking Nietzsche's crown, although his blood was used in forging the crown with which the other was crowned, needed and then forgotten.

Only through a posthumous indiscretion was a letter, written by Rée to a scholar who dedicated a book about Nietzschean philosophy to Rée, published. His judgment in the letter resembled that of all Nietzsche's friends and relatives. The comedy of fame began only when history was replaced by myth—better said when myth *became* history. It must be remembered that, in 1890, Nietzsche was presented as a student demonstration of paralysis in the clinic of Professor Binswanger in Jena (assistant physician Professor Theodor Ziehen).[28] In 1890 the German Rembrandt-scholar Julius Langbehn still dreamed of taking Nietzsche and looking after him.[29] Between 1890 and 1900 all Nietzsche's friends—Overbeck, Deussen, Rohde, Burckhardt—withdrew into the impregnable fortress called "science."[30] It was the same story: powerful stylist, superior poet, ingenious writer, but incapable of *science*. Someone whose exaggerated thoughts become European sensations, well received by some, considered less romantic or more austere by others. A controversial figure who *needed* friends now but had them only when he didn't need them. Paul Rée's opinion of Nietzsche did not differ from that of others. According to one of the bitterest opinions, Schopenhauer was a charlatan; Nietzsche was a philosopher who wrote like a charlatan.

Out of thoughts for which they had both given their heart's blood, Nietzsche's solitude gave rise to great fantasies, exciting prophecies, and apocalyptic visions of a new generation. In Rée's solitude these were stunted into dwarf wood: only 211 paragraphs showing the sober clarity of strong judgment and the dreary glaciation of his disenchanted soul.

On 28 October 1901 Rée set off on a hiking trip in the mountains. A worker found his shattered body at the foot of a glacier.

Notes

1. Paul Rée (1849–1901), German author and philosopher.
2. *Lessing refers to his inability to find a photo of Rée.*
3. Ferdinand Tönnies (1855–1936), German sociologist, economist, and philosopher.
4. Arthur Schopenhauer (1788–1860), German philosopher, best known for his work *Die Welt als Wille und Vorstellung* (Will and Representation) (Leipzig: F. A. Brockhaus, 1819).
5. The Battle of Gravelotte on 18 August 1870 was the largest battle of the Franco-Prussian War (19 July 1870 to 28 January 1871).

6. John Stuart Mill (1806–1873), British philosopher and economist; Francis Bacon (1561–1626), English philosopher and political figure.
7. Johann Jakob Bachofen (1815–1887), Swiss classicist and professor of law; Jakob Burckhardt (1818–1897), Swiss historian who was a founding figure in the field of cultural history. The interests of these scholars did not converge, sensu stricto.
8. Nietzsche later broke with Wagner (1813–1883), German composer, theater director, and polemicist, because, among other reasons, Wagner the antisemite objected to his friendship with Rée. "Nietzsche contra Wagner," written in Nietzsche's last year of lucidity (1888–1889), describes why he parted ways with his onetime idol and friend, attacking Wagner's religious views and philosophy.
9. Rée's friendship with Nietzsche disintegrated in late autumn 1882 due to divergence in their respective thinking and complications from their mutual involvement with Lou Salomé (see note 21).
10. In January 1889, Nietzsche suffered a mental breakdown. He was committed and died in an asylum. The cause of his insanity is generally given as tertiary syphilis, but this has not been convincingly proved. Rée died by falling into a gorge while hiking in the Swiss Alps. It is unclear whether this was due to an accident or suicide.
11. This is strictly speaking not true. Their friendship finally ended in 1882.
12. Lou Salomé.
13. Sigmund Freud (1856–1939), Austrian neurologist and founder of psychoanalysis; Alfred Adler (1870–1937), Austrian physician, psychotherapist, and founder of the school of individual psychology; Johann Friedrich Herbart (1776–1841), German scholar who was among the first to treat pedagogy as an area of intellectual inquiry; Theodor Lipps (1851–1914), German aesthetic philosopher, much admired by Freud. Both Freud and Adler were Jewish.
14. *A detailed critique of the logical and psychological advantages of so-called psychoanalysis and individual psychology can be found in* Europa und Asien, *5th edition, chapters 8 and 9.*
15. Here, the soul represents primary "living energy," which is immortal and eternal.
16. See note 13. From 1921 onward, Adler was a frequent lecturer in the United States during that decade and emigrated in the early 1930s. Lessing had a low opinion of individual psychoanalysis.
17. *Kesselstein.*
18. The first Bayreuth Festival, inaugurated 13 August 1876.
19. Malwida von Meysenbug (1816–1903), German writer, friend of Nietzsche, Wagner, and Romain Rolland.
20. *Parsifal* was Wagner's last opera. Torquato Tasso (1544–1595) was born in Sorrento.
21. Lou Andreas-Salomé (1861–1937), Russian-born psychoanalyst, writer, and world traveler.
22. Nietzsche's Übermensch is someone who overcomes himself, not others. His philosophy was perverted by the National Socialists.

23. The translator is not sufficiently qualified to comment on this point.
24. Baruch (Benedict) Spinoza (1632–1677), Dutch philosopher of Sephardi extraction. An early Enlightenment thinker who championed rationalism; Lev Davidovich Bronshtein (Trotsky) (1879–1940), Soviet revolutionary, Marxist theorist, and politician; Vladimir Ilyich Ulyanov (Lenin) (1870–1924), founder of modern communism.
25. Johann Wolfgang von Goethe (1749–1832), German writer, statesman, and scientist; Christian Friedrich Hebbel (1813–1863), German poet and dramatist; Friedrich Hölderlin (1770–1843), German romantic poet and philosopher; Stefan George (1868–1933), German poet and translator.
26. The words *Volk* and its derivative adjective *völkisch* are untranslatable in English. They denote exclusionary nationality. Jews were not part of the *Volk*.
27. This would have been possible only during the fifteen years of the Weimar Republic. Hugo Preuss (1860–1925), a German Jewish politician, wrote the first draft of the constitution that would come into effect in 1919. National Socialists referred to the Weimar Republic as the *Judenrepublik*.
28. Lessing means dementia paralytica (tertiary syphilis), although it is by no means certain that this was the cause of Nietzsche's insanity. The Wassermann test for syphilis was developed in 1906, six years after Nietzsche's death; Otto Binswanger (1852–1929), Swiss psychiatrist and neurologist; Theodor Ziehen (1862–1950), German neurologist and psychiatrist.
29. Julius Langbehn (1851–1907), German philosopher and art historian. His first book (published anonymously), *Rembrandt als Erzieher* (*Rembrandt as Educator*), published in 1890, was focused on initiating German cultural reform.
30. Franz Overbeck (1837–1905), German Protestant theologian; Paul Deussen (1845–1919), German Indologist and philosopher; Erwin Rohde (1845–1898), a leading German classicist.

Otto Weininger

On 4 October 1903, the 23-year-old philosophy student Otto Weininger shot himself to death in the Vienna Schwarzspaniergasse, in the room where Beethoven died.[1] How can we explain this?

A few months earlier, a powerful body of thought was published by Wilhelm Baumüller Verlag, based upon Weininger's doctoral thesis supervised by philosophy professors Friedrich Jodl and Laurenz Müllner.[2] It was entitled *Geschlecht und Charakter* [*Sex and Character*] and contained original research on the relationship of the elemental to the spiritual. The elemental was defined as "female-motherly," the spiritual as the "male-creative" sides of existence. Woman and man are thus navel and brain, or root and treetop, balanced against one another.

The success of this viscerally moving book was astonishing. The most significant thinkers of the time—Ernst Mach, Georg Simmel, Henri Bergson, Fritz Mauthner, Alois Höfler—read the book and began to dispute Weininger's astute thoughts in lectures and rebuttal publications.[3] Dissent outweighed agreement, but everyone agreed that this 23-year-old student was a genius.

The young man became an overnight sensation and seemed destined for greatness.

A dumbfounded world greeted the news that this young man had ripped the laurel from his brow, throwing his life away in the same room where Beethoven had breathed his last. Weininger had done the same as 37-year-old Philipp Mainländer, who hanged himself soon after publication of the first volume of his magnum opus *Die Philosophie der Erlösung* [*The Philosophy of Redemption*].[4]

During the generation that has passed since Weininger's suicide, many books have been written about him and his philosophy, correcting and improving his work. One cannot blame his friends—Emil Lucka, Hermann Swoboda, Oskar Ewald, and Moritz Rappaport[5]—for feeling forced, in face of the many wise diagnoses of oracular physicians and alienists,[6] to justify Weininger's doctrine. In truth, what is this doctrine if not a great natural game of morbid extravagance and brutal arbitrariness?

I mean the crude and rude doctrine of Judaism.

We begin from this vantage point because therein lies the key to the terrible destiny of tragic self-hatred.

Otto Weininger was a Jew. No child spat on his mother's womb or cursed her blood more than this young Jewish Oedipus.[7] His opposition to Jews and Judaism differed from all previous historical antagonism. We learn with a mixture of amazement and revulsion that *everything* is possible for the evil eye and that opposing concepts, which differ completely from one another, can be equally serviceable, provided the evil eye wills it so.

Important men have derived their prejudice against "Judaism" and "semitism" from a robust sense of life, from their German blood and German nature. For them Jews and the Jewish God were something sinister that appeared pale and abstract, diabolically bloodless, a cold logician, jealous poisoner, a bleak God of wrath, a paralyzing moralist. "Jahvism, jehovism, munism, monotheism, spiritualism, criticism, idealism, rationalism" were the slogans of the day for which the somber people were blamed. In any event, the God of anger and bile was the enemy and murderer of the lovely world of Greek gods[8] and Germania's lost wonders. Jehovah was opposed as the "destroyer of *form*." The logical opponents of the Jews always fought Christianity at the same time, because they saw in Jewish Christianity the secret instrument of division in soul and body and the destruction of both by that spirit.

An otherworldly Moloch[9] had forced itself between sensuality and sentiment in order to set body and idea against love and reason and thereby incurably corrupt them both.

"The body is thereby de-deified, the magic of nature has become incomprehensible. Dionysus is dead. The great god Pan is dead. The Magna Mater is drowned. Siegfried is slain. Baldur is murdered!"[10] So the lamentation went.

Who was victorious?

The unnameable God of fog and desert, revealed in dialectics, sophistry, and Talmudic hairsplitting, doctrine and word. That is the world of the Jews.

Most adversaries of the Jews still seize on these age-old issues. But a second, albeit smaller, group of no less significant thinkers—who in the pure and strict former sense must themselves be called Jews—base their aversion on an exactly opposite premise. Martin Luther accused the Jews of not becoming "sons of God," but remaining "children of the earth." "In their shroud and coffin, they still turn *earthwards* and pray to the sun and stars." The blind, rationalistic philosopher Eugen Dühring left countless similar statements: "The Jew is incapable of the factual and real because, as an Oriental, he is a teller of tales, who lives caught up in images and dreams, and thinks in parables. The Jew is a mythmaker. By comparison, the Nordic man, under the more austere and sober heavens, must fight this immoderate people with logic. We must counterbalance their religionist fables with a dose of healthy positivism."[11]

So, depending on one's point of view, materialism and realism could either be a *Jewish* Weltanschauung or a bulwark against "Jewish mythmaking fantasies." In a similar way, socialism and bolshevism, even capitalism could be called "Jewish." Maybe today's progress, radicalism, and revolution could be tomorrow's stalemate, stagnation, and reaction. Everything depends on the opinion of the moment. Either way, the Jews are responsible for everything.

Where does Otto Weininger's framework fit in? Where does his astonishing doctrine belong, that the Jewish essence is nothing but "amoral female lust, that drags down the spiritual father-God into indolent matter"?

Never have root and branch been more at odds. We must dig down deep, to find the diseased spot in the bone marrow.

In an attempt to divide peoples into the limited and the infinite, into peoples of statuary art and people of music, I would like to place the Jewish (and also by the way the German) people in the pathos of the infinite and rhythmic pulses of musicality, rather than the sculptural security of finite limits. This is made clear when we study the influence of Jews on mathematics.

About a generation ago, at about the same time that Weininger's work appeared, I published an essay on the psychology of mathematics. In this treatise, I tried to show that the then-robust geometrization of physics, arithmetization of geometry, and the then-recently advanced "theory of special relativity"[12] were closely connected to the Jewish soul. All were rapidly gaining scientific momentum, underlying the importance of this issue.

What is the origin of the entire body of Western logic, from Aristotle to Kant, which consistently states the same empty, self-evident fact?

It all originates from an acknowledgment of limitation! A limitation of what was thought once as set creed and accepted as a given.

One would like to say that logic was always a demand for *unity*. It was always the manifestation of what Aristotle called "a = a," his law of identity.[13]

But when thinkers of the Christian millennia made the irrational and imaginary into definitive sciences, destruction of logic and destruction of the cosmos *as a cosmos* began. Because the irrational and imaginary are not comprehensible as a unit. The infinite cannot end, the immeasurable cannot be defined. Even the proposition of identity, and with it reasoning, become futile as soon as finiteness and limitation of everything previously considered objective and tangible are disregarded. Is it not perhaps by means of its cosmos that mankind perceives and creates, sustains and maintains itself? Does the human race not disappear as a *living* entity when thought destroys the finite world?

In Plato's "Theaetetus,"[14] one finds the wonderful hymn to the "finiteness of everything perfect." According to Plato, beings in their essence cannot be infinite, because infinity is imperfect. Were the substance of life infinite, it could have neither form nor beauty. "Everything beautiful demonstrates the mystery of boundedness, because form thrives in all life's depths."

This doctrine of beautiful life as a *finite form* is the exact opposite of Spinoza's doctrine of transcendence, which prohibits the naming of life's substance as simply being, because the number of "God's" attributes are *infinite*, and "any limitation would be a denial."

And yet Plato, who was only able to see the divine in forms, dissolved the Greek form!

And Spinoza, who was only able to conceive of God as an impersonal being beyond space and time, imprisoned nature, forcing it into mathematical form![15]

Could it be coincidence that dissolution of the cosmos into the impersonal in favor of absolute mathematical norms has been mainly the acts of logicians of Jewish extraction?

The growth of non-Euclidean geometry has necessitated new fields of science: doctrines of numbers, quanta, set theory, dissolution of infinity-linked paradoxes, and the relativization of the last concreteness and clarity, all of these in favor of absolute calculus. And all these have been the work of Jewish brains such as Georg Cantor, Alfred Fränkel, Alfred Pringsheim, Arthur Schönfliess, Felix Hausdorff, Ludwig Kronecker, Alfred Sommerfeld, until finally A. A. Michelson, M. Minkowski, and A. Einstein forced the surmounting of the doctrines of Aristotle, Euclid, Newton, and Kant.[16]

It is as if this cohort had conspired to drive away the last poor remnant of manifest form, and steal away the last miserable small pieces of existence, to which man still can cling in the *tohu vavohu*[17] of "that which cannot be finished."

Thus, not only the "measurable world of space and time" faded away. But this happened as well to the process of "becoming":[18] fluidity, succession as a linear continuity, directedness, the beginning and the end.

Nothing remained out of the ashes of a world of manifest content except the will to *merit*.

In the late days of the Platonic school, there arose a concept that, even at that time, announced the dawn of a gray formless world: *apeirotaraxie* (shuddering in the face of immensity).

Is it not natural that life saved itself by withdrawing into its shell, behind armor and dam?

Should spellbound, ecstatic survivors (lured out with the greatest ease) not be the most afraid and on the greatest lookout for their own safety against flood and flame, whether in tower or prison?

In the midst of the thundering crash of waves and foaming whirlpools, a castle stands on age-old granite rock and opposes the boundless elements with a defensive *wall*.

Humanity has built its castle *logos*[19] on the rock of "spirit" and takes its stand against primeval confusion and chaos.

This castle has a multistoried superstructure, called *ethos*.[20] From its peak one can view the immeasurable sea, and over it the heavens and the stars by which man steers.

Our souls, hatchling birds of passage,[21] press on across the sea, but return after each journey to their secure *cages*—our anxiety, our strength, our yearning and renunciation. We forget that the world's all title page. The castle on the rock we call our *eternity*, and wrongly believe that the *spiritual life* is our true life ... Everyone who knew the young Otto Weininger relate that he was an open-minded, very receptive child. The fragrance of jasmine, the blossoming apple tree, the shimmering of a butterfly, could dazzle his tender soul. Faraway mountains were a promise of happiness, drifting clouds an adventure, and a moss rose bush a blissful rapture. Every sense was delicate, every nerve easily irritated. The death of a gnat easily could become a "problem."

With profound sympathy, this youth felt all life as if it were his own, and he drifted elfin-like through countryside and season, always in danger of lapsing into visions.

The boy grew into a young man and the young man became a poet, long before he became a thinker. His curiosity and hunger for life were limitless. His ability to interrelate and sense the *essence*[22] of everything made self-limiting form—something easily grasped by poorer and more rigid souls—the *most difficult* concept for him to understand.

For a long time it seemed impossible for him to decide on a profession—that bourgeois backbone of life—because no one thing gripped him sufficiently. There was nothing that he wouldn't have wanted to learn or experience.

His nature placed him in lasting danger of splitting himself into pieces, and his sole encompassing motivation became his single great passion: to raise himself above the many millions of creations, and find the common denominator for the searing abundance of his feelings.

That way leads to philosophy.

He never had been close to anyone. He was young, and every bird sang of wanderlust. This feeling can bring any young man to the edge of despair. So many unvisited countries that he would never see, hands that he would never shake, brows that he would never kiss.

Although he had a warm and faithful soul, it would have taken a firm decision to find himself.

He was the plaything of every breeze. For this reason his "moral character" was greater and more admirable than all life's gifts and riches.

Why should we be surprised then that Weininger fearfully locked himself up in the uppermost chamber "ethos" in the castle of "logos"? There he sat, a voluntary prisoner, using his powerful mental capacity to prove to himself that life in this glorious ivory tower was the only one worth living.

No one may slander his young idealism. It was an emergency exit, but no lie. It was the only truth he knew.

A memory from my own childhood appears before me. In the garden and forest, such a terrifying feeling gripped me (similar to what psychiatrists call "absences") that I had to slip into strange apprehensions. A terrible doubt arose: "Am I really here?" With my fingers I gladly grabbed the first available object I saw, in order that the sensation of resistance would affirm my existence.

I still remember the place and time when my companion of those days spoke of a different anxiety, one quite the opposite of my own: when he stood in front of a mirror at dusk, the feeling gripped him that his image might solidify and congeal in the glass, escape, and confront him as a solidified doppelgänger.

These are the two poles through which we steer as long as we live and breathe! On one side we always run the risk of becoming sponges, on the other of freezing into statues. The one danger leads to terror of the infinite, the other to the fear of the finite.

Otto Weininger had a Heraclitean nature that strove for posture and form.[23] The Protean[24] nature of his unfulfilled character provided a basis for the tragedy of his self-hate. But something else had to be added. Something insoluble and problematic: his birth as a Jew, but detached from Judaism.

No man has ever freed himself from the compulsion of his blood. No categorical imperative has ever eclipsed the voice of his blood.[25]

Weininger called everything that he was, and passionately felt, *Jewish*.[26]

At no other point is man more inextricably bound to destiny and eternity than by his sex. Because Weininger's agitated soul was masculine, and he regarded woman as a complement and antithesis that he could not do without, he called everything that both attracted and at the same time frightened him *feminine*.

Woman and Jew were therefore two different names for the *natural ground* that he both feared and avoided.

The course of study on which this still immature young man entered filled him with mental prerequisites that required a fulfilled, long life of philosophical thought if they were to be overcome and removed.

Western philosophy, from Descartes[27] to Kant, always has proceeded from the primal phenomenon of *consciousness*. It never occurred to them that consciousness and the entire content of consciousness (everything that we have ever called reality) could have emerged as *one* creative possibility from the vital element of life, out of millions of other possibilities. No! The conscious world was the *absolute* world!

"What is conscious is alive!"

As if livings things *could become* conscious!

"Life has existence, and the right to prove existence, as a thinking or conceived living thing."

And so, the poles were wrong: consciousness, logos, spirit became *real* life, and the sustaining element gained the character of a dark spiritual apostasy and its divine purity.

Weininger immersed himself in scholastics. He read Hegel[28] and Kant and fell under the spell of mathematics and phenomenology. The more he read the deeper he felt about the monstrous historical and moral arrogance of the judgmental personality who perceives his chthonic[29] underworlds and background worlds[30] as a disgraceful humiliation.

This is the conceit about which Kant said, "The mind creates nature," and which Hegel mocked, "If nature does not agree with reason, the worse for nature."

Weininger hated his Jewish blood. He hated women and the voice of the earth-spirit, from the moment sexual awakening began to make him uneasy.

In his surviving papers, no words crop up more than "crime" and "criminal."

His entire philosophy is based on brooding about the twin problems of sin and redemption, making it entirely Christian in its outlook. In Hindu, Vedic, and Buddhist philosophy, love stands in the center of all reasoning, encapsulated in *tat tvam asi*.[31] By contrast, the dark decline of man, and his inevitable guilt, are the central experience of Christianity. How can man be redeemed if he is born with original sin?

"Redemption" can come only from the sublimation of all human into the realm of the purely spiritual.[32]

Perfect reason, perfect morality—that would really be the end! . . .

Kant's "two world theory"[33] was set ablaze by this young philosopher.

He saw everything through the optics of an intellectual world.

The Bible, Veda, Buddha, Plato . . . everything proclaimed to him the glory of life completely different from a life in *this* world.

However, in a world dominated by indebtedness and self-destruction, the world turns gray and a monastic tendency grows, to sour the enticing *Frau Welt*.[34]

Frau Welt is beautiful, and all beauty needs love.

Weininger was afraid to succumb to this beauty and tried to abstain from it through disgust. For him, no term of abuse was sufficiently harsh enough in reviling the beautiful life.

The more beauty beckoned, the more horribly he painted its fall, and his own descent into horror and disgrace.

To sink into the womb of *Frau Welt* would have meant loss of his laboriously won self and philosophical repose.

Every self-destructive person revels in exaggeration. The sense of guilt of one who is ethically and morally sick is never proportionate to the act of remorse.

All this self-flagellation, for nothing!

Even as an old man, Augustine anathemized himself because he remembered that, as a boy, he stole a neighbor's apples.[35]

Sören Kierkegaard became a deep-thinking philosopher of regret, out of torment from his supposed fault for returning the engagement ring to his intended, having done so because of melancholy.[36]

Origenes atoned for an episode of self-abuse [masturbation] by castrating himself.[37]

Where nature turns against itself, man becomes defenseless, and nothing is simpler than to sacrifice the defenseless.

An ethically and morally obsessed person is, at a moment's notice, ready to sacrifice everything he has, including himself, to be able to *insist on* himself and his own demands.

If the same ethically and morally diseased person also perceives a feeling of self-guilt, then no responsibility is needed even for the most gruesomely irresponsible acts.

There are always malefactors—friends, loved ones—ready to make the first sacrificial cut. They kiss his hands and celebrate the slaughter. They do not think they have done anything wrong, bless themselves, and shrug their shoulders. "The wolf devours those who make themselves lambs."

But he learns (hopefully not too late) that it is more important to be a strong, courageous predator than to be a saint in this world.

Man is like a bird that may rise into the pure ether for a few moments, but cannot remain aloft and make its home there lifelong.

The more it wants to force its being into the empty air, the more it will fall to earth. The momentum of its wings will tiredly abate, and it will rise up lower and less often.

The spirit hobbles itself with execrable vows. It swears never to succumb to the alluring torch dances of figures. But a faraway odor, a singing laugh, a strand of blonde hair, a soft glance, quashes his oath.

He is gripped by the sacred yearning of night moths that during the hours of their procreation are seized by something transcendental, that forces them to wander into the light, because all life must die in order to be renewed. As Goethe wrote:

> Tell this to no one but the wise,
> for the masses will only ridicule it.
> I would praise the living thing
> that yearns for death in the flames.[38]

A general stands before a fortress on an impregnable rock, one that no one yet has taken by storm. He takes the ultimate risk, sending his daughter into the fortress and swears, "Tomorrow I'll fetch you back, or we'll both die."

He throws the palladium,[39] without which he cannot live, into the enemy's midst and jumps into battle in order to save it.

He burns his boats behind him and leaps over the wall. Now there is no turning back.

Otto Weininger, 23-year-old Jewish philosophy student, promised himself and the world an insurmountable doctrine of morality. He had to both create and destroy himself with this proud work, and thereby destroyed his innate self, Pascal's *moi haïssable*.[40] Born into light, he retained his innate self, Kant's "intelligible autonomous personality."[41]

He preferred to die rather than sink back from the heights he had reached into the banal community that restricts us all.

Then came success.

There is nothing more soul-destructive than success.

Europe's fame astonished the poor Jewish student. Honors, travel, money, power, proud women—never had *Frau Welt* assailed a man more enticingly. This young man had regarded himself as life's stepchild; now life entered his tower of famine and called him "my beloved."

The poor young man had a good heart and didn't wish to preach water while he secretly drank life's wine.

He practiced exactly what he preached.

His anxiety neurosis whispered that he was weaker than his message. He knew that he had set down firm rules of engagement that his blood could not withstand. He was seized by the obsession of criminality. And there was only one crime: to be untrue to himself.

Were he to break his own oath before the thousands who now looked on him as the young heir to the throne of German philosophy he would be *untrue to himself*, have to creep shamefully into a dark corner, and die worse than the worst animal. Otto Weininger said to his friends, parents, and teachers, "I am a criminal." While his praises resounded, he crept into churches or the Vienna woods, groaning, "I stand condemned of a crime."

What did this harmless young man want? How could this gentle boy, who couldn't harm a fly, feel like the guiltiest of the guilty?

Crimes stared out at him wherever he looked: from the eyes of flowers, the gaze of animals, even from crystal and stone. Joyful street colors, implements and fabrics in shop windows, paintings, the seductive magic of women, children's grace, every form of beauty accused him of being a criminal accomplice.

In the eyes of dogs he saw the tormented soul of humanity, half humanized, half still imprisoned in a wolf's heart and incapable of redemption. In the eyes of horses he saw the madness of a creation bred and transformed by man, bewildered by its natural power, and incapable or disdainful of using it. In the miraculous birth of the deep ocean—about which Goethe uttered the immortal words "How beautiful every living thing is, how true, how simple, how complete in itself"—Weininger's diseased, terrified mind saw the incarnation of greedy, torturing, blood-sucking, clawing, murderous rage. Sensuality became murder, and love guilt. What we call a miracle, he called a crime. The unheard of, the unknowable, the irrational, life itself—all were crimes.

The humiliating knowledge that we have not lived up to our potential does not always lead to remorse and disintegration. It also can lead to megalomania and hubris.

We all have the tendency to exaggerate demands that we ourselves cannot easily fulfill. So exaggerated that no one can fulfill them, we thereby spare ourselves many failures.

The cleverest foxes aren't the ones who declare the high-hanging grapes to be sour, but those who call them holy and untouchable. Every clever fox says, "We are all born sinners."[42] The deeper in the dust it sees its own soul, the more the spiritual being in us feels itself elevated above everything earthly,

Which psychologist has ever resolved the simultaneous problems of darkness and humility, inviolability and melancholy?

Otto Weininger was far too self-confident. His intellectual arrogance grew out of an overabundance of moral ideals, whose God-sent herald and disciple he felt himself to be. Although the vessel was made of bad clay, it nevertheless contained the oil without which no king can be anointed.

That is how he got lost. In order not to have to return, he broke his own mold.

Did any benefit bloom out of all this?

He fled once more to Beethoven's great heart. The *Eroica* symphony, that promethean hymn of the fate of the earthly bringer of light, told him what could not be expressed in words: "He who beholds the face of God dies."[43]

We think of him like Goethe's Euphorion, hardly born but destined for heroism, who boldly climbed the rock and tried to fly but failed and was smashed to pieces.[44] The words recited on Nietzsche's grave also apply to him:

> You put the dearest part of you to death
> Then reached for it anew with trembling hands
> And cries of pain as loneliness closed in.
> He came too late, the one who begging warned,
> "There is no way across those icy boulders
> Where fearsome birds await—the time is now:
> To step into the circle drawn by love," ...
> Whenever then that stern and tortured voice
> Rings out like praise into the azure night
> And limpid flood—lament, "This new soul
> Should have sung, but chose to speak instead."[45]

Notes

1. Otto Weininger (1880–1903), Austro-Hungarian philosopher.
2. Friedrich Jodl (1849–1914), German philosopher and psychologist, one of the most significant representatives of German positivism; Laurenz Müllner (1848–1911), Austrian philosopher and theologian.
3. Ernst Mach (1838–1916), physicist and philosopher of science; Georg Simmel (1858–1918), German neo-Kantian sociologist, philosopher, and critic; Henri-Louis Bergson (1859–1941), key thinker in the continental philosophical tradition in the first half of the twentieth century; Fritz Mauthner

(1849–1923), Austro-Hungarian novelist, critic, and philosopher of skepticism; Alois Höfler (1853–1928), Austrian educationalist and philosopher.
4. Philipp Mainländer (1841–1876), German poet and philosopher. According to Lessing, his central work *Die Philosophie der Erlösung* (*The Philosophy of Redemption*) was "perhaps the most radical system of pessimism known to philosophical literature."
5. Emil Lucka (1877–1941), Austrian writer; Hermann Swoboda (1873–1963), professor of law and philosophy; Oskar Ewald (1881–1940), Hungarian-Austrian philosopher; Moritz Rappaport (1808–1880), Austrian physician, journalist, and writer.
6. At the time of writing, psychiatry, as we now know it, did not yet exist.
7. Mythical king of Thebes who accidentally fulfilled a prophecy that he would end up killing his father and marrying his mother,
8. *Die Götter Griechenlands* is a 1788 poem by the German poet, philosopher, physician, historian, and playwright Friedrich von Schiller (1759–1805).
9. Biblical name of a Canaanite god associated with child sacrifice, through fire or war.
10. Mythological images. Dionysus: Olympian god of wine, vegetation, pleasure, festivity, madness, and wild frenzy; Pan: god of the wild, shepherds and flocks, nature of mountain wilds, rustic music, and companion of the nymphs. According to Plutarch (ca. 46–ca. 120 CE), Pan is the only Greek god who actually dies; the Magna Mater (Cybele) was an Anatolian mother goddess. Magna Mater may also refer to Isis, a goddess from the polytheistic pantheon of Egypt, or to Maia, one of the Pleiades and mother of Hermes in ancient Greek religion. Siegfried (Sigurd): hero of Germanic *myth*; Baldur: one of the most beloved of all the Norse gods, son of Odin and Frigg. When Baldur began to have ominous dreams of some grave misfortune befalling him, the fearful gods appointed Odin to discover their meaning. The blind god Höd, deceived by the evil Loki (Loge), killed Baldur by hurling mistletoe, the only thing that could hurt him. After Baldur's funeral, the giantess Thökk, probably Loki in disguise, refused to weep the tears that would release Baldur from death.
11. Eugen Karl Dühring (1833–1921), German antisemitic philosopher and economist who opposed Marxism. The statements are excerpted and summarized from Eugen Dühring, *Die Judenfrage als Racen-, Sitten- und Culturfrage. Mit einer weltgeschichtlichen Antwort* (Karlsruhe and Leipzig: H. Reuther, 1881).
12. The theory of special relativity was published by Albert Einstein (1879–1955) in 1905.
13. Aristotle (384–322 BCE), Greek philosopher and polymath.
14. The "Theaetetus" by the Athenian philosopher Plato (428/427 or 424/423–348/347 BCE) is an epistemological dialogue. Here, Socrates (ca. 470–399 BCE) and the mathematician Theaetetus (417–ca. 369 BCE) explore three different definitions of knowledge.
15. Baruch (Benedict) Spinoza (1632–1677), Dutch philosopher of Sephardi extraction. An early Enlightenment thinker who championed rationalism.
16. Georg Cantor (1845–1918), German mathematician and creator of set theory; Alfred Fränkel: probably Abraham Fränkel (1891–1965), German

Israeli mathematician; Alfred Pringsheim (1850–1941), German mathematician and arts patron; Arthur Schönflies(s) (1853–1928), German mathematician; Felix Hausdorff (1868–1942), German mathematician who was a foundational figure in modern topology; Ludwig (Leopold) Kronecker (1823–1891), German mathematician specializing in number theory and algebra; Alfred (Arnold) Sommerfeld (1868–1951), German physicist who worked on atomic and quantum physics; Albert A. Michelson (1852–1931), Polish-born American physicist; M. (Hermann) Minkowski (1864–1909), German mathematician and theoretical physicist; Euclid of Alexandria (fl. 300 BCE), founder of geometry; Sir Isaac Newton (1643–1727), English mathematician, physicist, astronomer, theologian, and author, widely recognized as one of the most influential scientists of all time; Immanuel Kant (1724–1804), influential Prussian German philosopher in the Age of Enlightenment.
17. Biblical Hebrew phrase found in the Genesis creation narrative (Genesis 1:2) that describes the condition of the earth immediately before the creation of light in Genesis 1:3.
18. *Werden*.
19. A term from a Greek word meaning opinion, reason, or discourse. It first gained prominence in Western philosophy when Heraclitus used it to refer to a basic epistemological principle.
20. A Greek word connoting a community's defining beliefs.
21. Lessing uses the word *Wandervogel*. The word was adopted by a popular movement of German youth groups from 1896 to 1933; they protested against industrialization by going to hike in the countryside and to commune with nature in the woods. Drawing influence from medieval wandering scholars, their ethos was to revive old Teutonic values, with a strong emphasis on nationalism.
22. *Wesen*.
23. Heraclitus of Ephesus (ca. 535–ca. 475 BCE), pre-Socratic Ionian philosopher, who maintained that strife and change are the natural conditions of the universe.
24. Proteus: early prophetic god of rivers and oceans, capable of assuming many forms.
25. Kant gives two forms to his categorical imperative: (1) behave in such a way that a reasonable generalization of your action to a universal rule will lead to a benefit to a generic person under this universal rule; (2) always treat others as ends and not means.
26. *Das Jüdische*.
27. René Descartes (1596–1650), French philosopher widely known for the statement "Cogito, ergo sum" (I think, therefore I am).
28. Friedrich Hegel (1770–1831), German philosopher and an important figure of German idealism. His notion of a "world-historical individual" shaped modern-day German historical thinking.
29. *Khthon* (Greek). Denotes deities or spirits of the underworld, especially in ancient Greek religion.
30. *Unterwelt* and *Hinterwelt*.
31. A Sanskrit phrase (translated variously as "Thou art that"; "that Thou art";

"that art Thou"), one of the Mahāvākyas (Grand Pronouncements) in Vedantic Sanatana Dharma.
32. Interestingly, Lessing does not state that, according to Christianity, redemption can come only from acceptance of Christ taking the sins of the world on his shoulders. Judaism argues for personal responsibility.
33. Kant argued that there are two worlds of reality, which he called the noumenal and the phenomenal worlds.
34. In medieval allegories, *Frau Welt* was a beautiful woman who embodied physical pleasure and worldly happiness. Some roughly equate the term with Mother Nature.
35. Augustine of Hippo (354–430 CE), Roman African early Christian theologian and Neoplatonic philosopher, whose writings influenced the development of the Western church and Western philosophy, and indirectly all of Western Christianity.
36. Sö(ø)ren Kierkegaard (1813–1855), Danish philosopher and theologian generally considered to be the father of existentialism.
37. Origen of Alexandria (ca. 184–ca. 253 CE), early Christian scholar, ascetic, and theologian.
38. "Selige Sehnsucht" ("Blissful Yearning") by Johann Wolfgang von Goethe (1749–1832), leading German writer, poet, statesman, and author of *Faust*.
39. Statue of Pallas; its preservation was believed to ensure the safety of Troy.
40. "Le moi est haïssable" (The I is hateful) is a dictum by the French mathematician, physicist, inventor, writer, and Catholic theologian Blaise Pascal (1623–1662) from his *Pensées* (Thoughts). The concept is sometimes translated in English as "the hateful I."
41. *Intelligible autonome Persönlichkeit.*
42. The Christian, but emphatically not the Jewish, point of view.
43. The fourth (last) movement of the *Eroica* (Third) Symphony opus 55 by Ludwig van Beethoven (1770–1827) is a set of themes and variations on the finale to his ballet *Die Geschöpfe des Prometheus (The Creatures of Prometheus)*. Prometheus defied the gods by stealing fire and giving it to humanity. The gods punished him by binding him to a rock where each day an eagle, the emblem of Zeus, was sent to eat Prometheus's liver, which then would grow back overnight to be eaten again the next day.
44. Goethe's *Faust*, part 2, act 3. Euphorion is the son of Helen and Faust, embodying a kind of synthesis of Romanticism and Classicism. He ultimately chases a radiant chorus girl into the sky, only to fall to his death.
45. Stefan George (1868–1933), German symbolist poet and translator of Dante, Shakespeare, and Baudelaire; Stefan George, "Nietzsche," in *Der Siebente Ring* (The seventh ring) (Berlin: Blätter für die Kunst, 1907), 12–13.

Arthur Trebitsch

Two school classes ahead of the brilliant Otto Weininger, in the same Schottengymnasium, another unique student, Arthur Trebitsch, was also educated.[1] As his teacher, the Jewish philosopher Wilhelm Jerusalem,[2] described him, he was an extraordinarily handsome, blond-haired, blue-eyed youth. Like the fathers of Ferdinand Lassalle[3] and Maximilian Harden [see below], his father was a wealthy silk merchant and had contributed greatly to development of the silk industry in Austria. He resigned from the Jewish community and—although his pedigree was unblemished—let his three sons grow up without any connection to the old tradition, instead filling their minds with German values.[4]

A midrash[5] relates a competition between storm and sun. "Which one of us will steal the wanderer's old coat?" The storm rattles and buffets, but the more icily it hisses and the more violently it tries to carry off the old coat, the more tightly the wanderer wraps himself in the old, salvaged garment. By contrast, all the sun needs to do is to smile calmly and shine, and the wanderer takes off his coat without being forced.

It is part of the nature of up-and-coming classes to shed the clothes of their years of service, forgetting about Judaism's profound commandment: "Remember that you were slaves in the land of Egypt."[6]

Who talks more about ideals and rights than the upscale bourgeoisie? Where else is such devotion practiced with more success and more materialism?

To understand the golem's societal power that people call "reputation" and "honor,"[7] all we need to do is make the grim comparison between certain men and a French army captain[8] who has gone down in history. The best men of his generation sacrificed themselves for Dreyfus's cause, demanding equal justice for Jews.[9] All this bourgeois patriotic Jew wanted to do was prove his loyalty to the leading men of his country and please the authorities (even if they were crooked). We saw what happened.

This type of pride in "reputation" and "societal affiliation" was prevalent in the highly respected, "good" Trebitsch family household: "We are all just as blond." "We are the best gymnasts." "We do not look Jewish at all." None of them had any idea of how tasteless it was to deny the soil that nourished their ancestors' tree for millennia.

The gist of his case history is as follows: Arthur Trebitsch, born 1879 in Vienna of a Jewish family, a talented poet, philosopher, politician, author of about twenty books and countless essays, was, until the day of his death on 26 September 1927, a virulent antisemite.

His life is an object lesson in Jewish self-hate. Since the time of Johannes Pfefferkorn[10] in the obscurantist era, there never has been a comparable case, so moving and hopeless at the same time.

A fantastic delusion germinated early in this flaxen-haired youth: that of a vast, secret Jewish conspiracy, metastasized all over the world, with plans for world domination that threatened Aryan nations predetermined to rule mankind. But he, Arthur Trebitsch, was destined to save the German *Volk* from the Jews.

In this delusion he served as sincere warrior and fellow traveler of General Erich Ludendorff and his wife, Mathilde, and of obscure National Socialist groups in whose charmed midst several Jewish antisemites such as Nikolaus Cossman and Ernst von Salomon danced their roundelays.[11]

It is an old truth that converts become zealots. Because they are unable to find explicit confirmation of nationhood, they are insecure in themselves. No purebred German could persecute a foreign word as pompously as Eduard Engel, that great Jewish guardian of purity of the German language.[12] No true German soldier could be more keenly aware of his Germanness than the German Jewish chauvinist Arnolt Bronnen.[13] Palestine's only antisemitic custodian gloried under the name Gabriel,[14] and it can be no coincidence that lists of patriotic parties in every country contain many names that denote immigration, origin outside the nation, or mixed Jewish race.

I do not mean to say that love of the German homeland and spirit is a "delusion." A Jew can certainly participate in these feelings of faith and love, even be completely absorbed in them. In ancient times, kings, heroes, and leaders almost always came from abroad. (It was often believed that they had migrated from other worlds and were almost never of "autochthonous" blood.) Men of Jewish origin such as Léon Gambetta in France, Benjamin Disraeli [Lord Beaconsfield] in England, Ludovico Manin in Italy, and Joseph Nasi in Turkey became representatives and role models of other nations.[15] Some, like Torquemada, turned into wolflike zealots of another faith.[16] The sights of a city are more meaningful seen through the eyes of foreigners than by natives, who see them every day and become blasé. National wonders are most deeply felt and incorporated into the psyche by those to whom the values and their distinctiveness still are fresh. One thinks of the biological law that microorganisms are ineffective and unnoticeable in hosts accustomed to them. By contrast, in the presence of a new foreign element, they revive and are detectable again.[17]

It is not my task in these pages to clarify the relationship between *Volk* and state—two concepts that I regard just as opposed as nature and organization. I want to state clearly that every state must be, from its very nature, *polynational*. *Racial inbreeding* within the heart and soul of the *Volk* should not be desirable or decisive unless there is a need initially to solidify an unsolidified, primitive life unit and protect it from the dangers of *random mating* (panmixia). However, when history and custom breed a good, strong race, racial mingling is not only desirable, but essential for the nation's well-being. Historical personages who best incorporate a nation's image cannot just be explained from a family tree. I remember an actress of pure Jewish blood who incorporated German maidenhood like no woman before her and a great singer who, despite her pure Jewish origin, became beloved as an expert in the art of the lied.

There can be no doubt that Trebitsch's consciousness of his Germanic mission spoke to his inmost soul as clearly and logically as if he were a pure Aryan. He felt German with every fiber of his being, a true repository of German ideals. But it was his fate that in wartime and postwar German *völkisch*[18] cliques and political, militaristic, and imperialist societies, few could believe the impartiality of his Germanness. In many scientific circles a man who holds true to style and speech, and does not accede to college jargon, is suspected of not being a true "scientist." Similarly, in certain German National circles, anyone with a reflective mind is suspected of being in league with a foreign enemy. Anyone who provokes mistrust in his own camp runs the risk of being treated crudely. Noble minds also fall into this category. Paul Lagarde[19] was insistent and unrefined in his Germanness whenever he wanted people to forget his French origin. Houston Stewart Chamberlain[20] used an exaggerated, opaque style when, during the war, he wanted people to forget his English birth.

Every anti-Jewish power finds a general staff of Jews to outdo their leader's prejudices. Arthur Schopenhauer's first antisemitic utterances were strengthened by his apostles Frauenstadt and Asher.[21] Richard Wagner, always suspected of having Jewish ancestry, had no obvious objections to his disciples Heinrich Porges and Hermann Levi, while at the same time insulting Meyerbeer, Mendelssohn, Halévy, and Bizet as destroyers of German music.[22] Friedrich Nietzsche's Jewish disciples Paul Rée [see above] and Siegfried Lipiner[23] were "antisemites," although Nietzsche himself esteemed Jews highly. Eugen Dühring, that wildest of all Jew-devourers, was confronted by the astonishing fact that the Jewish author Benedikt Friedländer, out of enthusiasm for Dühring's antisemitic writings, had made Dühring a beneficiary of a sizable fortune, before the testator committed suicide.[24] Jewry, which has lost its way and is dragged down, cannot bear its strongest souls (one thinks of Jesus and Spinoza) in flight from the exercise of balanced power.[25]

I do not regard Trebitsch as one of the leading minds of our age. But he was a deep and precocious thinker whose achievements have been hushed up. Even today [1930], few are acquainted with his method of thinking. This cannot be explained away merely by ill will; it was unavoidable. His was the fate of a prophet who was not only inappropriate for all parties, but also a national embarrassment. Some awkward thinkers cannot be denied openly even by their greatest enviers because everyone feels their inevitable power and resistance to attack. On the other hand, the foremost prevailing minds of the age would bite off their eloquent tongues rather than acknowledge such uncomfortable outsiders. Very few truly free souls are capable of recognizing something that impinges on their own sense of self. We all love and praise certain insignificant beings because their presence makes us feel better about ourselves. But how can we love and honor someone who constantly humiliates us?

Arthur Trebitsch had the disastrous peculiarity of continuously struggling with his own party, telling them what he considered to be the truth. He was naïve enough to believe that people would automatically recognize his high-mindedness, while he bashed their skulls in.

Trebitsch played himself against the leading lights of his own camp. He implied that he was a better, more genuine German than Adolf Hitler or Alfred Hugenberg.[26] By doing so he irritated their followers with the statement that he, Trebitsch, was "just a Jew." On the other hand, he irritated the Jews with the most outlandish insults. But everything he said, even the most preposterous, was based on such subtle thought processes and newfangled cognitions that no one could respond to him.

Very few had the mental requirements, objectivity, calm, maturity, and especially time and leisure to seriously deal with the broad scope of Trebitsch's writings. It wasn't deemed worthwhile to have anything to do with this eccentric. One shrugged one's shoulders with embarrassment and passed him by while he dug himself deeper and deeper into his mire of infelicitous thoughts.

Here and there a friend felt the need for companionship behind the lonely author of these unbalanced books. No equally talented man since Schopenhauer, Nietzsche, or Dühring ever has suffered so much. Jews passed him shaking their heads, and as a German Nationalist, he created nothing but disquiet and confusion.

The guiding thread through Trebitsch's colorful books was the thought that it would be good and fruitful for a thinker not to deviate into polemics and controversies. These are the thoughts of a two-fold cognition, which yielded a man who looked at things in a twofold way. First, cognition is the primary observation of pictures, which Trebitsch named the "fixative apprehension of the world." To this fixative-pictorial comprehension he added a second indirect reflexive thinking that redesigns adherent images into "objects." By this, in arithmetic coin, the mind and language can follow and conclude. Trebitsch called this second type of cognition, in contrast to the original pictorial cognition, "secondary, flexible thinking." This distinction between primordial observation and loose orientation is the same thing that, decades earlier, I called the *psychology of the original state*,[27] which I have developed throughout my life.

I believe it to be an important truth that we humans, as conscious thinking beings in possession of ourselves, always see the world *double*. Not, as Trebitsch meant, in two distinct "forms of cognition" that have arisen historically apart and one after the other, but rather in two interdependent conceptually distinguishable "functions" that always are *experienced* simultaneously: on one hand unconscious observation and the other (in the same act) conscious knowledge of "objects." In other words, our conscious, objective reality always has an undercurrent of another subject-object-free reality, a reality of the *original state* in which we are simultaneously what we think or what we do. This is a far-reaching discovery.

For Trebitsch this became the starting point of a riddle that could be solved only by metaphysics. This is the same riddle that I tried to describe in my chief work *Der Untergang der Erde am Geist* [Decline of the earth at the hands of the spirit].[28]

This intellectual problem (on one side thinking and logic, on the other will and ethics), which caused such mental agony to Western European thinkers and poets for hundreds of years, also tormented poor Arthur Trebitsch. Unfortunately, by labeling "primary observation of pictures"—in other words, *quiescent* cognition—with the ornamental byname "Aryan thinking," he prevented himself from penetrating the heart of his discovery. By contrast, he labeled "secondary flexible orientation," in other words objectification, division of the subject-object-based mind on which living experience and the original state can founder, dry up, and freeze, with the negative connotation "Jewish thinking."

By these means, Trebitsch found an Ariadne-like thread through all labyrinths.[29] Everything that he could not tolerate in himself or others, everything that was second-class, subordinate, oblique, born out of need, compensative, compensatory, he labeled with the simple, all-encompassing opprobrious epithet "Jewish thinking." This included the entire structure of European-American civilization and everything equivocal about it—machine culture, industrialization, mechanization, capitalism, automation, scientific management, abuse and economization of the world. And so Trebitsch combined the downfall of extra-human forms, human impoverishment, over-empowerment of the earth by the working economic class (we can prove this very easily), developmental history of *Christianity*, and finally global destruction and everything that dissipates life, in one satanic, metaphysical force, crystallized in the diabolical form of a certain irredeemable people. He called this "advancing *Semitism*" and fought against it, as well as what he deemed the threatening *Judaization of the world*.

This was his idée fixe.[30]

"Judaization" became the catchphrase whereby all more subtle questions were set aside and all perceptible shortcomings in the world explained. It was the old theory of the scapegoat. The theory of *primal evil*! Trebitsch was able to link up with the racial fanaticism of Édouard Drumont[31] and Eugen Dühring. This old antisemitic literature had previously unequivocally called for crusades and pogroms.

As Dühring stated, the "Nordic man who grows and matures under cooler skies has the duty to *exterminate* the parasitic races, just as one must exterminate poisonous snakes and wild beasts."[32]

Trebitsch's delusion grew out of a mythology reminiscent of Zoroastrian teachings. There is a good and a bad principle, Ormuzd and Ahriman.[33] The blond, beautiful, blue-eyed Aryan is the god of light, and the black-haired, ugly, animal-eyed Jew the night demon. This cultural battle will last for several millennia, but eventually light-bringing, radiant Baldur will overcome Juda's hellish onslaught.

Arthur Trebitsch's assembled works are like little popping candy verses. They have a nucleus of clear thoughts, poisoned and fogged over by a yellow cloud of ideas of interference and persecution. They resemble a lovely landscape, always lying under the coal haze of artillery fire. He does not see facts incorrectly, but, through the immovable yellow spectacles of his terribly diseased soul, sees everything colored sharply and hatefully at the same time.

For a long time his logical intellect was able to hide the worm gnawing inside his soul. But year by year the inner rot became more and more evident.

As was the case with Dühring, at first Trebitsch's intellectual achievements and sick feelings were *juxtaposed* with each other. His objective feelings did not reveal the *ressentiments* that lay behind his logical arguments.

Some bold minds who create systemic constructs (including Nietzsche) think that they can turn their doctrinal spirit of personal experience into universally valid concepts, in the apparent battle for universal truth. Only in small subordinate clauses or notes can one hear a telltale crackle and feel that a personal soul has been armored with icy logicisms.

As with Dühring, some of Trebitsch's scientific books were partly autobiographical. In them he unburdened his soul and let rip at his enemies (he acknowledged no one as a mere opponent). It was as if his natural purity deterred him from intruding personal feelings into the text of a good philosophical work. Such feelings were inserted only in small printed explanations. However, bit by bit all his writings became self-exposed outrage. Outrage is a weighty word. He who is outraged divests his own armor.[34]

More offshoots and new, small dualisms grew out of his great dualism of "Aryan vision" and "semitic actions." On one side noble Teutons, on the other excitable semites. Here self-possessed, modest simplicity, there uncontrollable weakness and hysteria. This Aryan/semitic interplay created a doctrine related to the Nietzschean *Sklavenaufstand in der Moral* [Slave revolt in morality].[35]

This *slave revolt* doctrine is the most important part of Trebitsch's last book published in 1925, *Arische Wirtschaftsordnung* [Aryan world economic order]. The book still contains some intelligible thoughts on money and finance but, as a whole, is nothing but a desolate remnant of a gruesome rubbish pile.

Although he does not want to believe it, in this last book Trebitsch goes even further than the theory of Leninism, because it posits the most extensive nationalization of all tools and provisions. Like his contemporary Leonard Nelson,[36] he preaches the "absolutism of *reason*" associated with selection of an aristocratic leader. But because he establishes the dictatorship of autonomous reason, he attaches the same national label to both dominant logical reason and to its most illogical counterpart. For him the rule of reason is the same as rule by a destined race and class. "Righteous world order" is the same as "Germanic world order." The victory of morality is the same as German world domination. Germans are the chosen master race, the German man the appointed personification of nobility. This book clarifies what was announced in all his previous writings: he combines the Jewish question[37] with questions of social need, democratization, proletarianization, workers, social and minority problems, and the morality of the poor and suffering. Trebitsch understands Jewry as a sociological process of continuing *emancipation*.

By these means he simplifies contempt for the Jews. He overlooks all individual aristocratic, conservative Jewish existence but characterizes every pitiful, miserable type who craves power as "Jewish."

In the same way as Nietzsche, in *The Antichrist*, regards Pauline theology and all post-Pauline Christianity (in contrast to Judaism and so-called primeval Christianity) as a "slave revolt in morality," Trebitsch regards the Jew as the bearer of feelings of compassion (*rachmones*[38]) and of all of the ultimate goals of slaves.

It is strange how this Jew who prays to Wotan, the god of war, accepts the painful fact that he himself has arisen from this hated plebeian class. Occasionally he allows us to see through how miraculously he has been saved from all Jewish bloodiness and blessed with pure Aryan blood. He throttles his inferiority complex with the doctrine that all third-generation baptized Jews can change into Germans. The emancipation of the Jews since 1800 was the same process begun by the emancipation of plebeians in ancient Rome.[39] At that time, one had to distinguish between different types. The *libertus*, or freed slave, and the *libertinus*, son of a freed slave, who already had become Roman. (The witty Trebitsch employs the same bold etymology as Nietzsche, who used the word *libertinus* in the same sense as the French sword *libertin*, in other words the degeneracy of sexual life.) But there was a third class, *ingenuus*—the already freeborn—in ancient Rome.[40] The poet Horace and philosopher Epictetus descended from slaves but were the most Roman of Romans and succeeded in ridding themselves of their ancestors' pariahdom.[41]

This reasoning, and many others, points to the sore spot in his unconsciousness. The more unsuccessful, stifled, and isolated that a fighter in a lost cause feels, the more unreservedly he maintains that his doctrine does not apply to himself. He cynically cites the ugly idiom "No matter what the Jew believes, the swinishness is in the race."[42] In the same way, irrespective of what Trebitsch believes or thinks he believes, he has been given the task to shed light on who he is. He understands that ten thousand years of national history cannot be erased by a single individual and that the distant past remains alive in the present. "I cannot completely dismiss the weariness of forgotten nations."

Trebitsch felt himself cursed, a "man in the shade." A man hungry for light, who always chases the sun. But his shadow follows him, and light eludes him. Despite his best efforts he remains imprisoned in night. He cannot escape the consciousness: *Et tu, Iudaee*.

This psychosis, this curse from whose grasp no Jew can escape, atrophies the great creative talents of the race. The insecure person would like to forget or make himself forget. He craves respect, begs for love. Instead of revealing himself, he disguises himself. He does not give of himself, but play-acts, even when he *is* naïve. His work is not his own skin, but a carapace. The born aristocrat does not purposely act aristocratically but naturally, as though he wants no special privileges and takes the destiny of the weak on his stronger shoulders out of a sense of healthy dedication and responsibility. A healthy sense of race does not puff itself up with blue blood, but rather unconscious good nature asserts itself. What does a happy, self-confident man care about the world's biased assessments? About *mythically infused words* such as Jew, Christian, semite, Teuton? Unbreakable self-esteem and the dignity of good nature yield invincible resources of strength. The happy and secure Jew—who in his prayers even in the darkest days thanked his Creator for having been born a Jew—could stand alone against the whole world.[43] But when being Jewish becomes an issue of insecurity and "toleration" replaces self-esteem, then one is lost. Such a Jew must always try to influence "public opinion" in his favor—by achievement, resistance organizations, flight into the common and universal, becoming a herald of his own virtues, which thereby become quite doubtful.

This is the situation with *many* Jews, including Arthur Trebitsch.

Arthur Trebitsch did not notice how tastelessly and (worse than any devilment) pitifully his apologetics affected his strong personal ego. He did not notice that the rebuff he suffered from German chauvinists was thoroughly justified. He apologized for being there and tried to justify his existence before people who knew and recognized nothing but the justification and necessity of their own existence. It sounds paradoxical but yet it is true: a Jew can only be a true representative of German culture when he is a conscious Jew. Lord Beaconsfield never could have become prime minister of England if he had constantly assured the world that he was a genuine Englishman instead of just being proudly Jewish.

Trebitsch sometimes suspected these connections and saved himself by blatant foolhardiness. He acted thick-skinned but became oversensitive. His monomaniacal fear of being addressed as a Jew drove him into silly disputes.

We now come to his life story.

The external life of this astonishing man appears like a senseless sequence of wild riots, duels, trials, ructions, and squabbles. One time he slapped a friend of his youth because the latter denied him entitlement to speak openly in the name of the German people. Another time, he brought suit and pursued it through all official channels because he felt insulted by Mr. someone-or-other calling him a "Jew"; Trebitsch felt that his Germanness had been impugned. Yet another time, he demanded a vote of confidence from his party friends and sent seconds to the homes of all who refused, with demands for satisfaction.

He fell out with all groups, annoyed National Socialists who elected him führer,[44] turned on the church, clergy, and Center Party. He threw Rome and Juda into the same pot, having discovered that Catholicism was the work of the Jews, and henceforth spoke about "Jews and Jesuits" in the same breath. Then he decided that Freemasons were Jesuits and preached against "Jews and Freemasons." Finally, everyone and everything—Luther and Loyola,[45] socialism, Christianity—fell under the opprobrious concept "Jews."

He traveled from city to city, regarding these lecture tours enormously important, and each lecture a manifesto to the German *Volk*. Every time he spoke to a few hundred undiscriminating people he felt that his appearance was like Luther when he burned the pope's bull of excommunication.[46] His successes stood in ridiculous contrast to his fantasy life. He exposed his soul with every speech, many times moving the audience to tears, some to ecstasy. Young men accompanied him, and women threw themselves at his feet. But, in general, he was just regarded as an "interesting case." It is rare when one likes to talk and be heard with a mixture of goodwill and alienation. No group took him very seriously, no party supported his undertaking, and gradually his small circle of adherents dissolved.

Like his fellow traveler Dühring, Trebitsch suffered from a severe eye affliction all his life, gradually inclining toward blindness. Perhaps this declining vision was related to the progression of his mental illness. During the war his eye disease prevented him—the passionate gymnast and well-known sportsman—from serving in the field. He made himself useful with war work, giving lectures and writing pamphlets in verse—demanding that the Baltic nobility join the German cause—that were received very well by the German kaiser.

The collapse of Austria and the revolution drove Trebitsch into a state of hopeless frenzy. He became ever more dogmatic, ever more indiscriminate and gullible in the service of his controlling quirk. Much more intellectual than the primitive heroes of fascism, he became even more ridiculous than this already ridiculous group because he was not at liberty to preach his fabrications unbiasedly. The deeper the feeling "The Jew must be destroyed,[47] even the Jew in my soul" agitated him, the more his secret fear increased: "A setback is coming: the Jews will take revenge."

Megalomania created paranoia.

Trebitsch found physicians, among them an assistant in the Vienna clinic of Wagner-Jauregg,[48] who testified to his mental state. I include just a few details from his life between April and May 1919. These appear to confirm the diagnosis of paranoia. But I must preface my remarks with a comment.

Arthur Trebitsch published some apparently sane works while mentally ill, recording the history of his paranoia, similar to August Strindberg's description of the illness of his later years.[49] Both cases have similarities. Both men had manic periods that led to collapse, followed by a calm period. During Strindberg's manic episode in Paris and Trebitsch's in Berlin, both men were certifiably insane.

A psychic compulsion, which has lately become well-documented, developed in both men—vague fear of disease and death rays, and conviction that unknown conspirators wanted to kill them with deadly extrasensory rays.

I append a few stories that Trebitsch himself told, in his manic search for self-exhibition.

On 2 April 1919 he arrived in Berlin to give a presentation on the theme "Wir Deutschen in Österreich" [We Germans in Austria] in the Blüthnersaal on 25 April. Trebitsch rented a room in Wilmersdorf. The renter had a wine restaurant in the house, where Trebitsch took his meals. The first night there he suffered from an attack of apparent poisoning, with parotid gland swelling, salivation, and precordial tension. Next morning he discovered two small holes above his bed, apparently originating from the impact of broken-off nails, through which he believed invisible high-frequency currents had been led into the room. In the restaurant, he made the acquaintance of a Jewish sculptor, whom he quickly discerned to be a conspiratorial agent. He was convinced that a secret society, which he called the World Chavrusa,[50] wanted to murder him. Apparently the innkeeper was in on the plot as well. A Jewish family living in the neighborhood was tasked to alarm and confuse him with noise while he was half asleep. He had a lock that could be opened only from the inside made for the door leading into his room and placed an alarm clock over his bed. When a visitor showed him that the new door lock could also be opened from the outside, he was convinced that the locksmith was a disguised member of the Chavrusa. He discerned that the lock had been sharpened on purpose, so that he could wound himself with it, and that nails had been placed in his bed, his room examined in his absence, and the holes above his bed modified.

At the same time, he had a confused love affair with a lady living in Charlottenburg, a Catholic officer's widow, who had approached him as a devotee of his writings. In March 1919 they had a falling out when she told him that she was expecting his child. He recognized his paternity but would not marry her;[51] however, he did promise her 100,000 crowns and subsequent adoption of the child. Notwithstanding, he withheld the money and paid for an abortion. He wrote the woman absurd letters, accusing her of working against him with the Alliance Israélite.[52] He left the letters with like-minded people, because he was convinced that the Alliance would get wind of and try to destroy them, ensuring that they would never see the light of day. However, these delusions did not stop him from continuing his relationship with a woman whom he considered to have betrayed him. He then accused her of deceiving him with a Jewish physician but still attended societal balls with them both.

On 5 April, three days after his arrival in Berlin, Trebitsch disappeared from his Wilmersdorf lodgings and went to the war ministry, seeking protection from a conspiracy that was threatening his life. Like-minded Nationalist friends offered him accommodation, and he lived with three independent German National families in succession. Each time, the same thing happened: during the night he suspected poisonous currents and accused his hosts of sheltering an informer from the Jewish World Chavrusa.

After having asked his first host for a sleeping powder the first night, he decided that they had given him poison. He looked for the toilet during the night: when he found it locked, he thought that his host wanted to force him to wake up a servant and to send him to an insane asylum. He soiled the wash jug and bowl and locked himself up. The next day he refused to open the door, forced the people to enter through the window, and threatened them with a revolver. They terminated their hospitality, and he went to another family.

He declared himself terminally ill to the second family and went to bed. During the night he wandered through the house and decided, when the bathroom door handle came off in his hand, that the family wanted to lure him into a trap and murder him. He locked himself up again and, when medical orderlies arrived the next day, jumped out of the window and ran off hatless and coatless, leaving all his belongings behind. He walked around Berlin for a day in the permanent delusion of being persecuted, acting in the most inappropriate manner. Finally he arrived, dilapidated and disturbed, at the third family, who contacted physicians and telegraphed his family in Vienna. His wife came to pick him up. Wife, brother, and closest friends had no doubt that he was mentally disturbed and took him back to their country house in Sulz-Stangau near Vienna.

He lived on another eight years after these incidents, during which time he published a number of antisemitic books, all with the old central delusion that he was persecuted by a secret society. He supported this delusion with citations from a laughable, stupid book, long since exposed as a crude fake—the so-called "Protocols of the Elders of Zion."[53]

It would be pointless to outline Trebitsch's life further. I merely include a few of his most absurd assertions.

The Vienna socialist and Trebitsch's good friend Engelbert Pernetsdorfer[54] was murdered by the black magic of the Chavrusa because he was too much of a German National.

Houston Stewart Chamberlain, who died of myoatrophy, was also murdered by the Jews. Trebitsch, who called Chamberlain's philosophy the "transition from Kant[55] to Trebitsch," drove especially from Vienna to Bayreuth to warn Chamberlain about this.

Trebitsch attributed his younger brother's suicide to the work of a Jewish hypnotist, who forced his brother to commit suicide by bringing him under his spell. A third brother, Siegfried, noted translator of Shaw's works,[56] kept as far away as possible from Arthur's delusions.

When his wife, Marie Trebitsch, died of meningitis and sinusitis, Trebitsch was convinced that the Jews really wanted to kill him with electric currents, but that his poor wife—since they had changed bedrooms—fell victim instead.

Jews intercepted his letters by maintaining spies in every post office and telegraph office; and all the world's telephone calls were overheard by the Elders of Zion.

Jews worked as secret racketeers inside his own antisemitic German National Party. He proposed the fantastic motion that inside his own "cultural confederation," a commission should be appointed to investigate whether any of its members had been circumcised, to prevent Jewish informants from sneaking in.

This sniffing out of Jews involved him in ever new undertakings. Jews used their women to seek destruction of politicians and poets whom they deem to be dangerous by luring them into their net. The writers Laurids Bruun and Arthur Dinter[57] were lured into mysticism by women in service of the Jews. Most statesmen are married to Jews through the Chavrusa. He himself had been infected by syphilis four times by women who wanted him to develop tertiary syphilis and dementia paralytica. Great quantities of such nonsense appeared in print.

If we assume that all Trebitsch's assumptions are true, there must have been many hundreds of independent people who knew of the plan by the World Chavrusa to destroy this unfortunate man. He asserted that he had been persecuted by about fifty people but was careful not to name names. But it is clear from his accusations that he regarded—at the very least—the following people as being influenced by a Jewish secret society: Dr. von Nordberg, the Munich neurologist; Prince Felix Lichnowsky in London and his wife, the authoress Mechtild Lichnowsky; Berlin physician Carl Ludwig Schleich; authors Ferdinand Runkel and Hermann Bahr; Munich publisher Beck; Grunow in Leipzig; Strache in Vienna; Borngräber in Berlin.[58]

The interpretation of these diseased notions is simple.

He placed his internal world outside, for all to see. His delusion of being continuously persecuted by the World Chavrusa rose out of the dark world of tragic futility of his own position. The compulsion to crow about being a pure "original Aryan," knowing that he himself was descended from the "Tantalidean house"[59] and indissolubly bound to its subterranean umbilical cord, secretly gnawed at his conscience. This led to exaggerated and enraged reviling, slander, and disparagement of everything Jewish, while having no clear notion of what being Jewish really meant. Because he persecuted the "Jew" in himself, he believed himself to be persecuted by them.

His delusion of being surrounded by deadly rays gave a pseudo-logical interpretation to his vacillating moods. When a mentally ill person has disagreeable thoughts, he experiences them physically and they make him ill. In hypersensitive people it often is unclear whether susceptibility to emotional influences is the result of an objectively justifiable disorder or, conversely, whether the suffering and disorder arise from a hypersensitive imagination.[60]

Trebitsch petitioned the government to ensure that experiments with waves that do not fall within the scope of human senses may be performed only by "Aryan physicists." This would neutralize an international Camorra[61] of Jewish technicians and engineers, dictating that divisions of physics potentially disastrous for future humanity could be investigated (in accordance with the decision of the Elders of Zion) only by Jewish physicists and mathematicians.

Appallingly, he invited "Aryan researchers" to experiment on him by measuring his dolicocephalic, Gothic, North German skull and his pure German blood.[62] His brain too was a pure German brain. The racial madness poisoning humanity had driven this gifted man *insane*.

A friend described his end as follows:

During the last years of his life, Arthur Trebitsch suffered from paranoia. This unusual delusion focused on a single issue. In other areas of the mind he was, until the last, a man of unusual clarity, sharpness, and logic. His thought processes were so enlightening that it was a pleasure to hear him speak. He was convinced that the Alliance Israélite was a secret brotherhood that wanted to assassinate him. Likewise, they wanted everyone else with whom they did not agree to disappear from the face of the earth. This society operated with secret resources: wireless streams and poison gases that they sent through walls. He asserted that he physically felt these currents and gases and wandered from one room to the next in his Vienna apartment for nights on end. His bed stood on glass feet, to insulate it. Rooms were covered with insulating wires, and he had a little glasshouse set up in the garden of his Sulz-Stangau villa, in which he slept. He was convinced that the Jews had slowly killed Houston Stewart Chamberlain, whom he revered, in this way. When he heard that the great man had fallen ill, he drove especially to Bayreuth, to warn him. He was terribly distressed that Chamberlain not only did not believe, but smiled at his warnings. His delusional arguments were so real and convincing that at times I myself began to believe them. In fact, all metallic objects on his writing desk were magnetic; one day his pocket watch stopped working, and his watchmaker told him that its components had become magnetized. What can one think of this? Those who were close to him often did not know whether he was delusional or extremely clairvoyant. He died in Eggersdorf bei Graz on 26 September 1927 from tuberculosis that had initially healed but reactivated and became miliary. The infection began in the oral cavity, spread to the tongue, and killed him quickly. Of course he did not believe the diagnosis and was convinced that, despite all his precautions, the Jews had succeeded in poisoning him. He died in the clinic of his longtime friend and physician Professor Hermann Schmerz,[63] a great man and excellent surgeon, and was buried Thursday 29 September in Sulz-Stangau. The death notice for the friends was signed by Hermann Müller-Guttenbrunn, Vienna XVII, Schulgasse 80.

We are faced with a tragic fate in whose presence we must remain respectfully silent. Nevertheless, I cannot but accuse Arthur Trebitsch's friends, wife, family, and brothers of not feeling how unworthy it is, without a sense of self-betrayal, of anyone who is born Jewish to behave so antisemitically. It is the opposite of both Christian and German attitudes to life not first to look for the blame in oneself before accusing others. If there sometimes are disadvantages in being Jewish—and who would deny this?—we must recognize and work to heal the wounds wherever it is *possible* to know the world and change something in it. The problem resides exclusively in one's own ego.

The fragile man reviles others rather than quietly plumbing his own depths. By doing so he shuts himself off from the world and comes to contradict it. Continuing to oppress the oppressed, beat the beaten, and vilify the vilified is ignoble and makes one look contemptible.

We have the choice to see Arthur Trebitsch as either despicable or unhappy. I choose to see him as unhappy.[64]

Notes

1. Arthur Trebitsch (1880–1927), Austrian writer of Jewish origin who nonetheless became a prominent exponent of antisemitism. Among his works were antisemitic tracts for the Austrian branch of the Nazi Party.
2. Wilhelm Jerusalem (1854–1923), Austrian Jewish philosopher and pedagogue.
3. Ferdinand Lassalle (1825–1864), Prussian political philosopher who argued for social democracy in Germany.
4. *The essay on Arthur Trebitsch came about through my acquaintance with the following books: 1. Geist und Judentum; 2. Arische Wirtschaftsordnung; 3. Deutscher Geist oder Judentum; 4. Wir Deutschen in Österreich; 5. Aus des Ratsherrn Johannes Teuffelerius' Lebensbeschreibung; 6. Geschichte meines Verfolgungswahns.*

    I am indebted to a friend of Trebitsch for a great deal of material that otherwise would have been inaccessible to me. He wrote: "It is up to me to see a worthy memorial raised to my poor dead friend. Although you opposed him, you did so chivalrously. What you describe is all so sad and true, because those who stand where Rée, Weininger, and Trebitsch stood—and where I stand—are completely beyond help. Only a Weltanschauung causes our own blood to rise up against us with clenched fists, and Weltanschauung is innate. Even as an opponent, you understand and acknowledge this tragedy, because you have love in your heart and are no enemy as are others to whom our unhappy love pertains."
5. A method of biblical exegesis that includes consideration of extratextual features and implied or tacit meanings.
6. Deuteronomy 15:15.
7. In Jewish folklore, a golem is a living creature conjured from inanimate materials. The term was also used in some premodern texts to refer to shapeless or unformed matter.
8. The treason trial of the French Jewish military officer Alfred Dreyfus (1859–1935) was one of the most significant and contentious episodes in modern French political history. Remembered today as *l'affaire Dreyfus* (the Dreyfus Affair), it had a seismic effect on the Third Republic and resulted in Dreyfus's exoneration. At the time this book was written, Dreyfus was still alive.
9. These included the novelist Émile Zola (1940–1902) and journalist Georges Clemenceau (1841–1929), future prime minister of France.

10. Johannes (Josef) Pfefferkorn (1469–1523) was a German Catholic theologian and convert from Judaism. Pfefferkorn was a vocal antagonist of the Jews; he called for copies of the Talmud to be destroyed.
11. Erich Ludendorff (1865–1937), German general and leader of the war effort after 1916, who played a pivotal role with Adolf Hitler in the 1923 beer hall putsch; Paul Nikolaus Cossmann (1869–1942), German Jewish journalist who converted and became a devout Catholic—conversion did not spare him from deportation to Theresienstadt, where he died in 1942; Ernst von Salomon (1902–1972), German writer and right-wing mercenary of the Weimar era. Lessing is incorrect: Salomon was not Jewish.
12. Eduard Engel (1851–1938), German language and literature scholar.
13. Arnolt Bronnen (1895–1959), Austrian playwright and director.
14. Sir Edmund Gabriel (1875–1950), civil servant who served as a British administrator in Mandatory Palestine. In 1919, because of his pro-Arab sentiments, he was forced to resign. Lessing is being disingenuous: there is no indication that Gabriel had any Jewish blood; in fact his name origin was Gabrielli.
15. Léon Gambetta (1838–1882), French statesman, prominent during and after the Franco-Prussian War; Benjamin Disraeli, Lord Beaconsfield (1804–1881), two-time prime minister of the United Kingdom, who was born Jewish, but his father left the synagogue after a dispute with the congregation; Ludovico Manin (1725–1802), Venetian politician and last Doge of Venice; Joseph Nasi (1524–1579), Portuguese Sephardi diplomat who wielded significant influence in the Ottoman Empire under Sultans Suleiman I and Selim II. The Jewish origins of Gambetta and Manin are apocryphal.
16. Tomás de Torquemada (1420–1498), first grand inquisitor of Spain and a leading proponent of expulsion of Jews from Spain. Torquemada came from a family of conversos.
17. Lessing is speaking about the phenomenon of premunity—the development of immunity in individuals exposed to certain infectious agents.
18. Exclusionary nationalists. Jews were not regarded as members of the *Volk*.
19. Paul Lagarde (1827–1891), German biblical scholar whose antisemitic writings were an important influence on Nazi ideology.
20. Houston Stewart Chamberlain (1855–1927), British-born Germanophile political philosopher whose advocacy of racial and cultural superiority of the so-called Aryan element in European culture influenced pan-German and German nationalist thought, particularly Adolf Hitler's National Socialist movement.
21. Arthur Schopenhauer (1788–1860), German philosopher and author of *Die Welt als Wille und Vorstellung* (*The World as Will and Representation*) (Leipzig: F. A. Brockhaus, 1819); Christian Julius Frauenstadt (1813–1879), German student of philosophy and disciple of Schopenhauer; David Asher (1818–1890), German educator and philosopher.
22. Heinrich Porges (1837–1900), Czech Austrian choirmaster and writer of Jewish descent who was close to Wagner; Hermann Levi (1839–1900), German orchestral conductor of Jewish descent and longtime friend of Wagner, who conducted *Parsifal* for the first time at Bayreuth in 1882; *Giacomo*

Meyerbeer (born Jacob Liebmann Meyer Beer) (1791–1864), German opera composer of Jewish birth; Felix Mendelssohn Bartholdy (1809–1847), German composer and pianist and grandson of Moses Mendelssohn; Jacques (Fromental) Halévy (1799–1862), French Jewish composer; Georges Bizet (1838–1875), French composer, who was not Jewish but was married to Halévy's daughter.

23. Siegfried Lipiner (1856–1911), Austrian writer who was an influence on Wagner and Nietzsche.
24. Eugen Karl Dühring (1833–1921), German antisemitic philosopher and opponent of Marxism; Benedik(c)t Friedländler (1866–1908), German sexologist, sociologist, economist, and physicist.
25. Baruch (Benedict de) Spinoza (1632–1677), leading philosopher of the Dutch Golden Age. For his heretical philosophical views, the 23-year-old Spinoza was excommunicated by his Amsterdam Portuguese Sephardi synagogue.
26. Alfred Hugenberg (1865–1951), German businessman and politician who aided Hitler in his rise to chancellor of Germany.
27. *Ahmungspsychologie.*
28. Theodor Lessing, *Untergang der Erde am Geist (Europa und Asien)* (Decline of the earth at the hands of the spirit) (Hanover: Wolf Albrecht Adam, 1924).
29. Cretan princess in Greek mythology mostly associated with mazes and labyrinth.
30. Leitmotif first used by Hector Berlioz (1803–1869) in 1830 to denote the repetition in his *Symphonie Fantastique.*
31. Édouard Drumont (1844–1917), French writer who founded the Antisemitic League of France in 1889.
32. See chapter on Otto Weininger, note 11.
33. Ormuzd, the good god and principle of goodness; Ahriman, an evil god and author of misfortune, sorrow, and death.
34. *Entrüsten, abrüsten.*
35. In *Beyond Good and Evil*, Nietzsche proposes a *Sklavenaufstand in der Moral* (a system of morals for subjects, opposed to morality of the master).
36. Leon(h)ard Nelson (1882–1927), German mathematician and socialist.
37. Use of the word *Judenfrage* in 1925 needs no more emphasis.
38. Yiddish. Hebrew: *rachmanut.*
39. *Secessio plebis* (withdrawal of the commoners) was a form of political protest in ancient Rome. Plebeian citizens would abandon the city in great numbers, bringing economic activity to a standstill and leaving members of the ruling class to fend for themselves.
40. This section is confusing and not strictly speaking accurate. Freemen (*liberi*) were either *ingenui* or *libertini*. *Libertini* were those persons who had been released from legal servitude (*qui ex justa servitude manumissi sunt*). A manumitted slave was *libertus* (that is, *liberatus*) with reference to his master; with reference to the class to which he belonged after manumission, he was *libertinus*. According to Suetonius, a *libertinus* was the son of a *libertus* in the time of the censor Appius Claudius, and for some time after, but this is not the meaning of the word in the extant Roman writers.

41. Quintus Horatius Flaccus (65–8 BCE), leading Latin lyric poet and satirist under the emperor Augustus; Epictetus (50–135 CE), Greek Stoic philosopher, who lived in Rome until his banishment ca. 93 CE.
42. *Was der Jude glaubt ist einerlei, in der Rasse liegt die Schweinerei.*
43. Part of the *pesukei dezimra* (initial prayers) of every morning service. "Blessed art Thou, O Lord our God, King of the universe, who has not made me other than an Israelite."
44. In the early 1920s, Trebitsch helped to set up and fund the Austrian branch of the Nazi Party, allegedly being considered its leader for a brief period.
45. Martin Luther (1483–1546), German theologian and seminal figure in the Protestant Reformation. Luther became very antisemitic when he saw that Jews were not going to follow his teachings; Saint Ignatius of Loyola (1449–1556), Spanish Basque Priest and founder of the Jesuit order.
46. *Exsurge Domine* (Arise, O Lord) was a papal bull issued by Pope Leo X. Luther refused to recant; instead he continued his attacks on the church and burned a copy of the bull in public on 10 December 1520. As a result, Luther was excommunicated in 1521.
47. *Tut nichts: der Jude wird verbrannt* (no matter what, the Jew must be burned). Gotthold Ephraim Lessing (1729–1781), *Nathan der Weise* (Berlin: Christian Friedrich Voss und Sohn, 1779), act IV, scene 2.
48. Julius Wagner-Jauregg (1857–1940), Austrian doctor who won a Nobel Prize in 1927 for his work on malaria inoculation in the treatment of syphilis.
49. August Strindberg (1849–1912), Swedish playwright and novelist. Strindberg reportedly battled with severe paranoia in the mid-1890s and may have been rendered temporarily insane. (Some have argued that this was a result of his engaging in psychological and pharmaceutical experimentation on himself.)
50. A *chavrusa*, also spelled *chavruta* or *havruta*, is an approach to Talmudic study in which several students engage in sustained analysis and discussion.
51. He was already married (see below).
52. The Alliance Israélite Universelle is an international organization devoted to protecting the rights of Jews.
53. The "Protocols of the Elders of Zion" (Протоколы сионских мудрецов) or The "Protocols of the Meetings of the Learned Elders of Zion" is a documented hoax that supposedly describes Jewish plans for ruling the world.
54. Engelbert Pernetsdorfer (1850–1918), journalist and politician.
55. Immanuel Kant (1724–1804), influential Prussian German philosopher in the Age of Enlightenment.
56. Siegfried Trebitsch (1868–1956), Austrian playwright and novelist who was a key translator of the works of George Bernard Shaw (1856–1950) into German.
57. Laurids Bruun (1864–1935), Danish writer; Artur Dinter (1876–1948), German writer and Nazi politician.
58. Prince Karl Max von Lichnowsky (1860–1928), diplomat who served as German ambassador to Great Britain, who prominently argued that German diplomacy directly led to the Great War; Mechtilde Lichnowsky (1879–1858), German authoress and wife of Prince Karl; Carl Ludwig Schleich

(1859–1922), German surgeon and pioneer in the field of anesthesia; Ferdinand Runkel (1856–?1946), German author, historian, and Freemason; Hermann Bahr (1863–1934), Austrian playwright, director, and critic; C. H. Beck Verlag, Munich-based German publisher established in 1763; Johannes Grunow (1845–1906), German bookseller and publisher; Dr. Karl von Nordberg, psychiatrist; Strache Verlag, Vienna book publisher; Wilhelm Borngräber Verlag, Berlin and Leipzig book publisher.

59. In the underworld of Greek myth, Tantalus was forced to stand in a pool of water beneath a fruit tree; both forever eluded his reach, leaving him tormented by hunger and thirst.

60. *The monomania about rays and waves that permeated Trebitsch's life is the only puzzling thing about him. I am inclined to believe in a real basis for his experiences. He possessed an extremely delicate sense of currents and influences that others did not notice and interpreted his experiences in the sense of this pervasive delusion. Unsurprisingly, real confirmation appeared to him from every direction. When a mentally disturbed man is continuously fixated on magnetic waves, he finds or creates them for himself. A similar case that has come to my attention is instructive:*

In 1926, I received letters from a certain Professor von F. in an insane asylum, calling for my help against a conspiracy of doctors and psychiatrists. On orders from his wife, they were making him artificially insane through undetectable waves, whose influence drove him to absurd obsessions. He could prove the existence of these waves.

The fact that (in another case) I had opposed the opinion of one of the professors, whom von F. considered an enemy, had led him to consult me in the expectation that I would oppose that same scholar again.

Written communications from Professor von F. showed no trace of disease or confusion. They were the documents of a richly educated mind, clear, calm, and objective. His knowledge of physics was outstanding. He made appearance of real streams seem quite likely and defended his point of view through solid study, including that of psychiatric literature. His theory was that of a vicious circle: I am not insane, but a group is interested in driving me insane. Insofar as they can manage it, I show signs of derangement, but this, in turn, reinforces their right and causes the number of my adversaries continuously to increase. Because I wished to remain independent of his physicians, I asked Professor von F. to make the journey to my home. I found a quiet, thoughtful man, remarkably sensitive, reserved and delicate. His only striking characteristics were severity, inability to express himself, and great irritability. He lacked any lightness of spirit or capability of a relaxed sense of humor. Such an incapability to enjoy a comfortable joke always is the first sign of mental imbalance.

I summarized the case as follows: We recognize the reaction to intangible physical influences in animals. Every animal feels at once whether we are friendly or hostile. Could such thoughts not have a physical basis? Streams that can be felt telepathically? I become ill in an atmosphere of hostile thoughts but feel an upsurge of strength in a gathering that is well-disposed toward me. This man, sensitive and in need of love, immediately converted feelings of rejection into disease-causing waves. Always in defensive mode, he made enemies everywhere. He turned humans against one another and was, in his turn, again irritated by waves directed against him.

This hypothesis is admittedly very vague, but nevertheless possible. It is confirmed by an astonishing discovery. It recently has become possible acoustically to capture electrical processes connected to our thoughts.

Professor von F. felt free of hostile streams in my presence, but only until I explained my view of his case and tried to show him that his suffering was objective, but its interpretation subjective. From that moment, he saw me as an adversary and counted me as a member of the physicians' conspiracy against him.

61. The Camorra is an Italian Mafia-type crime syndicate, or secret society, which arose in the region of Campania and its capital Naples. It is one of the oldest and largest criminal organizations in Italy, dating back to the seventeenth century.
62. A terrible indication of things to come a few short years later.
63. Hermann Schmerz (1881–1941), Austrian physician and surgeon. An ironic surname: *Schmerz* in German means "pain."
64. *I had intended in this book to add some evidence that would have explained to non-Jewish readers what pathology can develop when children are brought up with the myth of racial delusion and are incited against their own lives. As it turns out, that would have made this book too long and unwieldy. Also, the documentation of self-hate would have yielded an incorrect picture were it not accompanied by the opposing affirmations of pride, satisfaction, and plain heartfelt joy at being Jewish (as is increasingly seen in contemporary Jewish youth). The following documents serve as an example of thousands of similar pieces.* They are excerpts from the diary of a great woman—well-born, beautiful, healthy, and talented, but who suffered from ethical self-destruction arising from early youthful impressions.

From diaries (1920):

I force myself not to think about it. But what can I do? It thinks in me, thinks of itself, does not ask what I want or desire, the natural will to flee pain, ugliness, and death. It is always there, inside me. The knowledge of my ancestry. Like a leper or cancer-sufferer hides his disgusting suffering under his clothes but knows it is there every second of the day, I carry the disgrace and opprobrium, the metaphysical blame for being Jewish.

What are all outside sufferings, disappointment and restraints, compared to this inner hell? To be what you despise! To have to be! To have to be! Yet all of the possible cosmetic notions and intricate self-deceptions are of no help at all. It is mercilessly clear to me—Judaism is inherent in my being. It cannot be shrugged off. I can as little tear off the eternal ties that bind me to that level between man and beast—the Jew—as a dog or pig can shrug off its dog-being or pig-being.

If I were a murderer, a thief, if I had done the most disgraceful, cursed thing—I still would stand guiltless before the eternal in me. But no, as long as I live I can never absolve myself of the curse of my being. I can never deny my Jewishness, the metaphysical primeval guilt that weighs on me like a mountain. I am cursed and damned. The disgrace of my ancestry sticks to me like leprosy. I am one of those of whom the Candogya-Upanishad spoke: coming out of a "stinking womb," a "dog-womb, pig-womb, or Tschandala-womb."

There are moments when I want to open my veins, to shed the filthy blood that pollutes my body and spirit. Yes! I'd rather be an animal: I'd rather have the blood of a rat or snake in me than the blood of that wandering plague, that form and figure that has become the symbol of the anti-divine.

Sometimes I have the crazy desire to atone for my being *with a murder*. One, at least one, of those boys responsible for Germany's downfall. One of those shameless Jew dogs, who have had the audacity to rule the German people of Austria. I would like to give my life, and wash myself clean of Jewish blood.

I play with the idea, think it through ecstatically to the end, give myself to it, submissively. And then it plays with me, so that my breathing stops, my heart wants to burst, and my teeth gnash together. Murder! Murder! Murder! My blood boils in my veins, and the thought raises me off the ground. I am rapt, unconscious, fervent with hate. If only I could kill them all—all of them! Wipe them off the face of the earth, redeeming the world! If only I could exterminate them, destroy this plague, this epidemic with my own life! I see red—my blood boils. I think and think of the loaded revolver in my writing desk and that it isn't so far to Vienna. And then—then —.

Good—good! But I know that I will never do it, because I am not capable of the deed. I want to, but my will is not real, because I am nothing *in the true sense of being*, because I am nothing, because I belong to that nonexistent something that is called Judaism, that unholy Ahasaverism that has no substance behind it.

The Jew can do everything. That is certain. Everything but one.

He can want to, he can know and also do what he wants when he wants. But he cannot be. He also cannot have to, because in order to have to, you have to be. He does not have to come from inmost depth, from inmost being, because he himself has no inner being. But he can always do things differently—he is an expert in that.

Weininger's suicide was his last act of recognition. I do not really exist. He felt that he could be different, that he, the moralist, could also be a criminal. That he the metaphysician could also be a realist. Why not? "Write right and write left," that is the Jewish way. He felt that he wanted to be a moralist, that no iron "must" or "be" stood behind him, that he was only an apparition with no atman, no real essence. Weininger died from hopeless self-doubt.

What do mundane, superficial rabid antisemites, feeling nothing but natural, healthy, racial antipathy, with no clue of its true meaning, understand about the personal hell on earth of the eternal wanderer!? I personally have never done anything wicked or base, and yet in the dark of night it is as if I have perpetrated all the guilt of the world, and laid it on my shoulders.

Restless world-wanderers, inexpiable primeval guilt. Ahasver . . . Ahasver, the Jew.

The Jew himself remains unchangeable over time and reality. He is one pole of humanity. He always was, and will be as long as mankind exists. He is its shadow, Ahriman, eternal god of darkness. Since the time of the serpent, who beguiled and slandered the first humans against God's light, the Jew has been the spirit of impious mocking, god of discord and denial. The Jew is Loge, who directed Hödur's arrow into Baldur's heart. Loge, ferryman of the dead who, at the end of days, brings the wolfish night elf breed to fight against Valhalla.

From time immemorial, the Jew's duty has been to destroy, poison, defile—races, states, ideals, human hearts—they are all the same to him. He carries the curse of his unholy breed through the millennia of human history, and rules blindly over his destiny. Mildew on the blossom, frost on the harvest, poison in the blood, filth on purity, malicious laughing in a bloodless face. He must want to destroy the sanctity of humanity whenever he wishes. He must seek to extinguish the eternal lamp as often as he approaches it. Consumed by envy, he wants to defile the whole world and tear away what he cannot have and does not recognize. Therefore, he hates all purity and spits on everything great, because he cannot reach it any other way. Therefore he tears down what others have built and always strives for evil. With sure instinct, he tries to destroy all blond, blue-eyed, pure humanity together with all who find their own black-haired, animal-eyed, short-legged appearance revolting to behold. His face overflows with lust, and he stands crookedly, neck bent subserviently, squinting at the upright, well-born scion of the noble, Teutonic, Aryan race. He swears to himself that that "bright-eyed, naïve, boy," innocent and unconcerned, whose pure humanity overshadows him, should crawl on the ground and munch on dust, as he does.

No Jew, in his inmost heart, does not realize the superiority of the Teutonic race. But he lacks the humility that transforms and enhances everything that is meager, poor, and low and raises it metaphysically to a height that is unreachable, but recognized and affirmed. Because he is the boastful aristocrat of the low-born, all that remains for him is hate and the will to destroy everything that is higher, better, more beautiful. He cannot be any of these things, and therefore averts his eyes from them. Hence, his cries for equality, instinctive tendency toward social democracy, and communism, which are nothing but doglike hate of the subhuman for the higher order. In form and figure he resembles the parable of the godless. Ahasver the God-murderer threatens to stab mankind in the back and murder it. Powerless and invisible, as if extinguished, when the midday sun is high, his power rises in the evening. Today, when humanity's sun lies deep on the horizon, the eternal denier's ghastly shadow spreads under the sun's last rays, covering the whole earth.

As a child, unconsciously striving to rise from the swamp of my origin, I drank in German fairy tales and myths with ardent love. Just as I later lost myself in Wagner's creations, I found salvation from distress and coincidence in Aryan metaphysics and myth. A dead-straight, never-wavering path led me to where I felt I belonged. But—unfathomable, terrible absurdity!—I was not entitled to belong where I was all along, and am still not allowed to be.

I did not ask why, because the question itself was a rebuke and an unauthorized desire for love. This wish to know the meaning of one's destiny is a desire, attachment, self-assertion, and will to affirmation. It is a spirit of self-interest, the Jewish spirit to which life seems capital that is owed interest, not a borrowed sum that should be managed without purpose or advantage. Therefore I did not, and still do not, ask why. Because knowledge of one's destiny is itself a relief. The road appears less hard and long when one knows how long it is and where it leads. It is the Jewish way to make everything as easy and pleasant as possible. I want to carry the humiliation, and not ask why.

I feel that, if there was a right to suicide, my being Jewish would grant it to me. It would just be self-reprieve from lifelong imprisonment. But I also feel that this right does not exist, and that my suicide would just be the final act of the blood from which I want to escape, a last act of selfishness. Metaphysical guilt and atonement are not shaken off by interruption of empiric life. It would as Schopenhauer says, be a premature interruption of a painful cure, but the pain itself would remain, because pain cannot be stilled by extinguishing its appearance. It is a bill that must be paid, that I do not have the right to tear up, saying defiantly: "I won't pay it!" I? Who am I to take my suffering so seriously?

During many hours of deepest reflection and submission, I say to myself: "There are so many wretched, disgusting animals, toads, snakes, spiders, vermin, and they all accept their existence with humility and without unreasonable questions. Why can I not accept my being Jewish humbly, as something imposed on me?" Perhaps, perhaps my wild denial is my way to God the Eternal. I sometimes think in jest that I am a member of the Germanic race. I could then joyfully feel my "ego" and proudly, freely, and cheerfully affirm my Germanness, standing unshakeable, proud, and strong with both feet on my own soil. I shake my head—this could not be my way to perfection. My way must lead to self-denial and self-loathing.

Only one who knows himself can measure the enormous bitterness that comes with belonging where one does not *belong, and not daring to be, and ultimately never* being *able to be, what one is. It is true that I can never be* German, *no matter how much I love, know, and understand this nation. I can never be an Aryan, no matter how Aryan my thoughts and feelings are. My thinking and feeling, never my* being. *From an empiric point of view, Judaism is something that must be overcome, a developmental stage that is subject to becoming, that can be forced into a higher form with nobler nature. I myself have overcome Judaism, by denying the age-old Jewish character traits of selfishness and greed for gain.* Because I have never known, and do not know now, the search for earthly gain, *and am familiar with the* tat tvam asi *[Thou art that] that will always remain closed to every Jew, who knows no reality than his own, including his own family. Because I want self-deprivation for its own sake, not reward and advantage "that I may live long upon the earth." Because I understand the concept that is* most foreign of all to Jews—*the categorical imperative. Certainly, I am not a Jew anymore in the empirical sense of the word. I am less of a Jew than many Christians and Aryans. But what does empirical mean to me? I know better and do not want to lie to myself. In a metaphysical sense, the only sense that matters, Judaism is something other than a mere state of affairs and developmental stage. It is a symbol and earthly guise of primeval original sin and is inflicted on me like a hump or leprous rash, or innate blindness.*

I carry the torch, delivered to me by an unfamiliar hand in the darkness of the unconscious. I carry it faithfully and conscientiously, even if it smolders, the smoke takes my breath away and glowing pitch drips down and singes me. I carry it until I can hand it over to someone else, burning and well-protected. I must go my little way. If, as I am a Jew, I am ordered to go where these black, harsh fumes stick in my throat and suffocate me—I may not ask why. Because there is no causal relationship between fate and its bearer.

What do you know, you light elves, you blond, blue-eyed favorites of the gods—what do you know of Nibelheim's eternal, sunless night? And yet I do not harbor envy or hate against you. I love you, because I must love everything lofty, noble, and beautiful. I say "yes" to the higher form that is not my own and willingly stand aside in this life. But see how my content bubbles over and overflows my form. I do not grasp it, it is too narrow. My content does not stick to or belong to it anymore, and I therefore do not feel humiliated, but rather uplifted, by the unfamiliar height. I am not what I seem anymore. I have disappointed the appearance with my being. I have been liberated for hours, even days.

How bitter it is not to be able to belong *where I once derived my roots, to creep shyly past the gate behind which my homeland lies!*

Over and over, I feel how Germanic *my thoughts are. My experiences and thoughts rise up to me faithfully and blissfully from Indian metaphysics and German mysticism. I feel, breathe in joyfully: "I am that as well." But my fate mockingly says "no," gives my destiny a swift kick—"That is what you are"—and scornfully throws me back into the ghetto, into the disgusting society that I despise and deny with every fiber of my being. What does it help to clench my fists? What good is all my despair? I carry the* indelible *mark of Cain*—Jew. *Only he who has not personally known and suffered the eternal fate of Christ can sense or believe that anyone can have shrugged off Jewishness as completely as he who overcame it!*

Only someone who has survived a disease and become immune to it, who has experienced and survived bubonic plague, is safe from infection. If I really love Germanness, I must calmly want my destruction. I have no choice.

There is hardly a more tragic lot than the few who really have wrenched themselves away from their origin, and whom nobody believes or wants to believe. What is to become of us? Where should we go? *Behind lies disgust and loathing, in front the abyss yawns. No ground under their feet, homeless, rootless, mercilessly banished to a deathly rigid circle of hate.*

See how here and there they eye you from their houses,
And then they slam the window in your face.

At times, I temporarily forget, and shake off these thoughts when I take breath again in my self-imposed solitude. I seek refuge where there is no hate and no contempt flicks its serpent's tongue. A place where my best friends provide comfort and cognizance: Yajnavalkya, Eckhart, and Schopenhauer. But then it abruptly strikes me again and sinks its icy sharp claws into my neck: "Jew!" And then I feel as if I must carry all the faults of that cursed breed, whose poisonous incubus blood scorches my veins, on my shoulders alone.

I imagine that I must expiate all the crimes of the Jews against Germanness. It appears justifiable that I am greeted with contempt everywhere I go, as if it were true for all.

I would like to call out to the Germans: Stay hard! Stay hard! No mercy! Not even for me!

Your German walls must remain impenetrable. They should have no secret small back doors open only for a few. Because one day treachery will creep in through them. Close all doors, all windows, holes, breaches. Outside the plague is raging! If you want to save your house from infection, do not allow anyone in from the infected area. There is no more time to winnow out the few. It is much too late. Close, close all the cracks, because every breath brings in the plague. Close your hearts and ears to all who beg for entry. This is your last chance! You small final fortress of Aryanism: Stay strong and true!

No, no, no! It wasn't right that God wanted to spare Sodom and Gomorrah for the sake of one righteous person! Not even for ten or a hundred!

Away with the contaminated filthy puddle! Burn out the wasp's nest, even if a hundred righteous people are destroyed with the unrighteous! What is it to you? What is it to us? What is it to me? No! Have no mercy, I beg you!

Max Steiner

The afternoon of 22 June 1910, chemistry student Max Steiner from Prague was found dead on his bed in his North Berlin apartment.[1] He was dressed in a new suit that he had had made specially for his doctoral examination. He had passed his preliminary examinations and had only to take this final step to complete the process. He had submitted his dissertation on the chemistry of aromatic substances, which had been accepted by the University of Berlin chemistry faculty, and his final oral examination had been scheduled for 23 June.

He told his landlord that he wanted to schedule the customary "examination visit" with his teacher, the famous chemist Professor Emil Fischer.[2] While he was dressing for the visit he must suddenly have been overcome by extraordinary depression.

As a chemist he was in possession of poisons, with which he routinely experimented. Before he took poison, he wrote a short parting letter to his parents.

In the letter, he apologized for taking his own life. He could not give an actual reason for this and in fact did not have any. Never had he been so free as now, in the hour of his departure. He was completely unconcerned about his coming examination. The hopeless suffering of all humanity, not his doctoral examination, weighed heavy upon him. Life-weariness was his last awareness, and all he wanted was rest.

Steiner was born 21 May 1884 and died when he was twenty-six. He already had authored two strange books, published by Ernst Hoffmann in Berlin, which had caused some sensation in scientific circles.

The first book, 125 pages long and published in 1905, was entitled *Die Rückständigkeit des modernen Freidenkertums. Eine kritische Untersuchung* [The backwardness of modern freethinking: A critical investigation]. The other, 244 pages long, was entitled *Die Lehre Darwins in ihren letzten Folgen* [The final consequences of Darwin's theory].

The fact that Houston Stewart Chamberlain, the mostly widely read philosopher of his day, had sent a letter to the unknown student, caused a stir:

I note today that even the best-founded rule (or as our dear old Kant used to say, maxim) is well and truly confirmed by a properly applied exception.³ I write to an author whom I do not know, to thank him for his instruction, stimulus, enjoyment, even liberation. The physiologist Julius Wiesner made me aware of the second book. Although already overburdened with work, I read it through, line for line, in one sitting. I got to bed late because I could not tear myself away from the unexpected and unhoped-for joy of this book. If I had my wish, two hundred thousand copies of it would be distributed.⁴

Although this young man's talents had become known in scientific circles, very few knew why he died. As in the case of Otto Weininger's suicide, newspapers indulged in vague speculations. One spoke of examination neurosis: anxiety about his doctoral thesis suddenly had overwhelmed him. Others spoke of his lonely, secluded, ascetic life and that a recent tongue infection had made him even more morose.

Only a few friends knew the truth. One of these, Kurt Hiller,⁵ handled his estate. He found in it fragments of a third book, *Die Welt der Aufklärung* [The world of enlightenment]. Hiller published the collected notes in 1912, with an introduction and a 1903 photograph of Steiner.

The image of a rigid young man gazes out at us. He is stiffly tucked in a black frock coat with silk cuffs, in a stand-up collar and starched shirt. His young face has only recently begun to mature. He is a cool, distant type, with strikingly wavy, thick light-blond wavy hair and clear aquamarine blue eyes. His brow is as broad as it is high, and his severe nose is small and narrow. His remarkably narrow, closed lips lie just above a small sprouting beard. He has a broad chin and big ears.

His expression is laughing lively, ironic, cheeky, deeply sad. Although every detail of his face contradicts the Jewish stereotype, a physiognomist will recognize that it can only be that of a Jewish intellectual.

Three books, each of which spins the same thread, relate the development of this precocious young man.

Prague, where Max Steiner attended the Piarist School and Grabengymnasium, is Europe's most eclectic city. Its ancient Jewish community is the most intellectual in the world. Two cultures, Sudeten German and West Slavic, mingle together, and every child of the educated class speaks Czech and German equally well.⁶ The city has a thousand churches and chapels. Its many hundreds of baroque facades and gloomy incense-filled vaults tower over tombs in which the histories of all three peoples sleep.

Steiner experienced the first blossoming of Czech poetry: Otokar Březina, and the great poets of the proletariat Petr Bezruč and Jiří Wolker.⁷ The dark, decaying Catholic sweetness of old Catholic Prague drifts out of Rainer Maria Rilke's delicate verses.⁸

Max Steiner grew up in a world filled with tensions, the most intellectual of intellectuals. He had great logical-mathematic talent but no connection to music. He had little interest in music, lyricism, or poetry, but a great passion for knowledge and an unrefined mind that called thinking itself into question.

At age twenty he became a science student. Because he was destitute, he chose to study chemistry so as to be able to make a living, but his enthusiasm centered on philosophy and mathematics.

He passed his school-leaving examination in July 1903 and three months later arrived in Berlin, where he remained until his early death. In Berlin he entered a circle of young academics and intellectuals who spent nights discussing crime, religion, science, and social issues. Steiner was the most skeptical of the group of skeptical[9] logicians and ethical Marxists, but also the strictest in moral demands.

He was dismissive, abnegating, and harsh in the area of eroticism as well. He was inclined to adulatory friendships but, as far as one could tell, had no attraction to women. "Women and love are not tragic—only knowledge is tragic."

He was a harsh young man of utmost morality, awareness, will to validity, and ethical ambition. His only life ideal was that of the Greek gymnasts: "always to be first and win the race."

Kurt Hiller, himself characterized by engagement and shrewdness, reported, "The features that were immediately obvious to anyone who had contact with Steiner were terrible coldness, conversational acuity, unearthly freedom from sentiment, and the restless compulsion to achieve feelings of superiority, which made debates with him both torture and ecstasy."

The great fashion in the prewar Kurfürstendamm around 1900 was not yet—as it would be twenty years later after the World War had been lost—the comforting world of the "irrational," the "mythic," the "cosmic, the "astrologic." Then, the fashion centered on Haeckel's *Welträtsel* [World riddle], Bölsche's *Das Liebesleben in der Natur* [The love life in nature], and Carneri's *Der moderne Mensch* [Modern man].[10] Or (as a more striking counterbalance) Hermann Cohen's *Reine Logik* [Pure logic], Chamberlain's *Grundlage des neunzehnten Jahrhunderts* [Foundations of the Nineteenth Century], or Friedrich Albert Lange's *Geschichte des Materialismus* [History of materialism]. The young student wavered between the two camps of Darwin on one side, Kant on the other.[11]

From an Orthodox Jewish home, he was a very poor boy who paid for his studies by casual labor and hourly lessons and often lived on coffee and black bread in a back hotel room near the Alexanderplatz. Unworldly, and tough-minded, he was an honest provincial who gazed defenselessly into an urban world filled with all sorts of opportunists and scoundrels.

One saw important, distinguished Jews at the pinnacle of all intellectual life. At the University of Berlin the spirit of today already was dawning, defined by three Jewish names: Einstein, Bergson, Husserl.[12]

One man, however, was the living, all-formulating all-seeing eye of the city of three million people. He was the eternal Berlin *Privatdozent*,[13] studiously overlooked by Culture Minister Herr von Gossler.[14] A man regarded by his peers with a mixture of admiration and confusion, visited by his students as if he were a spiritual magician. The birth house of this giant intellect, who "surveyed" all, and the magical mouth who formulated all, stands on the corner of Friedrich- and Leipzigerstrasse, in the middle of Berlin's traffic vortex from hell. His name was Georg Simmel[15] and he was *the* most important tourist attraction for all intellectual connoisseurs in 1900 Berlin. The straightforward, coarse-grained young man from Prague hated Simmel from the moment he was astonished by him, and could not understand him. So this was the famous filigree weaver of the mind, the double and triple seer of the future, who seemed to use philosophy like an acrobatic ballgame with red, green, blue, and violet balls or tobogganing up hill and down dale! This was the invincible intellectual who could philosophize over a "waistcoat button" as if it were a problem over the existence of "God"! For Steiner, Simmel became a symbol of the luminous phosphorescence of dying Judaism, the all-decaying element-less spirit of 1900.[16]

Fritz Mauthner masterfully dissected belief in word and language.[17]

Max Dessoir destroyed the wonder of mysticism and spirituality.[18]

Ernst Cassirer lived in the giant corpse of transcendental philosophy.[19]

Maximilian Harden [see below], wisest of wise political climbers, reigned in the political sphere.

Irreverent psychology and weighty psychoanalysis destroyed what remained of classicism and romanticism.

Enough to set the entire world on fire! All this burned down as a daily feuilleton game for the leisure hours of smart wheeler-dealers and their lady friends.

With his gritty, superior talent, awkward seriousness, clumsy loyalty, and all-encompassing intellectuality, Steiner looked around and began to hate what he saw. People who were smooth and unassailable. Intellects who encompassed everything that they were not. Who created with blood without shedding their own. Chutzpah without simplicity. A mountain of ability, achievement, knowledge, printer's ink, and work. He himself, unfinished and unmusical, had nothing with which to oppose them but a heart filled with high-strung emotionalism and death-willing morality.

Because of his great intellect (he was in essence a man without a fate) he despised all art and intellectual games. Without sensing that he was trying to drive out one devil with another, he countered its wit with his ethos, by commanding a group of those who would attempt to "save the world." These he called "activists."

They dreamed of revolution and spoke of "goals." No word was used more than "deed," again and again! One would have expected Steiner to set himself practical and achievable sociopolitical goals, to give hungry children bread, and decrease the number of mothers dying from tuberculosis and men overwhelmed with filth, disease, and poverty, He might have chosen political goals such as communism or achievement of his great utopia as a faithful Social Democrat. But no—Steiner's intellectual steadfastness only directed him to theoretical crises.

He began as a morality activist, educating humanity. After a few years he became a nihilist and anarchist and ended as a convert to Catholicism. Marx, Stirner, Loyola [20] were all mileposts on his short life's pilgrimage. A typical career, exemplarily shortened. Before discussing the three-act tragedy of his life, some background is necessary.

The background is 1900 power-frenzied Berlin and the nouveau riche suburbs of Schöneberg and Grunewald. A few words about them are necessary. Enlightenment! Progress! An easy pathway for the industrious! These were the words to which Steiner's sensitive soul reacted like a provoked bull to a red rag.

Like his great teacher Karl Kraus (whom he never dared approach), Steiner hated timeworn literary Judaism, regarding it as the most dangerous carrier of the false ideals of power and success.[21] His hate of any irresponsible games became hatred of his own blood.

It was understandable, although unjust, that Steiner's anger first turned against Georg Simmel. Because everything that, for him, was a deadly serious matter appeared to the great conceptual artist merely as an object for cultured dialogue. Simmel was a master in the art of embossing ornamental Tanagra figurines,[22] and Steiner wanted to soak the marble with his own blood. Simmel's modest ambition was to see everything clearly from every possible angle. When a problem seemingly had been exhausted, he quickly, by sleight of hand, viewed the issue from a new and subtler perspective. "This thinker cannot be disproved if he likes the position he has taken, but then only if to do otherwise would make him late for lunch, he reconciles by refuting himself."

Two never-corresponding strata intersected here. The crude and the subtle were irreconcilable.

I fear that I might be misunderstood when I admit that (without being blind to his intellectual nihilism) I regard Georg Simmel as the more life-fulfilled thinker. He represented *earth* in an incomparably stronger way than Max Steiner. Simmel had a great, modest nature. As an agnostic, he was capable of great and varying insights. But he remained instinctually faithful to life and all of life's manifestations.

There were no cultural areas in which Simmel's opinions risked damaging his reputation. But there was nothing natural that he did not feel, and he never passed by the genuine and elemental. He was far more nihilistic in spirit, but also more fervent by nature, than Steiner. He lived greatly and died greatly, because he lived life to the full. Nothing was further from his belief than haughtiness of spirit. By contrast Max Steiner was arrogant. He needed the spirit. He cried out for the imprisonment of absoluteness, because his heart had become empty. He had to serve a spirit idol because he loved no one, not even himself.

Let us look at his three books, the three acts of his prematurely ended tragedy.

His first book, published when he was nineteen, provides the leitmotif that would become enriched in his two following books: critique of the Zeitgeist as a superstition of science. Two naturalists were the nabobs of the era: Ernst Haeckel and Wilhelm Ostwald;[23] besides them a thousand other junior luminaries: Bölsche, Büchner, Woltmann, Strauss, Bebel, Kropotkin, and who knows how many more.[24] What did the young man have against high priests of science of the day? With coldhearted logic he set out that all their scientific teaching was a religion, much more superstitious and implausible than medieval Christianity. He demonstrated the bombast of conceptual idols, energy, substance, material. The inconclusiveness of the usual questions such as relationship between soul and body. The naïve realism of premises such as assumption of "a thing in itself" such as cosmos or as spirit.

In short he mobilized the arsenal of Kantian criticism against presumptuous dilettantes who boasted that they were freethinkers and monists, without having learned to ask scientific questions.

Three years later he took a further step forward. He already had realized that humanity's scientific conceit was vulnerable only in one place: "giving meaning to the meaningless." Because basically the whole of humanity is grounded in one delusion: that of *history*. The three great shamans of this modern-day developmental craze were Hegel,[25] Marx, and Darwin.

Max Steiner was a natural scientist, and so he gathered himself for a giant leap against one of the three: Darwin.

It was easy for him to prove that the doctrines of vital or mechanistic biology override all hurdles of epistemology. But it must be said that Steiner was no stronger an intellect than Darwin. Anyone who speaks of development and history must properly explain the meaning of time, linear sequence, and progress. Steiner needed concepts such as development, developmental stages, and cultural process. He spoke of the strong, the weak, and the hierarchy of life, of eradication of the unfit and rise of the strong. However, what else could these phrases mean but "giving meaning to the meaningless"? If the anthill that is our nexus waxes lyrical about "progress" and "culture," that means nothing else but that we have succeeded and that he who succeeds *is right*. Steiner looked for norms and axioms, but he remained trapped in the natural history of values. He rightly saw that truth must be *absolute* but could not escape from "relativity." He had succumbed to a terrible "clever stupidity." The hopeless stultification of man by logic and ethics.

Although Steiner's philosophy was no more convincing than Darwin's, he was superior for his era in one point. He was the one who thought through false theories to their logical end, and he did not shrink from the final consequences. There is no better method permanently to disprove a theory than showing that it is built on false premises.

Max Steiner proved this in two main ways: the doctrine of "struggle for existence" and "ascent of the gifted."

Darwin and his successors proved that the weak and sick are displaced by the strong and healthy. Darwin taught that Need, that great master, guarantees a selection of the species and increasing fitness.

Well and good! But how can man interrupt this fitness? How can he lock himself up in the prison of morality? Should our recognition of natural selection not totally discard Christian ethics, socialism, and altruism? If nature brings about transformation of a unicellular organism to a human being by a competition against the weak, how can man sanctify the weak, thereby thwarting the law of evolution by a sentimental ethic of compassion? If nature really does have a history of ascendancy, this should not be disturbed. The ethic of Christian millennia is therefore counterproductive. It seeks to preserve what is given, not ascend higher. It makes an infirmary for spiritual beings out of the beautiful predator world. We call progress the mustering of countless weak beings against the few who are tall and strong, but in reality this type of human advancement stands in the way of natural progress.

In iron sentences of terrible coldness, Steiner shows that Friedrich Nietzsche[26] was the only real Darwinist. Only he drew the correct biological conclusions: the war against Judaism and Christianity. Replacement of brotherly love with the more distant/remote love of the creative process.[27] Reevaluation of all values, liberation of the necessary emotions from the spirit of suppression, and replacement by a new superspecies[28] with the necessary emotions, violent impulses, and blood instincts. In short, liberation of the *fittest*.

These sentences could have been written by Max Stirner, not Max Steiner.[29] Behind the old hatred toward freethinkers and the sentimentality of murmuring sighs of Christian love there emerges the flaming face of an even stronger hate. Hate of the Liberals and the Democrats, the Socialists and Communists, and the dictatorship of the majority.

Steiner admits that he is an individualist, anarchist, and nihilist. He justifies this by breaking the second pillar of the evolution doctrine with the power of Samson: the doctrine of transformation from an existing to a new species by virtue of variety.

He breaks it by thinking it out to its logical conclusion.

How does this work? Almost all natural science researchers declare that the difference between the lowest and highest man—a bush kaffir and a Goethe—is much greater than that between a bush kaffir and a well-behaved anthropoid ape. So why does one not extend the validity of moral law to an anthropoid ape? How can one speak of particular human rights—of a united humanity with *one* conscience, *one* logic, *one* moral law? Logically, the evolutionary theory must lead to paganism. "Animals and plants are our brothers. The commandment of love applies to *all* forms of life."

But instead of this, we proclaim human kindness! Are we not ashamed of this humanity, this belief in "equal rights for all"? Where one teaches in the same breath that the distinctive variety of all natural forms always has been the driving force of all progress and that only differentiation between species leads to ever higher biological forms?

Steiner the natural scientist plunged the logician's knife deep into these two sore points (first the necessary fight for feeding ground, second the necessary diversity of values). He showed that "natural selection" is irreconcilable with Christian charity and that the necessary "inequality of the species" cannot coexist with social democracy.

How is it that natural scientists had not seen this earlier!? Out of inertia, cowardice, mastery, fear of the opinion of the masses. This lie is now labeled "presuppositionless science."

The end of the book quietly announces a reversal of circumstances, and the third act. Steiner turns to the Catholic Church. He advises it to change tactics. They should no longer fight against modernism, progress, and development, but rather accord these words their meanings. The church must force modernism to be logical to the end, because then the puffball will burst and nothing can be germinated from an imperfect windblown seed.

We now come to the third act.

We do not know how the last turnaround happened. We hear that one day Max Steiner withdrew from his "activist" friends and displayed only derision for his previous plans of deeds and goals. He remained out of sight for months, reading and writing in his room. Finally modestly, and as though nothing had happened, he informed his companions that he had converted to Catholicism. Just as the beautiful young Jewish boy Pius Monteira had disappeared from his hometown Prague ghetto and mysteriously had reappeared later as a pupil of the Jesuits and zealot for the sole beatifying faith, Steiner suddenly had experienced his Damascus.[30]

He apologetically said, "Only the coarsest or more refined turn to the Catholic Church."

Steiner wanted nothing from his conversion. He looked for no help and no advantage. After his conversion he lived even more meagerly and wretchedly than before.

The Catholic Church has enchanted hundreds of thousands of Jews. Jesuits, Benedictines, Franciscans have given refuge to clever Jews in their quiet monasteries, and converted Jews have been allowed to become bishops and prelates.

What feeling can be more comforting than the certainty that two-thirds of humanity live in one community? We understand these conversions and know many examples such as of the insightful Laura Marholm, of the overpowering Theodor Haecker. We understand their path through the booklet by Theodor de Bussières about the conversion of the Strasbourg Jew Alphons Maria Ratisbonne and the monumental apostasy letters of Robert Kosmas Lewin. In that fashion he hereby found his haven.[31]

The great poet sings:

> *Coelum non animum mutaris*
> *Per mare currens.*[32]
> (You change your heaven but not your spirit,
> Even if you flee across the sea.)

We have seen in the stormy life of Max Scheler (a real Jewish Cain) that, for the spirit of the restless, calm harbors can be much worse than storm and sea.[33]

Max Steiner was no sooner in the harbor when he was driven onto his third circumnavigation. He wrote the following statement by Epictetus[34] about this third unfinished book: "What do I care whether the world is made up of atoms or any other material? What matters to me is that the good triumphs."

What did Max Steiner want? A universal ethic, a doctrine of blessedness as a scientific pinnacle. Is that the *religious* man's way? To be pious is to be quiet and rest in beauty. But one who languishes in need, sick, tired, hungry, born on the defensive, who carries millennia of suffering in his ancient blood, and thirsts for *justice*—how can natural, immediate life be gifted to the living without grief?

He must order, choose, wrangle, judge, be active. But it also means to bend nature, even one's own nature, under the power of the spirit. To be possessed by the spirit of utopia, even when one imagines oneself to be a realist. The ethical man is born to be an adversary of his dreams. He must dismantle, even if he builds wonderful syntheses from rubble. He must deny, even if every one of his conquests breathes possibilities. He must be a pessimist, even if he seeks joy for all. Because every ethic must (by its very act) overthrow the given. Every goal is negative, every form murder.

Every living thing is beautiful, not ethical. Only the merry and pious, loving and happy hold onto their quintessence. Never the oppressed, never the workers—they must attempt to extract the fullest measure of value from their situation!

But moral will, moral demand, moral preaching, moral lies, all exist and must exist, as surely as hate and rage, envy and distress, struggle and war. Because out of them grow nation and ethics. Culture is hate. Values are hate. Work is hate.

The Jew in eternal *galut* [exile] feels this moral frenzy more deeply than anyone. He is the prophet, that is, the non-religious man. Because prophecy—be it active or passive, wrestling with or inspired by God—is enthusiasm and liberation to the spirit. Religion, however, is salvation from the spirit. He who loves life learns from it. And only he who loves will be loved again. He is neither harp nor harpist.

Steiner was a chemist, slayer of myths, and knower of the farthest things of nature and life.

Once again his noble shadow enters his bare North Berlin hotel room. It is the morning of his examination. He has dressed in his new suit, tied his new cravat, and tried on his new hat. He steps ironically in front of the wall mirror, sees his image, and smiles bitterly.

"Good luck, Herr Doktor! . . . And then? . . . Privy Councilor Fischer mediates advantageous involvement in the soap industry. . . . And then? Marriage! Children! Obligations like everyone else! . . . My parents will say: 'He has become reasonable.'—Long live everything that I have hated. Is it still worth the effort? Is it worth all the drudgery and squirming? . . . 'Daily ten more leagues through the wilderness.' Did old Čermak not always say that in the Prague piarist school? Čermak, called *rosche* [cruel person]: 'Xenophon[35] chapter 8 . . . History of a descent.' On the way my nation dies. The new nation disgusts me. What remains? . . . 'The sacrifice of the intellect.' But to 'give up the ghost' is a little more difficult for me than for others, whose sacrifices are within reach. . . . So where are the gateways into life? No! . . . Tomorrow I will not be called 'Herr Doktor' but rather Mr. Dust, Mr, Wind, Mr. Tree, Mr. Stone. That is eternity, bliss, completion.

"At least the end of this distress."

The beautiful light of a lovely June morning crept from the courtyard onto the bitter sleeper in the narrow bed and illuminated the childishly delicate figure in the festive black suit. Three human faces looked at him from the wall: his three great masters Kant, Schopenhauer,[36] and Nietzsche.

No flower relieved the bare room. If only he had tended a few hyacinths or, while dressing, a cheerful little bird would have pecked at his blond curly-haired head.

Perhaps he might have made his way out of the cul-de-sac of his logic and ethics.

On one of the ten thousand modest ways of a modest, loving life.

Notes

1. The Prague-born Jewish student chemist Max Steiner (1884–1910) poisoned himself after writing two well-received treatises on free thought and Darwinism.
2. Emil Fischer (1852–1919), renowned German chemist and 1902 recipient of the Nobel Prize in chemistry.
3. Houston Stewart Chamberlain (1855–1927), British-born Germanophile political philosopher whose advocacy of racial and cultural superiority of the so-called Aryan element in European culture influenced pan-German and German nationalist thought, particularly Adolf Hitler's National Socialist movement; Immanuel Kant (1724–1804), influential German philosopher in the Age of Enlightenment.
4. *Julius Wiesner (1887–1916) is the well-known botanist, rector of the University of Vienna at the time this event took place. Although a Jew, he accepted the dedication of Chamberlain's* Grundlagen, *a crass example of lack of self-respect.*
5. Kurt Hiller (1885–1972), German Jewish essayist and political journalist.
6. Bitterly ironic. Lessing was assassinated in his study by Sudeten Germans in Marienbad (Mariánské Lázně), Czechoslovakia, where he had fled to escape the Germans just after Hitler came to power in 1933. History shows just how well the Sudeten Germans got along with the Czechs.

7. Otokar Březina (pen name of *Václav Jebavý* (1868–1929), Czech symbolist poet and essayist; Petr Bezruč (pseudonym of *Vladimír Vašek* (1867–1958), Czech poet and short story writer; Jiří Wolker (1900–1924), Czech journalist and poet who helped to found the Communist Party of Czechoslovakia.
8. Rainer Maria Rilke (1875–1926), Bohemian-Austrian poet who made the consonant-rich German language sing.
9. Lessing uses the word *"pyrrhonic."* Pyrrhonism is a school of philosophical skepticism founded by Pyrrho (ca. 360–ca. 270 BCE) in the fourth century BCE.
10. Ernst Haeckel (1834–1919), German zoologist, naturalist, philosopher, physician, professor, marine biologist, and artist who discovered, described, and named thousands of new species; Wilhelm Bölsche (1861–1939), German author, editor, and publicist; Bartholomäus von Carneri (1821–1909), Austrian poet.
11. Hermann Cohen (1842–1918), cofounder of the Marburg school of neo-Kantianism; Friedrich Albert Lange (1828–1875), German philosopher and sociologist.
12. Henri-Louis Bergson (1859–1941), French Jewish thinker who was a leading figure in continental philosophy in the first half of the twentieth century; Edmund Husserl (1859–1938), German Jewish philosopher who developed phenomenology as an area of inquiry. Bergson may have given lectures in Berlin, but he did not live, write, and teach there.
13. *Privatdozent(in)* is an academic title in primarily German-speaking countries. It indicates that a scholar can teach a given subject at a university.
14. Gustav von Gossler (1838–1902), German jurist and ministry official.
15. Georg Simmel (1858–1918), philosopher and critic who was an early German sociologist.
16. *My book* Philosophie als Tat *(Göttingen: Otto Hapke, 1914) includes a 1912–1913 essay entitled "Georg Simmel. Betrachtungen und Exkurse" (pages 303–342), a psychological study of the Jewish mind. It is much more detailed than I can present here.*
17. Fritz Mauthner (1849–1923), Austro-Hungarian novelist and critic who worked on the philosophy of skepticism.
18. Max Dessoir (1867–1947), German philosopher, psychologist, and theorist of aesthetics.
19. Ernst Cassirer (1874–1945), German thinker who attempted to formulate an idealistic philosophy of science.
20. Karl Marx (1818–1883), German philosopher, economist, political theorist, and social revolutionary; Johann Kaspar Schmidt, better known as Max Stirner (1806–1856), German philosopher whose work prefigured important developments in nihilism, postmodernism, and psychoanalysis; Saint Ignatius of Loyola (1491–1556), Basque Catholic priest and theologian who cofounded the Jesuit order.
21. Karl Kraus (1874–1936), Austrian journalist and satirist.
22. *Tanagra* figurines were a made from a variety of Greek terracotta beginning in the fourth century BCE, primarily in *Tanagra*.
23. Wilhelm Ostwald (1853–1932), German chemist and philosopher, who received the Nobel Prize in chemistry in 1909.

24. Eduard Buchner (1860–1917), German chemist and zymologist, winner of the 1907 Nobel Prize on chemistry for his work on fermentation; Ludwig Woltmann (1871–1907), German anthropologist, zoologist, and Marxist theoretician; Emil Strauss, German novelist, narrator, and playwright; Ferdinand Bebel (1840–1913), German socialist politician known today for cofounding the Social Democratic Workers' Party of Germany in 1869; Pyotr Alexeyevich Kropotkin (1842–1921), Russian anarcho-communist activist and philosopher.
25. Georg Wilhelm Friedrich Hegel (1877–1831), German philosopher and important figure of German idealism.
26. Friedrich Nietzsche (1844–1900), influential nineteenth-century German philosopher (see chapter on Paul Rée).
27. *Nächstenliebe, Fernstenliebe* (love of the future and love of furthest ones). The words are from *Thus Spoke Zarathustra*.
28. *Überart*.
29. See note 20.
30. Historically inaccurate. The Mortara case captured the attention of much of Europe and North America in the 1850s and 1860s. It concerned the Papal States' seizure of a six-year-old boy named Edgardo Mortara from his Jewish family in Bologna.
31. Laura Marholm (1854–1928), German-Baltic authoress; Theodor Haecker (1879–1945), German writer, translator, and cultural critic; Theodore de Bussières (1802–1865), French diplomat, traveler, and ethnologist, author of a book entitled *La conversion de Ratisbonne* (The conversion of Ratisbonne); Marie-Alphonse Ratisbonne (1814–1884), French Jew who converted to Catholicism and became a Jesuit priest and missionary; Robert Kosmas Lewin, author of *Apostaten-Briefe* (Apostate letters) (1928). As far I could find, neither Marholm nor Haecker was of Jewish extraction.
32. Exact quote: *Caelum non animum mutant qui trans mare currunt* (They change their sky, not their soul, who rush across the sea). Quintus Horatius Flaccus (Horace; 65–27 BCE), *Epistulae*, book 1, epistle XI, line 27.
33. Max Scheler (1874–1928), German philosopher known for his work in phenomenology and ethics.
34. Epictetus (ca. 50–135 CE), Greek Stoic philosopher, who lived in Rome until his banishment ca. 93 CE.
35. Xenophon (431–354 BCE), ancient Greek philosopher, historian, soldier, mercenary, and student of Socrates.
36. Arthur Schopenhauer (1788–1860), German philosopher, best known for his 1819 work *The World as Will*.

WALTER CALÉ

All the spirits that we have so far summoned up, no matter how different, have one thing in common. They strove from narrowness to vastness and extinguished themselves when their soul was consumed by thought or will—frozen, cold, empty, and disappointed.

Son of merchant Martin Calé, who died in 1893, Walter Calé was born on 6 December 1881 in Berlin and committed suicide there on 3 November 1904, at age twenty-three. Calé had nothing in common with the self-hate roundelay of tormented logicians and disappointed moralists described earlier in this book.

His life was not impoverished, but richly fulfilled. He did not strive into vastness, but retreated deeply into himself without wishing to be well-known. He was a beautifully consummate, blessed, sovereign human being. But sensitive as a mimosa plant, he was too tender for life.

There is no more touching femininity than that of young Jewish girls during the all-too-short loveliness of their fourteenth to eighteenth year. The dreamlike roundelay of our foremothers Rachel and Leah, Judith and Deborah, Miriam and Ruth, appears to us once more.

In Heine's "Rabbi of Bacharach" the lover says to his beloved, "Close your eyes, lovely Sarah," as soon as they encounter something humiliating, because the tender loveliness of her youth becomes tainted by a speck of filth.[1]

Walter Calé, like the precocious Otto Braun,[2] grew up shy as an Oriental maiden, but firm and healthy, a peach with an iron core.[3]

He sat at a richly appointed table, grew up in a happy home with a happy crowd of siblings, was beloved by his teachers and adored by his fellow students at the Friedrich Gymnasium. At age seventeen he entered university and chose law in order to live comfortably. He mastered the subject easily, without haste or difficulty.

He never was seen studying or having any problems. He learned as easily as breathing. The most important things in his life appeared to be celebrations with friends (male and female), walks, and discussions, hours during which youth opens up to each other and thoughts reach out from heart to heart.

He didn't attend many lectures and read only the very best books, always new. He anticipated his knowledge of the world and at age twenty was able to say:

> Events the times have brought to pass
> I knew them all ere time began.
> The source of all that lives has sprung
> As a great mystery from my breast.
> And when I read what Scripture says,
> I only learned what I am now.
> A darkness covers all that is
> But I am light and I am truth.

A handsome, healthy young man stands before us tall and slim, dark, dreamy, pensive. Soft reverential eyes, always turned inward, lie under his high forehead. His nose is big and bold. His lustrous, deep black hair is silky and wavy, but his defiant chin and tart, pinched lips show a wild energy.

What did he lack? He had everything that anyone could want. He enjoyed beautiful clothing and cultivated fashion. He collected bronzes, paintings, and fine old books. He spoke several modern languages fluently. He mastered Ancient Greek and Latin. He accomplished many things: a beautiful work about Plotinus,[4] novels in the manner of his beloved Gottfried Keller,[5] poems in the manner of Stefan George,[6] verse dramas reminiscent of the young Hofmannsthal.[7] All of this gave rise to a music of his own, and he was able to combine the simplicity of folk songs with the mature art of top masters. He created everything without ambition, for his own pleasure. Before he died he burned these papers. There remained only a small accidental remnant, which his friend Arthur Brückmann and the philosopher Fritz Mauthner[8] collected and published in fall 1906 (S. Fischer Verlag, Berlin) in the form of a small volume entitled "Walter Calé, *Nachgelassene Schriften* [Posthumous papers]."[9]

Nevertheless, we include him in the list of "Jewish self-haters."

The reason becomes clear when, instead of the more beautiful world he took with him, we speak of the bitter world into which, without regret, he let himself slip before death. We will speak in plain words, no matter how unpleasant they may be.

The era of ten thousand Jewish scribes has long forgotten what a poet is and how a nation's poets come into being.

Out of a great crowd of the simple, silent masses, fate raises up someone who speaks, sings, preserves memories, explains the unexplainable, makes the unsaid comprehensible. Perhaps he is a well-behaved youth who, in a fiery eruption, protects nature and nature's geniuses.

Maybe a woman's heart, penetrated by sword or arrow. Maybe a wise old man such as among the Finnish bards who only began to sing after their seventieth year. These "elected of God" open their breasts and turn their hearts into harps for the lamentations and lofty aims of their people. Their earthly concerns are soon forgotten and scarcely outlive them for an hour. They glow, speak their word, and sink. But enchanted ones recognize them, drink their blood, and elevate them into gods. By comparison, let us now consider passage of the "modern Jewish poet" into the "cultural conversation lexicon."

Papa has made a fortune on the stock exchange or earned a great deal in the dressmaking business, so his son Sigi (who is exceptionally talented—all crossbred products of marriage requests in the *Frankfurter Zeitung* and marriage offers in the *Berliner Tageblatt* are inserted by "frightfully gifted" men) can rent a country house and become a poet. He also could become a lawyer in District Court III or "devote himself to an academic career." But becoming a poet is so much more posh and also (if only he makes a fair amount of money) more "estimable."[10]

Sigi learns everything that has become easy to learn: write plays, tinker with cheap novels, stylize essays. Because culture consumes intellectual merchandise en masse. Those with fancy waistcoats and those who live in fancy villas shower the ten thousand purveyors of literature with compliments of "subtlety" and "intellectual wealth": true representatives of culture!

They sit in the leather armchairs of their editorial offices or in plush theaters and glide around in zeppelins, mammoth steamers, and luxury automobiles over land and sea. And everything—whether war or national collapse, a ball at the Kristallpalast or starving children of cave-dwellers, primeval forests or Okeanos[11]—everything is "material." As Flaubert, that genius of Sitzfleisch, opined:[12] *tout est matière pour nous* (everything is material for us).

And so they pile it up deceivingly, exchanging the genuine for its mirror image: paper, paper, more paper. Words, words, words ...

A million trees must be cut down, to provide enough paper for a world that must be "kept to standard" and consonant with "public thinking."

Wherever they go throughout the world they press the flesh of their peers. They tell nations their valued opinion, know the value of everything on the intellectual stock exchange. And opposite them—O terrible caricature of the austere earth mother-goddesses—their stylish women sit on their silver thrones, handing out laurels, laughing all the way to the bank.

That is the history of exploitation for the purposes of "culture."

This exploitation, by not concentrating on what is really good and important, has wasted the best material of the Jewish people in the pursuit of material gain. This *wastage* started the day Moses Mendelssohn turned from an oppressed Jew into a publishing Jew.[13]

Do you want the best directors? The most effective film stars? Dermatologists? Humorists? Acrobats? Psychologists? Industrialists? Communists? Lyricists? Just tell us and we will deliver! We lead everything. We can do everything. Do you want talent? We have plenty of talent. Do you want genius? We have that too.

It would make no difference—indeed it would only lead to ridicule or be counted as lunacy—if, in their bacchanal of "work and achievement," a live person would call out, "You are *dead*!"

How is it possible that all these men and women—so busy, receptive to the public, alertly eager, world-shaking—have turned into gasping corpses?

Worse! They have turned into murderers of our people, murderers of gods and singers, murderers of the soul.

Yes! It really is true. The elite of the history-making and of the history-regarded are abandoned, rubbish!

Expelled from both the German and the Jewish people.

The German *Volk* look on these talent drones as profiteers of their souls. The Jews must also reject their talents, whether in the "general public" or the "millionaire address book" where they are kings for a day and then forgotten in favor of newcomers.

Where will this lead?

It is a picture of a whirring flight of vanishing birds who have flown too high over the *graveyard* of the people.

Though well-perfused with the veins of concessions it's a hopeless world, in which the tragedy of Jewish self-hate plays out less frequently because people more often just shrug their shoulders and say: *Nebbach!*[14] or "Oh, well."

What did our little poet want in such a world?

He had early knowledge of his mark of Cain.

What could he become? A much sought-after lawyer, a famous professor, a valued author? Only not what he really was: a poet.

When the young Michelangelo boasted that he could knead figures like Phidias,[15] the cardinal laughingly pointed to the snow in the Vatican garden and said, "Knead!" Michelangelo tried to do so, calling out with tears in his eyes, "Give me marble!"

It is bitter for musicians to be born into a country without musical instruments. The only instrument on which a poet can play is the heart of his people.

They will be reborn again and again until the catastrophic end. Rare flowers, rare animals, rare hearts. Even if they are recognized by being plucked, coveted, and chased, no one achieves fulfillment anymore. At best, he may find compensation with honorable utilization of his abilities.

Calé could not do this! He was a "beautiful soul." Children and flowers are defenseless. If they are not looked after, they sicken and die.

He was a tree that gave forth fruit in the wilderness, but no wanderer came to use it.

He was a flower that bloomed in the abyss of beauty, but no eye was there to enjoy it.

All beautiful things want an eye to see them.

He was a princess who grew up in the forest in which worthy men do not get lost, enabling them to rejoice in her.

His was the life of a hermit who writes his will in the sand before he dies knowing that during the next few hours the simoom[16] will blow it away.

Walter Calé was comforted by the thought that he would remain only as long as he wished:

> There are red springs outflowing
> Around the place I dwell,
> An all-black rider waters
> His black horse from that well.
>
> A hundred years he's tarried
> Outside my rounded gate;
> He never loses patience,
> He'll simply have to wait.
>
> If I would take just three steps,
> I could be by his side,
> We could go off together
> Wherever I would ride.
>
> I am so glad to know that!
> I say a thousand times:
> "There is someone who's waiting,"
> And yet I stay inside.
>
> The rider sleeps in shadow,
> His coat of mail is bright,
> His steed is very sleepy,
> I think things are just right.

The ancient world believed that a poet, glowing briefly with the divine spirit, arises from the nation, blood, and countryside to give voice to a multitude. But there comes a time when a poet needs nothing more than protection from publicity. The concept of the publisher and of the publicist has become the antithesis of the poet terrified of self-loss.

Nations are not closed societies anymore. The people's community[17] has been replaced by the international society, the people's state by the class-state. This immense substructure, this swarming proletarian anthill, on whose back the class pyramid rises, each class carrying the other. One of these classes (in its opinion the highest but in truth nothing but the ornamental façade of state architecture) is the group of "civilization-producing professions."[18]

There is no doubt that today's poet does not grow like a field flower, nor does he sing like a bird in the bush anymore.

This situation can be saved by only one thing.

During the last several centuries an astonishing sociological miracle has been developing: *the circle.*

Trees no longer thrive in the open air. They need nurseries and greenhouses. Refined, tender teenage boys and girls do not yearn for publicity and space. They require their own "circle" to protect them from public life for as long as possible.

This process corresponds with emergence of religious orders within the church and is related to laws by which leading castes and estates have developed.

The heart of the matter is as follows: a group of people submit to their own strict norms and duties and, through this strict and difficult-to-access life, they declare themselves to be the "chosen people," the "better Germany," the "secret France," the "real England," the "coming America."

It is indeed a strange aberration that the bourgeois world regards this walled-off circle as formless and digressive—because it originated from familiar forms—attributing it to bohemians and gypsies. In fact, the contrary is true. The poetic circle with its iron bonds is the opposite of all groups who claim special rights without special duties. The more "exclusive," "distinguished," "more discerning" the circle is, the greater the possibility for outsiders to gather their collective intellect and will to explore and try to capture its forms and values. These outsiders are gnawed by the greedy worm of the excluded and stung by the envious scorpion of the ineligible and uninitiated. Ultimately, the circle, adversarial to the masses, is recognized if not supported, appreciated if not loved, by an entire people.

This seems the only *possible* way of allowing the poetic muse to attain power these days. Preoccupation with the extraordinary *individual* is awkward and embarrassing. Occupation with the exceptional *circle* is the favorite work of all academic minds.

This sociological process is secretly just a cult that hides the apotheosis of the *only-personal*. This can be most easily demonstrated with the "Parnassians" or "Symbolists," but especially the circle of Stefan George.[19] It is not driven by national symbols such as river sources or volcanoes, but rather fragile, vulnerable figures join company to practice a guild-like art or intellectual exercise such as that of a noble cenacle, literary coterie, Greek symposium, or *thiasus* (θίασος).[20] These forms are in constant need of protection and either incapable of or unsuitable for open battle. Just as a creation of exquisite handwork, a poem, book, play, painting, statue, piece of architecture, or (although less often) music, is cultivated, stylized, and pictured, chapter by chapter, strophe by strophe, line by line.

This is an entirely new type of art exercise that will without doubt triumph in the future. The end of naïve folk art. National songs and stories did not originate in the upper and *sink* into the lower social classes. Rather, all artistic expressions of the national community — weapons, domestic utensils, clothing, implements — originated, sleeplike and dreamily, unconsciously from the bosom of the elementary. Finally, however, enlightened craft work and clear objectivity have replaced all spiritless, man-made constructs.

In the beginning, individuals were not important: the most glorious primeval art is not attached to a specific name. Later, however, "personality" and ability created schools and cults. The poetry-cultivating circle may eventually reach a dangerous boundary, where experience of an eminent *individual* demands religious and symbolic consecration. A Caesar, who demands that his dead lover Antinous become a god and his favorite horse a consul.[21]

Walter Calé lacked the one thing he needed most: the *circle*.

He was one of those who "missed the connection." He was neither imperial ruler nor servant, and this tender Epigone[22] was much too weak to become a stubborn maverick and loner. He was a shade shrub with no sun in whose shadow it could grow.

He was much too genuine and genteel to write industrial-grade poetry and devalue his gold into popular currency, like ten thousand other writers. All he could do was, like a pale prince starving amid plenty, languidly play with the jewel with his slender fingers. He could make people both happy and unhappy, and in the evening sigh, "What is the purpose of all this?" After having worked extremely hard for eight days to polish a piece of prose, he became ashamed of its artificiality: he tore it up and sighed, "What is the *purpose* of that?"

In considering and making ourselves important, we need to reflect on the deep connection with human frailty. No one has said it more wisely than Buddha:

> Those who cannot heal themselves
> Try to save the world instead.

Each of these poor sufferers who have "missed the connection" (be it connection to church, party, Weltanschauung-community, school, orbit, or circle) is one day burdened by the near-sacrilegious delusion of an emergency exit. He inflates the *ego*, finds *himself* important, and his own suffering different and more important than all other suffering. He makes himself out to be a physician but cannot heal himself. He becomes a "benefactor of humanity," an individualistic aristocrat, a "blusterer."

That was not the way for Walter Calé. Anyone who saw him during his short life saw a correct, polite, modest, refined young man who always preserved form and posture and didn't thrust himself into the light. He opened himself up to male and female friends with increasing rarity, and only during hours of celebration. He hid his work. To the world, he was a well-educated young law clerk from a good family. He didn't want to be anything else.

But he had arisen from blood that seldom courses through the veins of pious hermits and beatific contemplative monks, but rather through those of countless people who are ready for physical and spiritual deeds. His blood said to him: "Our God is an all-consuming fire. I have come to ignite a great fire and see it burn." He looked around the western suburbs of Berlin, the market of Jewish vanity. Men with positions, offices, and adorned with high-sounding titles; women bespangled with rings, jewelry, and precious stones. And all alienated from the dream, from the night, and in the deepest possible loneliness.

And so: "Will you become like that as well?"

During one of a thousand nights of pondering, disgust overwhelmed him, and he simply left. As silently and thoughtfully as he had lived, among the few papers that he could not burn, Walter Calé stepped out into the night. The last thing that he wrote before he died was:

> Fingers curled, I'd like to begin playing
> But your strings are badly out of tune,
> And your body is as well all broken,
> Alas poor Lute.
>
> Burning a match I try to find your wicking,
> But the oil has lighted other evenings,
> And the wick itself is soot and ashes,
> Alas poor Lamp.

Outside the window clownish masks are waiting,
They stare and press their foreheads to the panes,
And scratch their fingernails along the glass,
Alas poor Soul.

Notes

1. Heinrich Heine (1797–1856), German poet, writer, literary critic.
2. Otto Braun (1897–1918), German author and poet, killed in World War I.
3. Otto Braun was the only child of the esteemed socialist politician and theoretician Heinrich Braun and well-known socialist leader Lily Braun, a daughter of the Prussian General von Kretschmar. Through her grandmother Jenny von Gutstedt, she was connected to the Goethe Circle, and she came from Napoleonic stock. Otto Braun, Jewish on his father's side, was like a messenger from another world. He grew up in the same house in which Maximilian Harden was born, and I saw him for the first time in the same room where I saw Maximilian Harden for the last time. His posthumous papers, edited by Julie Vogelstein, probably are the loftiest thing remaining from the Great War, and no more noble sacrifice was made to the Fatherland. I quote Richard Wagner's beautiful epitaph to a friend who died young:

    > Ripe now for dying, a lifetime's slowly ripening fruit,
    > Is brought to early harvest by fate's abruptly shattering force.
    > Was it your lot? Was it your courage?
    > We'll rue both your lot and your daring in our mourning.

    I do not want to leave the impression that Braun's terrible war sacrifice of raw warrior virtue and courage was not deeply genuine and true. Of course, it cannot compare with the elaborate scandals of "contemporaries" living the good life today (as fashionably "pacifist" as they were "warlike" then). I remember the lyrical phrase: "The war must be sustained as a war against war." A "famous novelist" wrote the following from his elegant desk and plush chair: "If Germany's heroic spirit can be preserved thereby, may this war last seven more years" (afterwards, he carefully eradicated such spiritual ecstasy from his "Collected Works"—his opinion had changed in the meantime). Otto Braun lived far away from this vaunted world of wretchedness. He paid for his opinions courageously with his flesh and blood. And yet—what nonsense! What a waste! I remember a mother who wrote and prattled her whole life in passionate books about the "redemption of the poor and oppressed," and whom a uniformed comrade eulogized as "the mother of a lieutenant."

4. Plotinus (204/5–270 CE), major Hellenistic philosopher who lived in Ancient Egypt.
5. Gottfried Keller (1819–1890), Swiss poet and writer of German literature.
6. Stefan George (1868–1933), German translator and symbolist poet.
7. Hugo von Hofmannsthal (1874–1929), Austrian novelist, librettist, poet, dramatist, and essayist.
8. Fritz Mauthner (1849–1923), Austro-Hungarian writer and philosopher of skepticism.

9. Walter Calé, *Nachgelassene Schriften* (Berlin: S. Fischer, 1907).
10. *Among my old papers, I found some notes from 1902. At the time, I was a teacher in a German boarding school. There were many Jewish boys at the school, most very talented and planning to become "poets."*

    > *And every year there came new men and women,*
    > *Each one of them hard-working, talented,*
    > *And capable of turning out a story*
    > *Or playlet just in time for Christmas eve.—*
    > *When I think how I struggled lonely nights*
    > *To write the single poem of my life,*
    > *Oh, how they got them easily together,*
    > *And so mature as they I'll never be,*
    > *The poet Speier and the poet Cohn*
    > *The poets Meier, Frank, and Mendelssohn.*

    A few years later, all these so-called talents really did "devote themselves to literature."

    The unnaturalness of the above-mentioned societal stratum was brought home to me when the school suddenly issued the following regulation: "Minor children, or children of Jewish extraction, are generally not allowed in German boarding schools." Self-evidently, I felt that I must respond to this shameless act by resigning my teaching position. I believed that all Jewish parents and pupils would be on my side; but something astonishing happened. I was the only one who resigned. All other Jews remained, reassuring themselves with the fact that it had not been decided to expel them but rather, in general, not accept any new Jewish pupils. I asked a Jewish mother whether a sense of honor did not dictate that, on principle, she take her son out of the school. I will never forget her answer: "I do not understand what you want, Herr Doktor. If boarding schools do not admit any new Jews but leave our own children where they are, they will be in really good company."
11. Keanos (Oceanus) was the primordial Titan god of the great, earth-encircling River Okeanos, font of all of the earth's freshwater rivers, wells, springs, and rain clouds. He was also the god who regulated the heavenly bodies that rose from and set into his waters.
12. Gustave Flaubert (1821–1880), French realist novelist best known for his book *Madame Bovary*. Lessing is being a snob, as befits a German writer. He is poking fun at Flaubert's prolixity with words.
13. Moses Mendelssohn (1729--786), German Jewish philosopher; untranslatable wordplay. From *gepresster Jude* (oppressed Jew) to *Pressejude* (an opprobrious epithet much used by the Nazis for a Jew who willingly accommodates commercial publishing priorities).
14. *Nebbach* (Yiddish): regrettable.
15. Phidias (ca. 490–430 BCE), Greek sculptor of the statue of Zeus at Olympia.
16. Simoom is a strong, dry, dust-laden wind (sirocco, hamsin). The word is generally is used to describe a local wind that blows in the Sahara, Israel, Jordan, Syria, and the deserts of Arabian Peninsula. Its temperature may exceed 54°C (129°F), and the humidity may fall below 10 percent.
17. *Volksgemeinschaft*. A prescient word, much used by the National Socialists. Jews and other undesirables were excluded from the *Volksgemeinschaft* and could not be *Volksgenossen(innen)*.

18. *Kultur*. German civilization and culture (sometimes used derogatorily to suggest elements of racism, authoritarianism, or militarism). Lessing is being sarcastic.
19. Parnassianism was a nineteenth-century French literary movement influenced by positivist thought; Symbolism was a late nineteenth-century art movement of French, Russian, and Belgian origin in poetry and other arts. Stefan George (1868–1933) was the main person of the literary and academic group known as the George-Kreis (George-Circle), which included some of the era's major young writers such as Friedrich Gundolf (1880–1931) and Ludwig Klages (1872–1956). In addition to sharing cultural interests, the group promoted mystical and political themes.
20. In ancient Greece, the symposium comprised drinking, music, or conversation following a banquet. In Greek mythology and religion, the *thiasus* was the often-drunk entourage of the god Dionysus.
21. Antinous was a favorite of Emperor Hadrian, widely commemorated and even deified following his death.
22. In Greek mythology, the Epigoni are the sons of heroes of the first Theban War.

Maximilian Harden

Dissatisfied, highly strung, and wistful, I sat at my school desk in a small German town, a youth seventeen years old. I was building castles in the air, dreaming into the blue sky, when one day in a forgotten weekly publication I was confronted for the first time with the name Maximilian Harden.[1]

The signature appeared underneath a series of passionate essays full of acuity and joking word games that unsettled and began to preoccupy those who read them. I became the first, but perhaps the keenest, of Harden's readers. One day I packaged up the first fruits of my immature garden of poems, plays, and novellas and sent them off to the dreaded critic with a description of my needs and request for advice.

Never in later life have I waited so fearfully for a response. Weeks passed before I received the reply, which exceeded all expectations. "You have more talent in your little finger than I have in my whole body and everything belonging to it. One day you will develop your own voice but it will take toil, sweat, and tears. Dare to throw everything else away, and begin an independent writing career."

Soon after, Pentecost 1890, I moved to Berlin with a little suitcase that contained more paper than linen and asked the way to Köthnerstrasse, home of Maximilian Harden.

A worldly, cheerful gentleman (perhaps the most captivating person I have ever met) received me. He was eleven years older than I, but greatly superior to me in worldliness, self-control, attitude, and wisdom. He observed the life-hungry high school student half-smilingly, half-respectfully, and treated me like a better-off elder brother. He brought me to Otto Brahm, Theodor Fontane, and Arthur Levysohn, editor-in-chief of the *Berliner Tageblatt*.[2] He listened half-moved, half-amazed to the endless declamations of the uncritical and pretentious young man until deep into the night. After eight days, my first flight into the open was met with disappointment, and the germ of our friendship died in the bud.

How could that have come about? Nothing happened. Nothing was said. All was decided in a half-conscious moment during which my infatuation suddenly died.

It happened on a bright summer morning during a lively debate about our respective lives, which were very similar. Both of us had an unhappy childhood, hated family and our parents' home. Both of us were alone and lonely and felt our Jewish origin to be a pressure, burden, and unpleasant duty. We knew nothing about the religion and had not learned a single letter of Hebrew. Both of us felt passionately German and couldn't understand how there could have been even the slightest doubt of our Germanness.

We decided to take a walk into the Tiergarten, to continue our debate in the greenery.

I went into his small anteroom, to fetch my hat and coat, while he dawdled in his room, getting dressed in front of his large mirror. We spoke through the open door. During our passionate conversation I stepped onto the threshold and, turning my head, saw my companion looking into the mirror trying on his summer hat without my knowing, fashioning a small Napoleon forelock out of his thick, wavy hair. Our eyes crossed for a moment in the mirror. My face might have expressed embarrassment at having caught a man whom I so admired in the midst of so unworthy an action. To my horror, *"enemy"* flamed out of Harden's steely blue eyes.

I know now that this was a life-changing moment for me.

My dark feelings about this may have been: "Flee! You are in danger! He has discerned my scorn at something he took very seriously. Flee!"[3]

We walked through the Tiergarten. We spoke about many things and developed the plan for opening a magazine. He promised me permanent employment, but there was already a rift between us. He spoke patronizingly, I timidly.

That evening, I informed him of my final decision. I wanted to return to school, to become a physician or teacher. I was not meant to become an author. The cutting reply came back: "You are not strong enough to fly by my side." Our parting was ice cold: both of us were disappointed. We did not see each other again until shortly before his death.

From then on, our paths diverged widely, my own through many labyrinths: distress, poverty, confusion, to eventual renunciation of impact and success. Only then did peace and joy come. The other road, Harden's, soon rose steeply to heights of impact and sway that no single man, in Germany or anywhere else, has achieved through the power of his pen. Riches and fame were showered upon him.

He belonged to no party, but all parties courted him. He had no official post, but all the authorities hung on his every word. He disdained titles and medals, but those who bore the most distinguished names and titles feared his judgment.

The same in the theater and literature as in politics. His verdict was crucial in the widest-possible circles. When, in America, a poll was circulated about Germany's most influential personality, everyone agreed that there was but one name: Harden.

Maximilian Harden was the youngest son of Berlin merchant Witkowski, one of the old "1848" freedom fighters and friend of people's tribune August Bebel.[4] Harden's father was apparently an upright man, full of character, but became ill with a progressive brain disease that gradually became a torment to him and his entire family. The family's integrity eventually was so shattered that it became better for the four sons to change their names. The marriage was destroyed, and the parents went to court for custody of their children. The youngest, Felix, was supposed to stay with his father but ran away to his mother. Felix was a particularly good-looking, talented, but peculiar child.

The Göttingen physiologist Max Verworn[5] related: "I went to school at the Lycée français de Berlin with Felix Ernst Witkowski, who became the well-known Maximilian Harden. He had radiant blue eyes and a girlish head with blond curly hair. He was generally popular, a stubborn, proud young boy. He carried the Homeric nickname 'Decider of Battles.' He did not participate in our great snowball battles in the school courtyard, but sat high on a wall in a safe place, where no snowball could hit him, and acted as referee. His word was law, and all parties deferred to the brash youngster."

Every evening, the youth sat in the gallery of the Royal Theater. His adored heroes were the bohemian, outrageous, demonic Albert Niemann, Adalbert Matkowski, and Friederich Mitterwurzer—geniuses of power.[6] Even before he finished school, the theater enthusiast ran away with a traveling troop of actors and cut himself off from his parents and siblings. Between 1880 and 1885 he led a life similar to that of Wilhelm Meister in Goethe's "apprenticeship years."[7] Actor Fritz Odemar[8] related:

> We played in countless places, mainly classical pieces. As was customary, Felix had to choose a stage name, and cobbled together the name "Maximilian Harden." In doing so he may well have thought of Maximilien Robespierre and the necessity to be "hard" in struggle with life's toughness. After beginning with small roles, he soon played the young lover, a role he enjoyed playing in real life. We often overnighted in small country inns, where Harden and I usually shared a room. Once we arrived in a

town where a circus had pitched its large tent. The circus troupe and our group shared the same inn. Harden, who was easily inflamed by the female sex, fell in love with a circus dancer. One morning I woke up to find that Harden's bed had not been slept in. After walking through the hall I arrived at the dancer's room. I saw that she was still in bed. Next to her was a youthful figure dressed only in a nightshirt. Upon my invasion of his privacy, he sat up and, bowing to the lady in a noble, knightly fashion, said: "Allow me, *gnädiges Fräulein*, to introduce myself. My name is Maximilian Harden."

Franziska Ellmenreich, the great tragedienne,[9] related: "In 1886 I toured through Holland. I chose a series of roles from Schiller, Goethe, and Shakespeare[10] and brought my own ensemble with me. Maximilian Harden partnered me, playing the lover's roles. He was a clever actor and loveable colleague, but couldn't achieve lasting success because his body wasn't sufficiently robust and his figure too petite."

In the meanwhile, the other Witkowski brothers had made their own way. The three eldest brothers chose the name Witting, while two founded a flourishing export firm in London. Another made a good living as a Prussian civil servant and, in 1890, became mayor of Posen.[11]

Through his older brothers Harden came into contact with the *Berliner Tageblatt* and the publisher of *Gegenwart*,[12] Theophil Zolling.[13] He settled in Berlin, started to study at the university, and was particularly taken with works of Heinrich von Treitschke, Ernst Curtius, and Hermann Grimm.[14] He became a critic and feuilletonist, providing regular contributions to Paul Nathan's periodical *Die Nation*.[15] He wrote gossip columns, small sketches, and sentimental novellas for the *Berliner Tageblatt*, but soon turned to criticism of the times and satire filled with splendid storms and magnificent malice. When under the nom de plume "Apostata" the first collection of his work appeared in book form, he already had become a successful, well-recognized writer. In 1888 he went on a long voyage to the Orient and in 1890 turned to high politics.

Harden's great blossoming occurred in 1891, with the founding of his own periodical *Die Zukunft*,[16] with meager resources provided by his brother Julian and railway station bookseller Stilke.

It was during the great conflict between Kaiser Wilhelm II and the old Reich chancellor Bismarck.[17] Harden placed his periodical at the service of Bismarckian politics but without thereby betraying his independence. Through articles and glosses Otto von Bismarck was made aware of Harden's writings. When Bismarck fell[18] and was abandoned by so many, he remembered Harden and invited the young author to visit him in Varzin.[19] Soon Harden became part of the small circle of friends in Bismarck's home. Kurt von Schlözer, the painter Franz Lenbach, and the physician Ernst Schweininger became close friends.[20] After 1892, the best anti-kaiser policy in Germany was brewed up in the modest brown volumes of *Die Zukunft*.

It is incorrect, however, to connect the history of Harden's *Zukunft* too closely to his association with Bismarck. Harden guarded his independence and incorruptibility with utmost care. No camp or party could say that they had exerted longtime influence over Maximilian Harden. Especially in the social political arena (similar to Pastor Friedrich Naumann[21]) he diverged completely from Bismarckian policies. He always emphasized his *opposition d'épouser les haines d'autre* (i.e., to carry on Bismarck's spitefulness). But there was one issue with which he agreed to the last with the old man in Sachsenwald,[22] and that was hatred for the kaiser. The exact origin for this hate is difficult to pinpoint.

Harden despised the kaiser's many fancy uniforms, volatility, and continuous meddling in affairs he did not understand. He originated the saying "The old, wise kaiser[23] has been succeeded by a traveling kaiser."[24] He feuded constantly with the kaiser's overbearing and unstable, volatile, show-and-catastrophe politics, the unpredictable and mercurial petulance of the strongman's pose. Everything that the kaiser said and did provoked Harden's jokes and taunts. Just mentioning Harden's name made the kaiser upset and vindictive. Insofar as they were critical and dissatisfied with the kaiser's self-aggrandizement, Reich officials, Prussian nobility, military parties, and administration gradually saw a safe, effective haven in Harden's *Zukunft*. By 1900 Harden had become the pet journalist of old conservative Prussians.

Out of a sort of equality or inequality of natures, two theatrical personalities, the power-motivated kaiser and the impact-motivated man of letters, cudgeled each other. Harden lived off the battle against the "Wilhelmine Era." When the glory of the Wilhelmine Reich ended, Harden ended as well. The kaiser and political malcontents[25] faded away in a neighboring country on the North Sea. But for twenty years beforehand they were in daily battle.[26]

Harden's uncommonly delicate, graceful body bore a head that, despite its attractiveness and gravitas, still was almost doll-like, a pretty face on a chocolate or cigarette box. A child's face that, when it chatted amiably and animatedly, looked like a lady's maid waiting for approval. But when he became angry, bitter, and resentful (something that quickly drove this highly disciplined man into seclusion), the courteous maid-like face changed into that of a malicious little devil.

The reason for his strongly split personality was his iron self-discipline and ever-growing consciousness of the dangerous excitability that constantly threatened to make him the plaything of strong impressions. Volatile in his feelings, he was at heart a good, noble, faithful man. Although his moods were changeable, his judgment could not be misled. He was a man of the moment with an instantaneous nature. Every new day, place, and impression could change him so that, without noticing it, today he praised what he damned yesterday, and willingly condemned today what he tenaciously defended yesterday. His stance was never defined by economic situation, advantage, or base purpose. Just the opposite: he had the tendency to abandon each opinion as soon as there was a chance that it would become generally accepted. He distrusted success. He was suspicious of anyone who was acclaimed, and his decisions always had moral underpinning. Even when he became carried away, he was solidly convinced that he, and only he, was in the right.

He was genius-vain, with advocating, diplomatic, theatrical intelligence, concrete and practical, never philosophical. His intellectualism was determined by day and time. He sacrificed the world of eternity to the moment, and wrote a feuilleton for some unique but now-forgotten purpose or other with a seriousness and fervor sufficient for a weighty life's work. His manners of working and acting had something kittenish and playful about them. The style and way of thinking of contemporary politicians such as Rochefort and Clemenceau[27] clomped around on elephants' feet, compared to Harden's butterfly-like sentences. He seemed only to lay mosaics and sketch a small picture out of a thousand dots and dashes. One could have imagined that he collected material in a card index and was particularly proud to be the only one to know this or that detail before anyone else had a clue of its existence.

One can find this practical political acumen in many professions and social strata. In its most noxious excesses it is reminiscent of the "prognosticators and fabulists" who clutter up the contents of history's waste baskets. But even in its best and noble form, it creates *médisance*[28] in the general public and in the envious tattle of one about the other.

Political talents such as those possessed by, for example, Joseph Fouché, Friedrich Gentz, and Karl August Varnhagen von Ense,[29] as different as they were individually, had in common the fact that all of them were masters of the "sniffing out" of small facts (*petits faits*). As such, they fatally resembled "professional association lackeys," who failed in their careers. Maximilian Harden also possessed a smalltime curiosity about human frailties. He knew the life history, alliances, traits, and intimate aspects of all those in leading positions, sitting like a spider in his web of "connections." Ever coming and going, countless personalities of rank and power brought him significant inside information. Probably all of them hoped to channel his conceit of being the best-informed journalist for *their* own purposes. In fact, however, the enterprising writer used everyone and everything to compile, every Saturday, the best-informed and most astonishing articles in the busy day-to-day world.

It was not that he undervalued so-called ideals, principles, and ideas, but rather that he saw behind them only *people's* needs and faces. Flawed, limited people who had to be seized by their passions if one wanted to understand how to steer the great affairs of the Reich. The divisiveness of this world can be truly understood only through the fact that vulnerable people—with *needs* for falsehood and comfort—stand behind every event.

Nations and peoples appeared to him like competing firms that struggle for advantages. But his firm was called Germany. In his quietest hours he dreamed of becoming Reich chancellor. He deliberately loudly proclaimed himself a "self-made man," nothing but a man of theater and the best in European culture. He learned foreign languages, browsed through countless books (all of which had to deal with reality, contain concrete historical facts), and developed judgment and taste in many arts. He knew each country's business and economy and eventually possessed a practical knowledge about people and facts of his age that no practitioner, no statesman irrespective of branch or country, could hope to match.

But this over-consciousness became his curse.

Always inclined to brag with moderate vanities, mystery mongering, and meddling, he was willing to appear in the know and superior to all. He encumbered his writing style with lights that were too brilliant, too many innuendoes, citations, and witticisms. He became what antiquity called a colossalist[30] (aesthetic zealot).

Because they see things invisible to others, those who are ahead of their time are not recognized. They are always separated from the masses by a wide fog-filled gap. Happy is the man who stands now where the great majority will stand in the future. He always will be seen at the summit and is a born forerunner and leader.[31]

Harden's insubordinate tenacity gave him many proud moments, for example when the great Bismarck invited him to share the bottle of Steinberger Kabinett that the kaiser sent him for his birthday. Because he shared the wine, a gift from one whom they jointly hated, with the founder of the Reich, he could drink to the well-being of the German Fatherland. Another proud moment was when the powerful conservative party, nobility concerned with them, and the agricultural sector called on him to lead their press and he was able to decline with a grand gesture. This was the most sought-after glory for other writers, something unreachable for a Jew since the time of Friedrich Julius Stahl.[32] Yet another proud moment was when the German Writers Association honored Harden with an honorary pen, as the only man who, on his own and as an independent private citizen, had become Germany's leading literary light. Also, when the spidery intriguer Holstein[33] crept out of his lair carrying political secrets and information to Harden, who forthwith harnessed the old power-addict to the wagon of *Die Zukunft*.

But certainly Harden's greatest pride was that he, the most envied, was able to decline so many offices, titles, and decorations.

His pugnacious nature craved fame only in a great battle to gain the martyr's wreath of the bold truth-teller.

The following narrative from the philosopher Wilhelm Wundt[34] shows how far a gesture could be extended:

> Harden was sentenced to imprisonment for lèse-majesté, found in an article entitled "Grandfather's Clock." In novella form, the story described the story of a capricious heir who, having inherited it from his grandfather, allows the clock that regulates the Reich to gather dust in a corner. The allusion to the relationship between the kaiser and Bismarck was unmistakable.[35] Reich Chancellor Bülow,[36] whose person and politics Harden opposed, was personally sympathetic to the writer and would have liked to modify the court's sentence. Harden's friends built a plan around this, to obtain a pardon for him. A petition to set aside the remainder of his sentence was circulated. In Leipzig the historian Karl Lamprecht,[37] a close friend of Harden's, solicited signatures. Many professors signed it. Then came a surprise. The petition was published but, at the same time, *Die Zukunft* published an essay entitled "Bismarck and Bülow," mocking Bülow. Bismarck and his mastiff Tyras comically confronted Bülow and his miniature pinscher Mohrschen. The satire must have caused more irritation than all previous criticisms combined. But why did Harden permit the petition for pardon to be set in motion, allowing so many prominent people to try to free him, in that he himself made this impossible? Perhaps he just wanted to boast: "See, German science and culture stand behind me, but I remain independent and am not for sale. Do not believe that I'll ask anything of you. I demand justice!"

His was the life of a public man who through a generation and week by week provides all the events of the time together with his marginal notes, and intervenes in the lives of ten thousand people, offices, parliaments, banks, journalists, leaders of commerce and captains of industry. The entire life of his people, from music to logic and from the production of potatoes to beets comes under his sway. Such a public life is overabundant with lawsuits, crashes, controversies, and continuously changing human relationships.

There was a time when Harden's every spat, slap, and insult, every intimate story about women, love affair, or theater scandal, every stock market crash, all stirred by his adroit paw, held thousands in thrall. No one was more the talk-of-the-day in cafés, salons, and office spaces, from Königsberg[38] to Basel, from Moscow to Paris. But paper-fame yellows as quickly as wood-paper. What do names that once thrilled our hearts mean now? Names such as Kanitz and Mirbach, Bamberger and Lasker, Windthorst and Singer, lawyers Fritz Friedmann and Erich Sello, writers Paul Lindau, Franz Mehring, and Karl Bleibtreu, amorous actresses Elsa von Schabeltzky and Jenny Gross,[39] influential stockbrokers, leading professors—all of whose deeds and adventures were taken so seriously by us at the time.

In any event, a certain court case out of an endless series of Harden's dealings etched itself into posterity. It was the Harden-Eulenburg case that made large waves in the years between 1906 and 1909.[40] The court case originated, like all allegedly important issues in world history, from minor human frailties. Harden possessed, in large measure, what Nietzsche described as "an aesthetic joy in maliciousness." Not that he had become malevolent or took joy in other's misfortune. Rather, *la taquinerie est la méchanceté des bons*.[41] Good-natured, gentle natures have in them this enjoyment of entrapment and titillation.

From his years of friendly relations with Bismarck, Harden knew the intimate traits of everyone at court. He knew their sensitive spots, secret sins, and sometimes enjoyed threatening and showing his claws. The threatened usually easily reconciled him by deference or clever obsequiousness. Harden got wind of the fact that homosexual eroticism—what Bismarck called "the main sympathy"—in high levels of the administration affected many minor political decisions. It played a role in shake-ups and advancements, decided promotions, led to agreements among envoys and diplomats, and cast its shadows over treaties and alliances in weltpolitik.

In some of his essays Harden risked the inclusion of mocking intimations that only a small clique of intimates could understand. But this caused great unrest around the kaiser's table. A Hohenzollern prince fell out of favor with the kaiser because of homoerotic activities that turned into a scandal. He defended himself with the assertion that others, close confidants of the kaiser, had done much worse, and referred to insinuations in *Die Zukunft*. The crown prince handed the relevant articles to the kaiser, who was surprised and demanded an explanation.

Harden's articles made fun of Prince Philipp von Eulenburg und Hertefeld, a brilliant personality at the imperial court. Bismarck hated him, but the kaiser continued to admire the prince. He and his nearest friend

Count Kuno von Moltke (both were already nearly sixty) had, according to Harden's parody, exchanged over-effusive letters in which court confidences were gossiped about and people in the kaiser's vicinity called by pseudonyms known only to a chosen few. The kaiser himself was referred to as *Liebchen*. This correspondence was real. Harden knew that over the past forty years, Moltke had kept his friend Eulenburg current on all events at court every day the latter was absent from Berlin. He also knew that these two men had had an intimate relationship.

Eulenburg tried to compel Harden's silence. In response, Harden boldly demanded that Eulenburg—whose politics he regarded as dangerous—abstain from all interference in Reich affairs and retire voluntarily. Eulenburg, confident of his proven power over important people, risked a desperate gambit. He induced his friend Moltke to sue Harden for libel and swore to the court that he had never engaged in homosexual activities. Harden was convicted, but the prince remained in the court's good graces.

Extremely irritated, less by punishment than by the defamatory treatment that impugned both himself and his journalistic motive, Harden proceeded to open attack. He asserted that an obscure German camarilla linked to homosexual friendships acted as an irresponsible side-government and had surrounded the kaiser with their romantic and nebulous ring. Mystics, spiritualists, sweet-talkers, theosophists, ailing and effeminate men secretly directed Reich politics. By an extremely clever ruse an esoteric lawsuit was tacked onto an arbitrary one. Testimony under oath revealed that Eulenburg had committed perjury. The prince was put in the invidious position of having to sue Harden personally. With this new lawsuit, the accuser gradually turned into the heavily burdened accused. He was convicted, collapsed, and retired to his Castle Liebenberg for the remainder of his life. Only the kaiser's intervention prevented him from being tried and found guilty of perjury. A whole series of court personalities—Counts Hohenau, Lynar, Wedel, Moltke, Baron Wendelstaedt, French embassy councilor Lecomte[42]—were hard hit as a consequence of the Harden lawsuit. As curious as his actions were, it still must be said that Harden, as a powerless private citizen, fought the battle he thought necessary against the most powerful clique at court. He fought not only cleverly, but with peculiar grace.

Max Bernstein, Munich's most distinguished lawyer, who represented Harden, later related:

> When I was to represent Harden in a libel suit against the mentally ill King Otto of Bavaria,[43] one of my comedies entitled "Girl of My Dreams" was performed. Harden asked by telegram what my costs for represent-

ing him would be. When I replied, Harden sent me a one-word answer: "Girl of my dreams."[44] Harden was always ready to give satisfaction man to man. He stood for his allegations body and soul. It was neither his intention nor his fault that so large a circle of people at court and in the army were heavily damaged by the lawsuit. Despite the gravity of the matter, he divulged no more than the need dictated.

In hindsight, the fight against Philipp von Eulenburg became an exaggerated historical memory in Harden's mind. Perhaps this was because, subconsciously, he was ashamed of it. The historical law that I call "the meaningfulness of hindsight" (logification post factum) applies here as well. World history has labeled Prince Eulenburg a python threatening the German armed forces, an irresponsible secret regent felled by the devout Harden's shepherd slingshot.[45]

But suppose that Bismarck's circle of "romantics"—Waldersee,[46] Eulenburg, Moltke—really did unduly influence German history. What would be inferred? That politics should never be left to the mercy of private individuals no matter how powerful and clever they may be. Every political conceit that sees in the state and the state's good sense anything but a *growing* protection against individuals and independence of national destinies from the quirks and personal feelings of mortals is false and meaningless.

Harden had—consciously or unconsciously—a vital need to give outline and world-historical interpretation to his ever-changing and often private sympathies and antipathies. Those who revered him, and whose praise he appreciated, were regarded as genies and light elves. But those who were afraid or even critical of him appeared to him as envy-swollen serpents.

He did not stop to ask whether he himself had not done harm to countless people. He said of his judicial writings, "I do not negotiate, I enforce."

The time has come to discuss the strange stance of *Die Zukunft* vis-à-vis the Jews and the Jewish question.[47]

Although the best Jewish minds of the age contributed to the periodical, its stance was almost always "antisemitic." Around the turn of the century, a powerful movement had developed among German Jews; it was based on assimilation, mixed marriage, and mass baptism. A high jurist, Eduard Simon,[48] published a widely disseminated booklet "The Thoughts of a Jew." In the *Preussisches Jahrbuch*, an influential official writing under the name Benediktus Levita published an admonition to the Jews. Both affirmed that the older generation could not give up their being Jewish, but saw it as their duty to preserve reverence for their faith, preventing it from being changed for economic advantage.

By contrast, there was not the slightest reason why minors should be compelled to remain in the faith and set themselves apart from the majority of fellow Germans in a voluntary ghetto.

Around 1900 Walter Rathenau[49] published the call "Hear O Israel," which he later regretted, in Harden's *Die Zukunft*, unmistakably inviting mass baptism. Rathenau believed that preservation of Judaism only out of pious memories, with endless rites and laws that have become meaningless, is just a remnant of the ailing Orient in the midst of flourishing Western cultures. Jews should finally end the insoluble and unnecessary tension and simply immerse themselves in Germanness.

This was the unsaid opinion of the German Jewish majority. They had achieved equal rights (or so they thought), and this would have led to dissolution had Zionism not gathered the Jewish youth capable of revival in the years to come.

Harden's genial mastery of the intellectual game had never really taken anything seriously. Metaphysics, morals, world history—all appeared somewhat doubtful to him. But in one point he was in deadly earnest. There he felt completely responsible, dealing with lofty people as a loyal servant. It was called: Germany!

When his fiftieth birthday approached and his then hundreds of thousands of appreciative readers wanted to mark the occasion, he thanked them with a kind of public oath. He swore and presented his well-wishers with the glorious thought that he would, for as long as he could and with all his knowledge, serve "the good of Germanic man." This was (even if delusional) the final norm in his ever-active life, according to which he expressed judgments on Jews and the Jewish question. "What do you really want from me?" he called out to the Jews in *Die Zukunft*. "State clearly: whose business are you really conducting? Germany's or Zion's?" Another time: "One would think that if the battle against semitism were conducted with conviction it would not, in and of itself, be more contemptible than battles against Catholicism, capitalism, junkerism, and socialism." Harden was wrong. There is a difference whether I deny mankind on one hand as a creation of nature or on the other hand as a bearer of principles. At any rate Harden's disinterestedness in such a distinction is evident.

When he spoke about Germany his style became solemn and formal and resembled that of Jacob Grimm.[50] Some of his political thoughts had much in common with the Germany-worship of Paul Lagarde[51] and Heinrich von Treitschke.

I must confess that I fought against Maximilian Harden all my life.

After his death and toward the end of my life, I ask myself: why did I reject him? It appears to me that that moment in our youth was symbolic of my attitude. *Il s'était une tête.*⁵² Not that he lacked responsibility or that his satire was a game and his fury mere theater. He was serious, ponderous, loyal, and deliberate. But he never would have sacrificed himself to the cause; had he, would he not first have sent for the photographer? I wrote in 1900: "For Harden there is no true and false, but only clever and stupid. He criticizes world history as if it were a theater critique, but he would never go so far as to become impersonal."

I reflect back on a thorny life. Such an all-powerful, successful person without a single word of encouragement or appreciation for me. He knew of me and my achievements and often could have helped and enlightened me with a few encouraging lines. Far from assistance, over a period of forty years all I got from him were abuses and insults, worse than anyone of my rank should have to bear. Harden refused to say anything about it. Had I flattered and begged, he certainly would have remembered the promise he made to me when I was still developing. But I always saw the look in front of his mirror: "Player of greatness, ape of ideal, comedian of historical swindle, painted face, painted word!—Flee!"

Our relationship remained this way for many years. Then the hour that comes for us all once during our lives arrived. I asked myself: "Which of your goals have been good and true?" It was the hour when the World War broke out, July 1914.

The World War ended our youth, and everything that came before it had no genuine reality. However, in retrospect, when I occasionally thought about the possibility of a world catastrophe during the years of my youth, I was comforted by the following hopes: The power of the Internationale was far too great to be mutilated by the political impulses of nationalist jingoism, as if by drunkards scuffling in a china shop. The solidarity of the distressed, poor, and suffering in all countries would be stronger than the ministries' and Capitalists' greed for expansion and booty. No Socialist would ever approve war credits, and there could be no war without approval by the Social Democrats. In addition, there was the justifiable issue of women's suffrage and equal rights for women in Western Europe. The power of women would make Antigone's⁵³ word a reality: "I am not here to hate, I am here to love." Mothers and young girls never could turn into hyenas "thirsting for the enemy's blood." Finally, if the world's fifteen million Jews, scattered among all the nations of the earth, had any sense, they would build bridges and weave webs uniting different nations. It did not seem likely that a group of people—told everywhere that they were only tolerated and did not belong—would turn into wild "patriots" overnight and turn on each other, country against country, in service of their oppressors.

But it really happened! The Socialists betrayed the poor, the mothers betrayed love, the Jews betrayed their right and proper mission *of lo bechayil velo bekoach, ki im beruchi* ("not by might and not by power but by my spirit").[54]

Until the end of my life I will never think back on August 1914 with anything but the revelation of how delusional human ideas can be. Ideals became crutches, progress is just a mirage, history a lie.

It was as if everyone had just one fear: to be left out of the "great experience." Everyone imagined that they could become heroes overnight, even if yesterday they still haggled over success. Individual freedoms ended. There was no conscience, no evaluation, no deep inner examination, only a mix of rowdiness, high-mindedness, stupidity, profit-seeking, cowardice, herd mentality, greed for adventure, religious faith—in short all the best and worst in human nature combined in one concept: national destiny. Everyone felt as did his neighbor, and everyone copied his neighbor. If it became *fashionable* to die, everyone died. Anyone who said what people wanted and needed to hear at that exact moment became leader. Everyone wanted to become leader. Everyone imagined that his hour had come and that the world was waiting for him.

Only half-humans were really happy. Finally, what they regarded as abhorrent and obstructive—the need for a tender conscience and pure heart—had been dropped from national consciousness. Animal instinct now ruled, and anything that did not serve the animal in man was ready for death.

In the midst of this great emotional torment, suppressed and isolated as never before, I clung to a foolish idea. I hoped that Maximilian Harden would help in its execution—what a childish delusion! At this decisive moment the most acknowledged and best-known leading spirits in every European nation should speak publicly: "We, the appointed guardians of the eternal world kingdom, refuse to accept what now passes for the truth or follow history's bloody delusion. You can martyr and murder humanity only over our dead bodies. We are your leading lights, of which every country is proud."

If only the leading lights of every country would stand together with this "call to the spirit": George, Hauptmann, Dehmel in Germany; France, Rolland, Bergson in France; Shaw, Galsworthy, Wells in England; Mynski, Andrejew, Brjussow in Russia.[55] If only a European periodical with the broad influence of Harden's *Zukunft* could introduce this "call to the spirit," surely there would well up a wave of light that might blot out this war passion. It would be a tremendous historical example in an hour of extreme need, and its spiritual leader would be a Christ-like figure.

That was my delusion. The awakening was terrible.

The exact men whom I believed would be examples and educators of common sense turned into fanatics,[56] with Maximilian Harden as lunatic-in-chief and chief war agitator. His periodical *Die Zukunft* turned into an organ of the greediest expansionists and Pan-Germans.

This carried on for four terrible years, from victory to defeat, and defeat to victory, with only one goal in view: success. At first Harden conducted a campaign of violent frenzy. Then, when the situation deteriorated, he began to search for an advantageous peace. Then, from 1916, he tried by backdoor politics to salvage something for Germany from a ruinous war.

Finally, in fall 1918, and five years too late, came the German Revolution.

The country was exhausted, the army destroyed. The kaiser fled, the Bismarckian state was broken into pieces, and all kings and princes exiled. Never was a nation so disoriented, so willing to relearn and rebuild. But where did Harden stand?

His periodical became less and less influential with every passing year. Finally, he wrote it completely alone, with scarcely a thousand subscribers who had remained loyal and followed his thoughts—the monologues of a time-estranged lone wolf. The moment his hated imperial glory disappeared, the periodical became superfluous, because its only theme had been to tell Germany what the imperial economy should *not* be, and its only audience was now deprived of power. There are always too many lazy characters, seemingly destined by nature for mediocrity, who loll around on the upholstered easy chairs of power in well-kept homes, while millions of decent good people wither away in dishonorable conditions. Is it any wonder that we are inclined to be unfair to property and rank?

Harden liked to cite certain Bismarckian remarks such as "Someone who cuts fish with a knife should not become minister of cultural affairs" or "Many people think that they can keep Germany in order without being able to keep order in their cabinet drawer." For him, privileges were tolerable only when justified by a higher and greater humanity.

In vain did he look for grandeur and greatness among Germany's new rulers. For him, Noske, Ebert, and Scheidemann were parvenu petits bourgeois, none of whom stood out above bustling mediocrity.[57] They were men without tradition, history, education, finesse, happy heirs to the revolution. His hatred for social democracy's valiant emissaries who set themselves up as Germany's shining light was so great that he developed a feeling of real love for Russia—a silent hope that bolshevism would triumph and that German rule by small-minded mediocre men would be swept away.

The fact that chairs on which descendants of old noble families, encrusted with gold braid, orders, and ribbons, had sat now were occupied by coarse, boorish men who couldn't even write a decent German was unbearable to the graceful, witty actor. He showed how dependent he was, in his heart of hearts, on feuding princes, dukes, kings, and their courts, who had previously competed for his attention.

But then came events that made the blood run cold.

There was nothing—I repeat nothing—that Harden's genius for intellectual games took seriously. Metaphysics, morals, world history—all appeared to him somewhat doubtful. But he was in bitter earnest on one point. He, a man of noble endeavors, saw himself completely responsible as a loyal servant of—Germany.

An insolent race of people now cackled around the aging man. They knew nothing of what he once had meant and achieved (or thought he had achieved) for Germany. Nothing remained from the great past but thirty years of yellowing periodicals. He sat there like a faded opera diva under gilded ribbons of faded laurel leaves in their silken growlery. Younger, happier schoolmates—Emil Ludwig, Paul Wiegler, Stefan Grossmann[58]—had overtaken him. He remained the silken wordsmith, the clever charmer, the great foil fencer, who knew how to polish the finest intellectual damascene blade. But now he drifted, helpless as a child, in a coarse crowd who only knew how to fight with pitchforks and truncheons.

His beautiful well-groomed doll's head became angry and sad. His visitors described him as "a quiet, very courteous, bitterly angry, little marquis in exile."

When the old Reich began to totter, the kaiser asked his mortal enemy to conduct peace negotiations. Chancellor and prime minister both tried to conciliate the man who had written in the *Zukunft* issue celebrating the twenty-fifth anniversary of the Kaiserreich on 18 January 1895: "If things carry on this way, one fine day there will be formed a league of nations that will overthrow this great power and do away with everything for which the German people have worked so hard."

The prophecy was fulfilled, but the prophet forgotten. Like his love, his hate applied to all. None of the newcomers to political power (not even Rathenau and Stresemann[59]) pleased a man who had developed such political acumen over the years. Everything seemed eerily foreign to the man who belonged to no party or office.

Whenever people err, they retreat into naked survival mode. The Socialist Republic and democratic ideal were backdrops to the terror that reigned inside. The tragic farce that marked the end of Harden's remarkable career was so grotesque that future generations will find it difficult to properly comprehend.

The revolution bred confusion, and out of confusion came reaction. Jews had trustingly reefed white flags over the ruins of the people's aspirations for power: the venerable flags with the tantalizing inscription *Liberté, égalité, fraternité*. Now, where the onslaught of the proletarian masses was crushed, and the new possessors wanted nothing more than to secure their own power, Jewish firebrands quickly were swept away in the process. After the war they were labeled foreigners, of alien blood, outsiders.

The era of racial antisemitism began with the murder of far-seeing Karl Liebknecht and high-minded Rosa Luxemburg.[60] Bavarian prime minister Kurt Eisner too was murdered.[61] His murderer, Count Arco, had a Jewish mother.[62] That great and noble man Gustav Landauer[63] was literally trampled to death. Then Leo Yogisches was sacrificed, and the best minds of the revolution—Eugen Leviné, Mühsam, Toller, and Fechenbach—were imprisoned.[64] German foreign minister Walter Rathenau was assassinated by a murder conspiracy of romanticism-inculcated youths.[65] Suddenly, newspapers proclaimed that a degenerate character in the pay of a coterie of nationalists had attacked Maximilian Harden from behind in the dark of night and had beaten his skull in eight times with an iron bar.[66] That same brain that had, for three decades, been regarded by prominent men as one of Germany's shining lights.

And one merely allowed this to happen? No! People cheered, they rejoiced! The villainous deed was regarded as an honorable act in service of the Fatherland. It turned out that tens of thousands had envied or benefited from Harden or feared him but that no one loved him. In the perspective of Germany, he was a stranger.

Thanks to the skill of a famous surgeon his life was saved, but he became a broken man. However, he remained brave, capable of fighting, and mentally strong to the end.

Understandably he expected that his would-be murderers would be held to public account. But the attorney general prosecuted the case so casually, the trial took so long, and the press and public opinion were so disinterested that trial of the hired cat's-paws became a Via Dolorosa for the injured man. The real perpetrators long since had escaped to safety and covered their tracks completely. Astonishingly, in the end instead he stood before his nation not as the accuser but as the defendant.

His would-be murderers were given credit for having tried to destroy a pest. Everything that seemed appropriate to make the cowardly act appear noble was bundled together. The outrageously wronged and injured man was made to feel that the republic would not really have minded had he been murdered.

He figured in contemporary history as "Isidor Witkowski from Galicia," someone occasionally employed by Bismarck as a scribe. Malicious writers created the name Isidor out of nowhere. This was not his name, nor did he come from Galicia, but it would have been useless to try to correct these fabrications.[67]

Harden stood defenseless as a child against this sudden flare-up of personal bloodlust. He did not understand how this could happen, because this smoldering hatred in large parts of the population pressured him to the side that he rejected, and where he had never felt at home.

The name Harden commonly had been encountered as a prominent "nationalist" in contemporary French, British, and American political newspapers of the past few decades. In countries outside Germany he was regarded as a fanatical German. But now, in a free and democratic German republic, he had to defend his past as the past of a "Jewish parasite." A coincidence, or clever psychological trick, had filled the tribunal who sat in judgment over Harden's case with German-nationalist Jews. The chairman, who under German law was all-powerful, was the baptized son of a rabbi, and two Jewish lawyers were found to defend the murder conspiracy and accuse Harden of being an un-German pest. These two baptized Jews, Berliners Bloch and Schiff, represented the kind of smooth, coy Jewish assimilationism that never will be sufficiently German or Christian.

Once again, Harden gathered his formidable strength for a speech that would justify his life's work in plain words. But they had no effect whatsoever on a tribunal of Jewish antisemites, The curious situation was as follows: A Jew who had believed himself to be German his entire life and been regarded by millions as a representative of the German Fatherland now had to defend himself as a Jew. He must lead the Jewish cause before a tribunal of baptized Jews who, for the sake of their own success and power, had made the cause of this murky German-nationalist murder conspiracy their own. A miserable end to Harden's thirty years of service to the German people.

An excerpt from Harden's defense speech clarifies the impossible situation:

> I understand that these young men are being defended as requested. That must be so. But I, who became their victim, I, who at midnight, soaked in blood from head to toe, shoved into an ambulance, torn away from my professional activities of thirty years, with resultant huge financial

losses—that now you are trying to defame me—that is something new. Until this morning I was determined—because I find this entire business unbearable and outrageous—to step back and say: "There is a shorthand record of these proceedings and that is sufficient—the verdict speaks for itself!" I did not do so because early today I received a letter from a European politician who told me: "Wherever I go in neutral countries I am told: You Germans are going under because you make common cause with your murderers." State sovereignty and legal jurisdiction require that this act must be punished, irrespective of who the victim was. Nothing can be changed in this case, even if I were the monster you make me out to be. The heart of the matter is the following: If these men were named Rosenstock and Feilchenfeldt, and the person who was attacked had an old, stereotypically Germanic name, can you believe that this case would have been conducted in the same way? I do not think so! I was born a Jew, but always have had very casual links to the religion. Almost forty years ago, as a very young man, I converted to Christianity. At that time, German racial antisemitism was still unknown, otherwise my conversion would have been a kind of apostasy, and I wouldn't have done it. I understand antisemitism, but what I do not understand is why in Germany we do not realize more often that accusations made against the Jews are exactly the same as those made against Germans by a large part of the unfriendly outside world. I am no angel, but never in my entire life have I consciously done anything low and mean. It's bad enough that I need to proclaim this here. There are very few places in the world where this would be necessary.

Could anyone who heard these words not have the impression that here was a man who simply demanded protection, wanted to defend himself, and only solicited goodwill? It stabbed one through the heart when he turned to his persecutors in anguish: "Till the last moment, I had hoped to detect even a tiny speck of humanity and repentance from the other side. But there was none. It is very hard for a sick man to see these smiling, jolly men! In the long run, it is unbearable and impossible."

At the end of his speech, a great farce played out. Harden warned the tribunal that acquittal of his would-be murderers would harm the German people abroad. "It will encourage, provoke, and give everyone who thinks badly of us the right to do so." Suddenly, however, he interrupted himself:

No, my thought processes have slipped. I will not say of *us*, but of *you*. They will think badly of *you*. If you do not approve of me because I was born a Jew, well and good! I said often enough to Rathenau: "Why do you always write and say: we Germans? No one wants to count the Jews among the German *Volk*." I love the German people but do not force myself upon them. Germany must defend the way it conducts its legal procedures before the country, its children, and what I have called the world's conscience. If you acquit these hirelings of a murderers' fraternity, and dine in the Prytaneum[68] as reward for a patriotic deed, go right ahead.

As regards the actual facts of the case, could anything be more crass than to mix the law up with extralegal issues such as nationalist sentiments and supranationalist legal *norms*?

A German tribunal, on which baptized Jews sat, pandering to the murderers[69] of another baptized Jew, assuring the murderers that they wanted to murder only in the name of, and out of a sense of, pure German sentiment. Because one behaved as an extremely "German" German, they drove the other, who until now had been even more "German" than they were, back to "being a Jew."

Knowledge of the attack on Harden's life changed my attitude toward him in an astonishing way.

I thought that I had hated him for nearly forty years. But hate is love that has been destroyed, like thorns are withering buds. Compassion gives love that has died new life.

When I saw how this man had been, in front of the German people, struck down by a hired thug, without open support from any one of his million admirers, my attitude changed. All my previous disparaging and negative written comments about him disgusted me. I wrote to him out of a sense of immediate outrage, and his thanks showed me he was pleased by the concern of someone sharing the same fate. Because I too was being insulted and mistreated, to the acclaim of German public opinion.[70]

I saw Harden again one last time.

It was in his little house in the Grünewald. The little marquis's face had become old, his features sharp. He walked feebly. Only the steely blue eyes still retained their youthful luster, and his nature the same delicacy and magical grace of his youth. A hundred images and destinies that each of us had survived passed before my eyes. I said, "I would have fought you to the death, had you remained in power." He answered, "I would have fought Bismarck to the death, had he remained in power."

He recalled our previous conversations and remembered that once we had debated our fate-less state as both Germans and Jews. While I wavered, he had made the solemn demand to me: "German par excellence!" I had jumped up tormentedly and quoted a few lines to him. His amazing memory had not dimmed after thirty-six years:

> *Quo semel est imbuta recens*
> *Servabit odorem testa diu.*

> (The first scent you pour in a jar
> lasts for years.)[71]

He often had thought of this verse from Horace, and now in his old age the same thing was happening to him as with the author whom we had visited. Theodor Fontane too had felt that he was the singer of Prussia and of Prussian glory. But, on his seventy-fifth birthday not a single person about whom he had sung thanked him for it. The wicked little marquis had declaimed, half with pathetic seriousness, half impishly amused:

> But those who came to the celebration
> Were all from decidedly different nations.
> Meyers arrive, a battalion at least,
> And Pollacks and those living yet farther east.
> They gave me more than second looks,
> All of them had read my books,
> To them I long had been well known.
> And that is the main thing . . . Come in, Cohn.[72]

When toward evening we parted under the garden trees, I had the good feeling of being rid of a bilious burden that had oppressed me all my life. But now I would have liked to show him some sympathy. But how? I painted a picture of his personality, as it had appeared to me so many years before: sovereign, wise, and transfigured. In a foreign newspaper I found a sketch and sent it to him. It said that he was suffering and that he had traveled to Italy. A few weeks later I received his reply. As I had never dealt properly with the unpredictable, he still did not agree with me. He answered, "You paint me as a small Buddhist sage who prepares himself for death with nobility and resignation. I am neither resigned, nor Buddhist. I am a fighter, and you will see how alive I am when *Die Zukunft* reappears. This periodical is more necessary for Germany now than ever before."

Shortly thereafter came the news that Maximilian Harden had died. The ceremony took place in the Wilmersdorf crematorium. Beethoven's music echoed, and a young actor spoke a few words from Goethe: Thanks to nature that she was taking her child back to her great bosom.

The flames swallowed up the picture of the young boy who played "Decider of Battles" in the schoolyard. They took back the beautiful youth who had won hearts and women. They devoured the restless worker, Germany's most powerful man in words and writing. They devoured wisdom and words, injustice and blame, fame and history.

About fifty deeply moved people absorbed the beautiful, disappearing images. Most were Jews.

Notes

1. Maximilian Harden (1861–1927), influential German journalist and editor.
2. Otto Brahm (1856–1912), German drama and literary critic, theater manager and director; Theodor Fontane (1819–1898), German realist novelist and poet; Arthur Levysohn (1841–1908), German journalist.
3. See Psalm 39:9.
4. The anti-monarchist German revolutions of 1848–1849 were among several that took place across Europe around the same time. Aimed at expanding democracy, they were largely a failure, resulting in a monarchist constitution and weakened legislature. August Bebel (1840–1913) was a German politician who cofounded in 1869 the Social Democratic Workers' Party of Germany.
5. Max Verworn (1863–1921), German physiologist and native of Berlin.
6. Albert Niemann (1831–1917), German opera singer; Adalbert Matkowsky (1857–1909), German actor; Friedrich Mitterwurzer (1844–1897), German actor and director.
7. *Wilhelm Meisters Lehrjahre* (*Wilhelm Meister's Apprenticeship*) is the second novel by Goethe, published in 1795–1796.
8. Fritz Odemar (1890–1955), German film actor.
9. Franziska Ellmenreich (1847–1931), German stage actress.
10. Friedrich von Schiller (1759–1805), German poet, philosopher, physician, historian, and playwright; Johann Wolfgang von Goethe (1749–1832), leading German writer, poet, statesman, and author of *Faust*.
11. Poznań (Poland).
12. "The present," the most important art and literature daily newspaper of the time.
13. Theophil Zolling (1849–1901), German journalist, publisher, and critic.
14. Heinrich von Treitschke (1834–1896), German antisemitic historian and political theorist; Ernst Curtius (1814–1896), German archeologist and historian; Herman Grimm (1828–1901), German academic and writer, son of Wilhelm Grimm (1786–1859) and nephew of Jacob Grimm (1785–1863), compilers of *Grimm's Fairy Tales*.
15. Paul Nathan (1857–1927), German Jewish social politician.
16. "The future."
17. Otto von Bismarck (1815–1898), German politician who led the country's unification in 1871 and served as its first chancellor until 1890.
18. Wilhelm II's dismissal of Bismarck on 18 March 1890 also meant the end of Bismarckian Realpolitik, and his reinsurance treaty with Russia. Henceforth Germany was ruled by chancellors and foreign ministers of greater or lesser degrees of incompetence. These, together with Wilhelm II's mercurial nature, eventually led to a situation where a two-front conflict (something Bismarck dreaded and tried his best to avoid with his web of alliances) became inevitable.
19. Warcino (Polish Pomerania), site of Bismarck's estate.
20. Kurd von Schlözer (1822–1894), German diplomat and historian during the imperial era; Franz von Lenbach (1836–1904), portrait artist known for his depictions of leading figures in German public life; Ernst Schweninger

(1850–1924), German doctor who developed a method for combating obesity.
21. Friedrich Naumann (1860–1919), German politician and Protestant religious leader.
22. A forest near Hamburg given to Bismarck in 1871 for services to Germany.
23. Wilhelm I.
24. *Reisekaiser*. Also wandering or itinerant, flighty and impetuous kaiser. A dig at Wilhelm's inability to stay in one place for long, or possibly his unstable, volatile, and meddling policies.
25. *Frondeurs* (political rebels).
26. Despite the kaiser's bellicose, dictatorial attitudes, there was relative freedom of the press and opinion in Wilhelmine Germany.
27. Victor Henri Rochefort (1831–1913), French journalist and anti-empire politician; Georges Clemenceau (1841–1929), French statesman who served as prime minister of France during World War I.
28. Scandal mongering.
29. Joseph Fouché (1759–1820), French politician and minister of police under Napoleon Bonaparte prior to his becoming emperor; Friedrich von Gentz (1764–1832), German diplomat and writer; Karl August Varnhagen von Ense (1785–1858), German biographer, diplomat, and soldier.
30. Greek: someone obsessed by the good, beautiful, and perfect.
31. Lessing uses the word *führer* for Adolf Hitler in the 1920s, seen from Hitler's point of view.
32. Friedrich Julius Stahl (1802–1861), German politician and legal thinker. Raised Jewish, he later converted and became an ecclesiastical lawyer.
33. Friederich von Holstein (1837–1909), head of the political department of the German Foreign Office, who played an influential role in foreign policy after Bismarck's dismissal in 1890.
34. Wilhelm Wundt (1832–1930), physician, philosopher, and a foundational figure in modern psychology.
35. Published 1901 in *Die Zukunft*, the story relates the sad adventures of a magnificent clock bequeathed by a grandfather to his degenerate nephew. The grandfather was Wilhelm I, the nephew Wilhelm II, and the clock Bismarck. The inquisitive nephew gratified his idle curiosity by taking the clock apart to see how it was made inside. In this way, Harden paid homage to Bismarck and pointed out to the German people the folly and dangers of Hohenzollern policy.
36. Bernhard von Bülow (1849–1929), politician who was the German foreign minister before becoming chancellor of the German Empire in 1900.
37. Karl Lamprecht (1856–1915), German historian who specialized in German art and economic history
38. Kaliningrad (Russia).
39. Felix Kanitz (1829–1904), Austro-Hungarian anthropologist, archaeologist, and travel writer; Wilhelm von Mirbach (1871–1918), German diplomat, who was appointed ambassador to Russia in April 1918 and was assassinated at the German embassy in Moscow as part of a Socialist plot to incite a war between Russia and Germany; Ludwig Bamberger (1823–1899), German economist, politician, revolutionary, and writer; Emanuel Lasker

(1868–1941), German mathematician, who was world chess champion from 1894 to 1921; Ludwig Windthorst (1821–1891), German politician who was a prominent antagonist of Bismarck's during German unification; Singer (?); Karl Edmund Friedrich Friedmann (1852–1915), German writer, jurist, and journalist, who was the model for attorney Breslauer in Thomas Mann's *Buddenbrooks*; Erich Sello (1852–1912), German jurist and criminal attorney; Paul Lindau (1839–1919), German dramatist and novelist; Franz Mehring (1846–1919), politician who was a leading figure in the Social Democratic Party of Germany during the 1918–1919 German Revolution; Karl Bleibtreu (1859–1928), German naturalist writer; Elsa von Schabeltzky: Elsa von Freytag-Loringhoven (1874–1927), German avant-garde, Dadaist, actress, and poet; Jenny Gross, German actress.

40. Philip Prince of Eulenburg and Hertefeld (1847–1921), German diplomat who was a friend and confidante of Kaiser Wilhelm II; Kuno von Moltke (1847–1923), adjutant to Wilhelm II and military commander of Berlin. The Harden-Eulenburg affair was a controversy surrounding a series of courts-martial and five civil trials regarding accusations of homosexual conduct, and accompanying libel trials, among prominent members of Kaiser Wilhem II's cabinet and entourage during the period between 1907 and 1909. The affair centered around Harden's accusation of homosexual conduct by Eulenburg and Moltke. The reader is referred to Norman Domeier, *The Eulenburg Affair: A Cultural History of Politics in the German Empire*, trans. Deborah Lucas Schneider (Rochester, NY: Camden House, 2015).

41. Victor Hugo (1802–1885): "Teasing is the mischievousness of good people."

42. Frederick of Hohenau (1857–1914), German nobleman; Johannes von Lynar (1859–1934), German nobleman; Botho von Wedel (1862–1934), German ambassador to Austro-Hungary; Wendelstaedt (?); Raymond Lecomte, French chargé d'affaires in Berlin.

43. Otto of Bavaria (1848–1916). Although king from 1886 to 1913, he never ruled because of alleged severe mental illness.

44. German: *Mädchenträume*.

45. In reality, Harden later came to the conclusion that the affair was the greatest political mistake of his life, regarding it as the root cause of the World War and the fall of the Second Reich, inevitable without Eulenburg's moderating influence (James D. Steakley, "Iconography of a Scandal: Political Cartoons and the Eulenburg Affair in Wilhelmine Germany," in *Hidden from History: Reclaiming the Gay & Lesbian Past*, ed. Martin B. Duberman, Martha Vicinus, and George Chauncey [New York: Plume, 1990]).

46. Alfred von Waldersee (1832–1904), chief of the Imperial German General Staff.

47. Again, Lessing uses the word *Judenfrage*.

48. Eduard von Simson (1810–1899), German lawyer and liberal politician, born of a Jewish family who converted to Protestantism when he was twelve or thirteen years old.

49. Walter Rathenau (1867–1922), German Jewish business leader and politician who helped manage the German economy during World War I. He was assassinated in 1922.

50. Jacob Grimm (1785–1863), German philologist, jurist, and mythologist. He is known for formulating Grimm's Law, which deals with changes in pronunciation over time.
51. Paul Anton de Lagarde (1827–1891), German biblical scholar, Orientalist, and vocal antisemite.
52. He had a head.
53. In Greek mythology, Antigone was the daughter of Oedipus and his mother, Jocasta. Subject of a tragedy written by Sophocles on or before 441 BCE.
54. Zechariah 4:6.
55. Stefan George (1868–1933), German symbolist poet and translator of Dante, Shakespeare, and Baudelaire; Gerhart Hauptmann (1862–1946), German dramatist and novelist; Richard Dehmel (1863–1920), German poet and writer; Anatole France (1844–1924), French poet, journalist, and novelist; Romain Rolland (1866–1944), French dramatist, novelist, essayist, art historian, and mystic; Henri-Louis Bergson (1859–1941), French Jewish thinker, who was a key figure in twentieth-century continental philosophy; George Bernard Shaw (1856–1950), Irish playwright and music critic; John Galsworthy (1867–1933), English novelist and playwright of works including *The Forsyte Saga*; H. G. Wells (1866–1946), English writer, notably of *The War of the Worlds*; Nikolai Maksimovich Mynski (1855–1937), Russian mystical writer and poet; Leonid Nikolaievich Andreyev (1871–1919), Russian novelist; Valery Yakovlevich Bryusov (1873–1924), Russian poet, prose writer, dramatist, translator, critic, and historian. Hauptmann and Rolland were Nobel Prize laureates.
56. Strictly speaking not true. Both Shaw and Rolland were vocally antiwar from the start.
57. Gustav Noske (1868–1946), German Socialist politician, who was the first minister of defense for the Weimar Republic; Friedrich Ebert (1871–1925), Socialist politician, who was the first president of Germany from 1919 to 1925; Philipp Scheidemann (1865–1939), Socialist politician, who proclaimed Germany a republic during the revolution of 1918–1919.
58. Emil Ludwig (1881–1948), German-Swiss "biographer"; Paul Wiegler (1878–1949), German writer and translator; Stefan Grossmann (1875–1935), prominent Austrian left-wing journalist.
59. Gustav Stresemann (1878–1929), German chancellor in 1923 and foreign minister from 1923 to 1929. His premature death dealt a grave blow to the republic.
60. Karl Liebknecht (1871–1919), cofounder of the Spartacist League and the Communist Party of Germany with Rosa Luxemburg, with whom he was executed following the failed Spartacist Revolution; Liebknecht was the only non-Jew of the group; Rosa Luxemburg (1971–1919), Polish-born Marxist theorist, philosopher, economist, antiwar activist, and revolutionary Socialist.
61. Kurt Eisner (1867–1919), journalist and critic, who helped to lead the Socialist Revolution in Bavaria in 1918.
62. Anton Graf von Arco auf Valley (1897–1945), German nobleman, who assassinated Kurt Eisner.

63. Gustav Landauer (1870–1919), political theorist, who was a leading exponent of social anarchism and avowed pacifist and who was the father of the kibbutz movement.
64. Leo Y(J)ogisches (1867–1919), Lithuanian-born Marxist revolutionary and key figure in the Spartacist League, murdered by Freikorps forces; Eugen Leviné (1883–1919), Communist who briefly led the Bavarian Council Republic before his imprisonment and death by firing squad in Stadelheim prison; Erich Mühsam (1878–1934), German Jewish anarchist and literary figure, who fought for a federated Bavarian Soviet Republic; Ernst Toller (1893–1939), German expressionist playwright, who led the Bavarian Soviet Republic for six days; Felix Fechenbach (1894–1933), German Jewish writer and activist, who served in Kurt Eisner's regime.
65. Two months after signing the Treaty of Rapallo on 24 June 1922, Rathenau was assassinated in Berlin by the right-wing terrorist group Organisation Consul.
66. A few days after the murder of Walter Rathenau, Harden was attacked by two Freikorps members, Bert Weichardt and Albert Wilhelm Grenz.
67. Goebbels used the name Isidor to mock the hated Jew Bernhard Weiss, who was police vice president of Berlin (Peter C. Appelbaum, *Loyal Sons: Jews in the German Army in the Great War* [London and Portland, OR: Vallentine Mitchell, 2014], 289).
68. The Prytaneion was seat of the Prytaneis (executive), and so the seat of government in ancient Greece. The term is used to describe any of a range of ancient structures where officials met (normally relating to the government of a city).
69. Potential murderers. Lessing uses the term "murderers."
70. Lessing made the mistake of calling President Hindenburg a zero and stating that a zero could become a Nero.
71. Quintus Horatius Flaccus (Horace) (65–27 BCE), *Epistulae*, book 1, no. 2, line 69.
72. Theodor Fontane, "An meinem fünfundziebzigsten," in *Gedichte in Prosatexten. Gedichte aus dem Nachlaß*, ed. Joachim Krueger and Anita Golz (Berlin: Aufbau Verlag, 1995), 162.

VAULT

1

Do you know the Jewish song "Does the World Ask an Old *kasha* [question]?" "Tra-la, tra-di, ridi, rom?" one person asks. The reply comes: "Tra-di, ri-di, ri-lom." And if you wish, one could also "traj-dim." It's the same as the rabbi with the two litigants. "Present your case," the rabbi says to the one. When he has heard him out, he decides, "You are right. Now present *your* case," he says to the second man, who describes the same issue in the exactly opposite way. The rabbi listens carefully and finally says, "You are also right." The first man exclaims in surprise, "It isn't possible that both of us are right." The rabbi ponders again, and finally decides, "That is right *as well*."

When a Zionist spends hours and hours arguing that Jewry is not only a theoretical concept, a human society, a Weltanschauung, but a life and death reality, a Socialist declares, "It doesn't matter that peoples exist. The only thing that matters is *why* they are there and what purpose they serve. We have the right to exist only as bearers of eternal human values."

The opposite applies as well. A Socialist expounds for hours that the supranational community is more deeply committed to truth and justice than all incidents of birth and that no national question—not even that of nationalities themselves—is soluble on the basis of nation-states. Instantly the Zionist counters, "Blood is more real than spirit, and you cannot run counter to nature. We too have a right to self-preservation."

And so the battle of words roars on. For this book about self-hate, how can we build a vault, an overarching connection? How can we build the final bridge?

2

The author of this book has, if anyone has, striven with might and main to fulfill his deeply felt belief in supranational values. I am deeply convinced that only class struggle, not today's politics of nationalism, will solve humanity's problems. Judaism and "nationalism" are unbridgeable. But yet I wish that everyone could feel "I am who I am and have the right to rejoice in who I am." It would be fruitless to reflect: Am I more German or more Jewish? Am I both, or neither? We should grow and become fulfilled utilizing the potential with which we are born. If a country doesn't give you rights and wants to violate you, leave and live in another! *All* national questions are insoluble! But we must pose these questions ourselves. One day they will be solved, because in a few centuries these questions will not exist, as they do now.[1]

3

Two leading German Jews minds permit Judaism only to have an exclusively supranational role: the philosopher Constantin Brunner and social reformer Joseph Popper-Lynkeus.[2] Both renounce any sort of biologism. "Israel," they teach, "is a miraculous people whose historical mission can be preserved only when it gives up any specific, detached form and builds unlimited bridges of all kinds between nations. Israel must be supranational, like the spirit, mathematics, logic, and ethics, and is the eternal bearer of the one spirit in all of humanity."

How do we respond to these great teachers of ultimacy and succinctness? We cannot, because they are quite right! "If *life were spirit*," if a *doctrine* could make world history, then preservation of a special people among other special peoples would have no more significance than whether an ant species that has become rare is encountered in all anthills or in one particular spot in the forest.

But, O great philosophers and theologians! Have you ever seen a nation, society, or "representative" of nation or society who could *not* say, "We are the chosen ones!"?—Every anthill considers itself the center of the forest. Every species of animal and plant, *every* nation would eat the others up, if it could. There are no obvious *reasons* for the existence and preservation of any living thing. If we were asked why we wanted to survive, we would, if we were honest with ourselves, have no other response—like any other living creature—but "because we *are*."

It would be gruesome, terrible, and deeply problematic if humans were to give any other answer. Because then "mission," "rank," and the soul-destroying arrogance of the "universal" would have to be invoked.

The entire vital question of the Jewish people seems to me to hinge on whether their spirit of self-regard can be negotiated. Can they be satisfied with the most personal and the most proximate?

We know well that planting a forest or orange grove, draining a swamp, clearing a field, building an electric power plant are not great national goals. We also know well that in light of "the eternal value of truth and justice," the presence of a particular people, even the entire human race, makes no difference at all. Because it doesn't matter whether we exist, but rather that we are *worthy* of being there. That is very clear.

But the "spiritual" so overshadows the "ideal" that nothing remains of nature, soil, blood, and people. We don't live to be healthy. But for what purpose could a man live if he didn't, first and foremost, strive to be healthy or, if he isn't, to become healthy? If a Jew can give his life any meaning at all, he must, first and foremost, be a *Jew*, happily and willingly. But Jews must not only be *spiritual*. They are not just a number of individuals who stand together in the telephone book or company register. They are millions of burden-bearing distinct creatures of ancient blood. When they are treated unjustly in Russia, Ukraine, Romania, or Samarkand, we should never imagine that it doesn't concern us. Everyone, even the smallest Jew, should sense that his destiny always is the same as ours.

4

If we Jews had remained in Palestine we would today be just another Middle Eastern people like Greeks or Arabs. But we were expelled, caged in heaps of stones under different stars, and kept behind walls. Additionally, we were subjected to wrenching forces, overbred, and sometimes even destroyed. But with all that, we anticipated a development that, several centuries later, would become the destiny of the proletariat, and the masses locked up in the machinery of labor economics in Europe and America.

The heart of our national pathology is forced unnaturalness and alienation behind walls and under learned tomes. For several centuries our people lacked the regulators of healthy life, forest murmurs, trickling springs, sea waves, singing wind, and contact with plants and animals. Our people led unnatural lives. Pale children had never seen the countryside, wheat fields, oaks, or pine trees. It is well-known that the only occupation permitted to the Jews was the merchant trade. They couldn't be farmers, hunters, or soldiers. Theirs was a homeland of the mind, paper was their earth, the brain their anchor. This changed only in the so-called age of emancipation. Until then, our people's task was to provide ourselves compensation for the loss of opportunity to connect directly with the world of nature and the land.

Whenever a community (in the sense of the natural community) loosens, society (in the sense of conscious association of common thoughts and will) attempts to find a substitute. If nature cannot provide commonality, societal goals and ideas must prevent the splitting apart of the natural community. Jews joined common law instead of common earth, spiritual instead of animal subsistence. That is the core of Jewish destiny.

This destiny, this loosening of roots, alienation from nature, dissolution of national elements during the past generation, has become the fate of the entire European-American world, the more we replace those things with technology, industry, and finance. I cannot emphasize this point too strongly.

Great cities of the world, without plants and forests, swamped with coal dust and industrial quarters where pale children of the proletariat labor over machines for two-thirds of their lives, are nothing but giant, modern ghettos. Millions of industrial slaves are involuntarily banished to such ghettos.

This transition of still-unspoiled people to the triumphant modern monetary and industrial economy has coincided with emancipation of the Jews from discriminatory laws. At the same time that Jews were freed from their imprisoned lives, the great masses were locked up in industrial dungeons.

Here is the key to all current Jewish achievement, the solution to the riddle of their successes, and explanation for the special status of Jews in the modern world.

Jewish will and intelligence have made them into leaders. Why? Certainly not because they are more talented or even gifted at all. But simply because they have past experience with the same disease that is now suddenly attacking the rest of the world, especially old Europe. The Jewish people is currently in the position of an organism that has survived an epidemic or an infection and become immune to a poisonous sickness, which is running wild among younger peoples, and whose overcoming is just now becoming the life-or-death question for all the peoples of the earth.

That is the key to Jewish leadership in coming generations of the social revolution. It is not a particular inclination to revolution and radicalism, but simply an old experience of suffering.

The suffering that now threatens all the people in the world is an old experience for the ancient Jewish people. They already have had to think through and reconcile many questions that have appeared later to younger and happier peoples. Jews have not only found solutions for themselves, but they benefit all future sufferers. Therein lies not only the significance of the Jews, but also the danger of dissolving into the realm of the supranational and purely spiritual.

5

> There in the bone-white wasteland stands the flame.
> It drinks from all the purple of your blood,
> It drips from all the juices, oil, and wine.
> The hottest midday suns melt down inside it
> To rigid flame, the flame that gives no heat,
> Which brazen stands, stands clear in speechless air,
> All while the bone-white wasteland grows and grows,
> The massive graveyard crumbles down around,
> Till all is bone-white graveyard, bone-white light.

The noble poet Karl Wolfskehl[3] has given us the terrible vision of icy flames that radiate no warmth but give only *light*. He intuited it as the destiny of a people who exist only in the spirit, a people of cultural achievements. It can be expected that, during the course of the next century, many Jews will be leading lights all over Europe and America and that in every nation the most important proofs and achievements will come from their Jewish fellow-citizens.

Let us not be blinded by the glitter of this *achievement* destiny. We must close our eyes and admit that this is our shame! This is our people's only real danger. Our talents are our danger, just like an army with only officers, and no soldiers to obey them.

It is not true that "peoples are only a digression of history on the way to one or two great personalities."[4] It is not true that a great personality *makes* history or is history itself. History, nation, and blood are the billions of simple people who labor in obscurity. The heart and soul of every nation—ours included—is neither teaching nor teacher. Even if the Torah were a thousand times more sublime, the expression of pure knowledge and of God himself, we must not become mere shadows and ghosts. We must always reinvent ourselves into all the simple, joyful forms that know nothing of truth or falsehood. Children and women, farmers and soldiers, pack-bearers, workers, artisans, artists, and all the obscure, simple people who are the substance and fabric of our lives. We must not overstep the power of the mind, which conquers the world but destroys nature.

To a national people belong joyful games, pious customs, modest, small everyday acts, lovely simplicity, balance and rhythm of life, and the seasons. Peoples also include the superstitious and foolish, millions of sick and wayward, hardscrabble and weighed down.

Nations are characterized by good cheer in themselves and a decided yes to their own limits and to human weakness. A sense of humor is also essential.

Every healthy nation liberates itself from the danger of self-hate by laughing at itself and being happy in its own troubles. Every nation has figures and parables through which it rises above its worst misery. National humor loves its misfits and fogeys. Stubborn people recognize their rough edges, miscreants recognize the humor of their peccadillos, errants, recognize the puniness of their private destiny—everyone learns to laugh without pain.

Jewish humor is ironic and sentimental, its self-judgment is caricaturing or melodramatic. The Jew has never been happy with himself, but one day he will learn to love his limitations. He will become less proud of his wit and happier through humor.

The glittering sparks and fire of Western culture will spread out and, through it, primeval nature will be exhausted. After a few more hundred years the idea of a "cultured people" will exist only in the national almanac.

We don't want (as our great minds do) to be the "salt of the earth." We want to be a human among humans, to fulfill ourselves simply, like a tree does.[5]

6

This book has drawn the course of six tragic, struggling lives from Germany. Where can we find their equal anywhere? And yet, the possibility of such tragedies and struggles must exist in simple lives as well. The solution to the puzzle is as follows:

Every circumscribed life, therefore everything living, turns against its own limitations, and therefore against "itself."

Life not only means "self"-*fulfillment*, but also "self"-*destruction*. Not only self-preservation, but also suicide is the "meaning" of the world.[6]

Our entire life is a continuous balance between self-affirmative and self-destructive urges.

A curious law seems to combine the fact that the more securely the all-bearing ego is decided and absorbed in an *infinite* community, the smaller the danger that the ego stunts its own growth by self-inflicted wounds. Everyone lives from everyone else. The isolated one consumes himself.

Only the limited can live, but every limitation leads to death. Shape mutates, form kills.

We have portrayed the pathology of the suppressed, self-denied "consciously" scourged life.

But we have not been satisfied with outlining sickness; we have also depicted the nature of the all-too-human disease of self-hate, described its origin, and the possibility of healing.

In the Talmud we read that the wisest rabbis argued for three and a half years over the following question: Would it be better if the world of the spirit did not exist and that the spirit awakened in man would again dissolve into the unconscious and extracorporeal? Or would it be better if the unconscious and extracorporeal were completely transformed and uplifted to an alert mind and knowing humanity? The rabbinic schools argued for three and a half years. The solution, in which they combined the "spiritual" and "elemental" into one, was the following: There can be no doubt that it would have been better if the world of our conscious reality was absent. There is also no doubt that the end of humanity, its re-dissolution into the limitless, is the more desirable goal. But because we are humans and must live through this episode of "world history," it is our task to complete it as best we can with our most honest insight. It would be nonsense, indeed a crime, were we to complete this episode of "humanity" with the continuous complaint that our knowledge and conscience come only from suffering. The elemental, in the richness of its extracorporeal form, is eternally unknown to us. All we can do is to decide to be what we are. That is the way it is here as well. For true healing, all the Jew needs is determination to be what he is. He may ponder over the "nationalities question" for another hundred, another thousand years, may read and write hundreds of thousands of more books . . . There are questions that never will and never can have a solution.

So let us determine to be what we are!

Notes

1. *Those who know the author's philosophical writings will find that several apparent contradictions in this book—especially the ever-critical attitude toward "spirit" while at the same time giving an ethical meaning to life—have lost their ambivalence.*

   For those not acquainted with my philosophy, I wish to add a short reflection about the meaning and limit of ethics, and with it the theme of tragic self-hate.

   I refer mainly to my book Studien zur Wertaxiomatik: Untersuchungen über Reine Ethik und Reines Recht, *Verlag Felix Meiner in Leipzig, 2nd ed., 1914.*

   I deny the "natural'" existence of ethics and morals in the past, present, or future. If that fiction, "the philosophy of as if" has a meaning by which man—to preserve himself as a man—is forced to pretend that the rational-meaningful is the nature of reality, then this "general hypocrisy" must be necessary and advantageous to morality as well.

My denial of morality as an experental component of the real world doesn't in the least exclude the absolutism of ethical judgment.

My Wertaxiomatik *attempts to show that moral laws are fully as unconditional and vivid (evident) as the laws of mathematics. The fact that we are not and cannot ever become "moral beings" does not hinder us from having* moral judgment.

Every judgment is at heart moral (i.e., value-ranking). I call the narrowest circle of normative laws, to which every judgment must necessarily refer, "the axiomatic of value."

I cannot admit to such ethics being "absolutely valid but purely formal," because I do not know *the difference between material and formal logic or ethics. I absolutely dispute the doctrine of a material spiritual life that, in and of itself (i.e., independent of an ordered world of judgment), can be good or bad, moral or immoral as, in my opinion, love need not be "better" than hate, magnanimity better than revenge. My teaching that any state of mind can be, according to its classification, moral or immoral, has been disputed by Max Scheler. But I cannot convince myself that kindness and love are always, and in all circumstances, "better" or "more moral" than, for example, vindictiveness or envy. The above is followed by a second train of thought concerning the "unreality" of ethics.*

Human life, in contrast to nonhuman nature, is incurably tragic. It is tragic because it is compelled to judge and act according to a norm the full implementation of which would be nothing but the end of humanity itself. Guilt, and with it self-hate, is the never-ending, inevitable accompaniment to all our thoughts and actions.

The secret words "know yourself" were written over the Temple of Delphi. But we live only because we don't know ourselves. Life would be completely impossible if it were linked with a clear self-image.

We can tolerate ourselves only because the eye of ethics is unspeakably weak, but also attractively colored. We do not see that everyone, even the noblest and best of us, commits, and must *commit, crimes at every turn. In the end, the assembled dialectic of theologians and national educators lies to us in the most plausible and beautiful way about the fact that, at heart, we are an evil race of wolves. Not specifically we Jews, but* all humanity. *A race of wolves who will, one day in the far distant future when they can tolerate,* consider *each other and stand together, be able to achieve great things. Not because they have "love and kindness in their heart for all humanity." (Those hopeful people without our life experience will await this for a very long time). No! The reason will be simply that all so-called progress of the human race will come from growing external suppression and nationalization, to solve the problem: how can each person be* protected from *others and also from himself?*

Even the demand that the extra-human and higher animal world be protected from humanity appears completely utopian to me in the coming European-American world. Because this would mean the obvious renunciation of conscious animal killing, overconsumption, and exploitation.

The phenomenon of self-torment, self-contempt, and self-hate that I have (in its narrowest Jewish sense) outlined in this book seems to serve as an almost mirac-

ulous symbol of an other-earthly world. We see everywhere in what a bestial world we live, where selfishness is taken for granted and narrow hearts and heads are the order of the day.

Perhaps only one person out of one hundred thousand sees and stands up to this. All the while, millions go on secure in their godlike sensibilities. They apparently regard it as the most natural thing in the world that they live in a warm home with good food, while hungry craftsman pass by them in the rain, the calf is driven to the slaughter, and the unemployed starve in the streets.

Our self-recognition should be based on the fact that we are guilty with every piece of bread we eat, every cigar we smoke. However, it seems that humanity has a constant need and expectation of robustness, obliqueness of conscience, self-righteous mendacity, of not looking too carefully, and the power to gild happily everything that is deficient. We say with Shakespeare, "T'were to consider too curiously, to consider so," or with Goethe, "To be fair to all sides only leads to self-destruction."

The paradoxical fact of ethics is the following: All moral demands arise from lessening of suffering in this world. On the other hand, the world is propelled only by suffering. Suffering is the only active force in this world. If we extinguish adversity, we extinguish life. If we remove hardship, we have brought the world to extinction. This is the secret purpose and meaning of all logic and ethics. "Stagnation of the world, which is based on injustice and immorality, and could not exist without crime and guilt."

This spells the doom of the renowned Jewish optimism, which is nothing but a fiction, never a real truth.

If Jewish ethics were directed at a negative end goal, it would be less capable, but also less tragic.

Insofar as Jews constitute an ethical society, it is their fate to have to live until the end of their days under the yoke of a law by which no man (in other words no Jew), provided that he is a true man, can properly abide. Even if he stopped being a man, no righteous man would be left!

In conclusion, I can only speak in a banal, human way. We want to do good as much as we can, but still we do too little.

2. Constantin Brunner (1862–1937), pseudonym of the Jewish philosopher Arjeh Yehuda Wertheimer, who argued for a community centered around intellectual exchange that would expand democracy; Josef Popper-Lynkeus (1838–1921), Austrian Jewish philosopher, inventor, and social theorist.
3. Karl Wolfskehl (1869–1948), German Jewish author and translator.
4. Thomas Carlyle (1795–1881).
5. *If one wishes to categorize plants and animals by merit and rank, our bias and human egocentricity immediately become clear. But our cultural arrogance classifies the races of man into higher and deeper, more primitive and advanced peoples without being quite aware of the subjectivity of our norm.*

    I don't wish to assert that all current racial research is nothing but dilettantism. In my "Prinzipien der Charakerologie" (published in Deutsche Psychologie, *Verlag Carl Marhold in Halle, 1926), I have laid down the principles for sound racial research. The textbook* Symbolik der Gestalt *by Carus-Lessing (Verlag Niels Kampmann, Heidelberg) [Carl G. Carus,* Symbolik der menschlichen Gestalt, *co-edited and expanded by Theodor Lessing, 1925], contains a wealth of racial study observations obtained by physio- and pathognomonic experiences. Because the body is soul, national psychology can only be based on and knowledge of expression and form.*

However, I believe that all racial science based upon judgment and linguistic antithesis is dilettantish and arbitrary. This includes, for example, division of peoples into sedentary and transient, dreaming and acting, farmers and hunters—opposites that have never really existed in pure form. The long since dead antithesis of "Aryans and semites" should no longer be taken seriously. The science of linguistics (from which this contrast was taken, to characterize inflecting language groups) doesn't use it anymore. This dates from the time when research into the so-called Japhetite languages demonstrated what nonsense it is to characterize Teutons and Germans as "Aryans."

Wherever such cheap antitheses ("here" "we," elsewhere "the others") remain alive, self-assertion is the mother, and the will-to-legitimacy the father, of ideas.

What can recognition *gain from this?*

It makes no difference whether Jews are rejected or defended by such "science." The perspective in both cases is all too practical and wretched.

Any Jewish-friendly real researcher easily can refute the Jewish scare doctrine of O. Hauser and H. Günther by the following: "Without the research of Richard Willstätter, hundreds of thousands of German soldiers would have been killed by poison gas. Through F. Haber's research, German harvests so increased that uncounted numbers of Germans were saved from hunger."

What amazing racial science! This racial science is the sidepiece to the population theory that converts people into money—how much each man can profit or cost the state. As little as we may ask whether the nightingale should be exterminated or the bird of paradise preserved, so little can we interpret the value of the Jewish race by how "useful" the gentlemen Willstätter and Haber are to Germany.

6. According to the theories of Maximilian Weber (1864–1920), one of the founders of sociology.

Afterword
Paul Reitter

> The best author will be the one who is ashamed of being a writer.
> —Friedrich Nietzsche

In the spring of 1931, Theodor Lessing traveled to the Middle East for the first time. He was fifty-nine, and the journey had been a long time in coming. Lessing was a feminist, a socialist, and an anti-noise and anti-imperialism activist, who earned his living mainly as a kind of philosophical feuilletonist. But he was also a Zionist and had been one for more than thirty years. To his delight, Lessing discovered in Jerusalem that his work had preceded him there. A letter to his wife excitedly conveys the news: "Not far from the Wailing Wall, a Jew recognized me and addressed me by my name. He had just bought my 'Jewish self-hatred book'—all the bookstores in the city have it."[1]

If Lessing was glad to see his latest monograph being sold in Jerusalem, he wasn't surprised. Why should he have been? *Jewish Self-Hate* was a project that important Zionists had backed. Siegmund Kaznelson, the director of the Jüdischer Verlag (or Jewish Press), had made Lessing's study part of the press's new Zionist book league series. Robert Weltsch, a leader of the Zionist movement in Germany, had encouraged Kaznelson in this. Not that he had needed nudging: both men, and especially Kaznelson, thought that *Jewish Self-Hate* would serve the Zionist cause extraordinarily well. Upon reading selections, Kaznelson spoke of the book as being a "Zionist propaganda coup" and of how it would be "sensational in the extreme."[2] He predicted, moreover, that Lessing's work would "in its effects far surpass" whatever else he might opt to include in the Zionist book league venture.[3]

To say that he was right isn't saying much, since infighting at the press soon killed the series. But Kaznelson and Weltsch also came close to being on the mark about the impact of Lessing's volume. If the book failed to create a sensation, it succeeded in causing a stir, quickly popularizing the catchy young term in its title. Furthermore, with its mix of pathos-laden homily, colorful theory, and concise biography, Lessing's text won over a parade of Zionist readers. Writing in *Self-Defense* in 1930, Felix Weltsch, a cousin of Robert, gave this gushing appraisal: "the well-known philosopher" has "brought forth a deep-reaching psychology of the Jewish spirit," which "shows us how to find the way that leads out of negation and decline, and to healing and freedom."[4] Kafka's friend Max Brod, whom Lessing had propitiated for years, would take the opportunity to flatter Lessing back, hailing *Jewish Self-Hate* as a stroke of "genius."[5] According to an anonymous reviewer for *The Voice*, Lessing deftly illuminated the "tragedy of the Jew who tries to flee from himself and his Jewishness."[6] In the *Jüdische Rundschau*, perhaps the most respected organ of German Zionism, an unnamed author enthused over the "liberating force" of Lessing's words, as well as their ability to open up "new perspectives on a great Jewish future."[7] Meanwhile, a less mainstream Zionist newspaper thanked Lessing for revealing—"with uncommon acumen"—the "deep psychic abyss that is Jewish self-hatred."[8]

Anti-Zionists, on the other hand, tended to be harsh in their assessments, though they weren't the only ones to express scorn. Freud famously disliked Lessing's book, in which psychoanalysis figures as a consequence of Jewish self-hatred, but he stated his disdain curtly and informally.[9] It was the newspaper of the integration-minded Central Association of German Citizens of the Jewish Faith that felt compelled to carry out a thorough public reckoning. Its upshot wasn't so much that Jewish self-hatred didn't exist or warrant scrutiny as that, with their anti-rationalist bent, Lessing's ideas about Jews and Judaism were misguided to the point of making little sense. Lessing had hardly gone out of his way to head off such doubts. To the contrary, quite a few passages in *Jewish Self-Hate* read like attempts to speak the effusive language of Jewish renewal that Gershom Scholem dubbed "Buber-deutsch," after the Zionist philosopher Martin Buber (and his rhetorical excesses). Lessing's book proclaims, for example, that Jewish self-hatred won't abate until there are Jews who "spend their time praying before the trees and the clouds."[10] Summing up his or her objections, the reviewer for the Central Association's newspaper dismisses such lines as absurdities. They have, according to the reviewer, nothing to do with the Jewish *Geist* [spirit], which spends its time before nothing other than *Geist*.[11]

When we set up the reception I just described as I have—namely, as a series of Zionist and anti-Zionist responses to an ardent, officially sanctioned Zionist work, outfitted with a fresh label for what its author treats as the given of Western Jewry's malaise—then the reception unfolds as we might expect it to. But if I had begun with an overview of more recent accounts of Lessing's book and proceeded from there to survey the early debate about it, the tenor and the dimensions of the debate would be less self-evident. Indeed, they would likely come as a surprise. This isn't simply because over the past half-century Lessing's readers have been scholars, who have, naturally enough, transformed the meaning of his study by bringing to it their own questions, concepts, and interpretive strategies. Here the gap between early and later understandings also has to do with a tendency to misrepresent both the historical place of Lessing's signature usage and its explicit content, and the gap is therefore a problem.

One of the main sources of confusion is Lessing himself, or more precisely, his earlier contributions to the general discourse of Jewish self-hatred, which scholars have too often treated as of a piece with *Jewish Self-Hate*. As Lessing would write in his posthumously published autobiography *Once and Never Again*, his goal around 1900 was to be the "scourge of Jewish degeneration," and he worked toward that end with such truculence that he could, and did, appear to partake of the very syndromes he wanted to expose. In both private correspondence and rebarbative essays on the shortcomings of "intellect Jews" (Lessing's phrase) like the writers Ludwig Jacobowski and Samuel Lublinski, Lessing employed an array of phrases that may seem almost synonymous with the one for which he is known today. Indeed, decades before *Jewish Self-Hate* appeared, Lessing wrote of Jewish "self-splitting," of "self-dissection," of "self-incrimination," of "self-blaming," of "self-accusation," of "self-humiliation," of "self-negation," of "self-skewering," of "self-dissolution," of "self-destruction," of "self-tormenting," of "self-betrayal," and of "self-contempt."

It makes at least some sense, then, to understand Lessing's notion of Jewish self-hatred as stemming from fin-de-siècle discourse networks, which is what scholars often do in their reckonings with Lessing's *Jewish Self-Hate*. One of them writes of the key term "Jewish self-hatred" that its "prevalent use was typical of a certain particular phase in the history of German Jews, following the completion of their formal emancipation, especially during the years immediately preceding World War I."

But the specific notion of Jewish self-hatred that Lessing works with in his book didn't enjoy prevalence or prominence before the Great War. The earliest instance of it I could locate dates back to 1918, and while it is certainly possible that the locution had already been coined—and become a part of oral discourse—I have my doubts. After all, the Viennese satirist Karl Kraus, who had his language-obsessed ear to the ground for such things and was one of the first secular Jews to deploy the appellation "Jewish antisemites," didn't speak of "Jewish self-hatred" until 1921. But the trouble with genealogies of Jewish self-hatred isn't simply that they conflate "Jewish self-hatred" with similar-sounding tags and, as a result, present a misleading chronology of that specific term. We might say about genealogists of Jewish self-hatred roughly what Nietzsche said about genealogists of morals: they have missed the dialectical movement of their object. The logic behind folding "Jewish self-hatred" into a complex of earlier formulations is that the term's meaning approximates theirs, when, in truth, it was forged largely to oppose them. "Jewish self-hatred" entered public debate as part of a self-consciously post–World War I undertaking, whose aim was to reorient the existing discourse of Jewish self-hatred. The concept seems to have been designed and first implemented, that is, as a kind of oppositional measure, as a sort of expressionist, anti-bourgeois counter-concept.

When Lessing introduced the term "Jewish self-hatred" into his vocabulary in *Jewish Self-Hate*, he was picking up on this shift and the positive—indeed, redemptive—meanings that went along with it. Often characterized today as a "polemic," Lessing's "Jewish self-hatred book" comes close to being a self-help manual, where your sufferings give you opportunities for self-transcendence and improving the world. Certainly the book stands much closer to the genre of self-help than anything Lessing produced either before it or afterward, when, tellingly enough, "Jewish self-hatred" all but disappeared from his work. Perhaps Lessing thought that in 1930 German Jewry could use some uplift. Or maybe he wanted to experiment, to try out a position and a voice more optimistic than his usual ones. Maybe it was a combination of those things that motivated him. Whatever the case, in his study *Jewish Self-Hate* Lessing, more than before, took up the idiom of philosophical self-help writing.

Lessing, in all likelihood, opted for the phrase "Jewish self-hatred" because its meaning back then was such that it suited his purposes and fit his affirmative message better than any of the terms he had been using and would go on to use, such as "Jewish self-contempt," "Jewish self-tormenting," "Jewish self-destruction," etc. Neither earlier nor later, after all, did Lessing trumpet lines like "Whoever does not love himself will be loved by no one," "Do not run from your destiny," "Love your destiny," "Follow your destiny," "There are questions that never find a solution—except through a strong resolution," and, to cite one more example, "Be whatever you are, and always try to live up to your best potential." By contrast, in the earlier text he adverted to as "his chief statement on the Jewish question," Lessing had conjectured, "Today's Jewry in Western Europe is a non-Jewry that is probably too far gone to be saved by Zionism." An essay from 1932 accepts, and even declares, that the "Jewish question is unsolvable."

That Lessing forayed into the genre of self-help, while promising readers that he would not short them on philosophical heft and would still be taking them "deep into the deep," is also what finally explains the rapturous welcome the self-hatred study got from its Zionist reviewers. For isn't the bulk of their emphasis on the book's practical value, on how it might "heal," how it might open "new perspectives on a great Jewish future" and thus "help set free"? People didn't say analogous things about Lessing's earlier reflections on Western Jewry's "self-splitting" and "self-humiliation" because that had hardly been the point. In those fin-de-siècle writings, Lessing had not held up much hope that the Jews would overcome their practice of "self-censure," which, in his estimation, engendered special acuities but also caused chronic and seemingly insurmountable psychic duress.

The crucial procurer figure here is Anton Kuh, who, to the best of my knowledge, coined the term "Jewish self-hatred" in a series of speeches that he gave between 1918 and 1920 and published a little later under the title *Juden und Deutsche—Jews and Germans*.

It is likely—very likely, in fact—that Lessing read Kuh's book about Jewish self-hatred before writing his more famous volume, for a shared main theme was hardly the sole link between the two works and their authors. Both Lessing and Kuh were frequent contributors to the *Prager Tagblatt*, which ran a long review of Jews and Germans, and when Lessing was pushed out of his teaching post at the University of Hanover in 1925, Kuh stuck up for him in print.

In the end, however, what makes some direct influence seem probable in this case is that despite the pro-Zionism/anti-Zionism divide separating Lessing and Kuh, Lessing's theory of Jewish self-hatred bears striking affinities with Kuh's.

Kuh was born in 1890, into a family of Viennese Jewish journalists. Well-connected and witty, Kuh had no trouble establishing himself. By the beginning of the World War I, he had published hundreds of essays and anecdotes, many of them caustic little musings on Vienna's coffeehouse culture, which back then no one ever seemed to tire of writing or reading about. The war changed that, amid so much else, radicalizing Kuh in various ways. Indeed, toward the end of the conflict, Kuh did one of the most drastic things a Viennese intellectual could do: he switched cafés. Having been a regular at the Café Central, where he had sat at Peter Altenberg's table, Kuh went over to the Café Herrenhof. There one of his two main interlocutors was the anarchist critic of patriarchy Otto Gross, who was also the father of Kuh's sister's child. The other conversation partner was Franz Werfel, who was, to paraphrase Kuh, "the storm from Prague that blew away the culture of Viennese breeziness."

But the breeziness was, again, already on its way out. Often overshadowed by the towering cultural accomplishments of Weimar Germany, the culture of "Red Vienna" was formidable in its own right, and it abounded with instances of artistic and intellectual innovators acting as serious agents of social reform. It was very much in keeping with the moment, for example, that Ludwig Wittgenstein signed up to become a provincial school teacher and compiled a dictionary for children. Alfred Adler took psychoanalysis to the streets, setting up free clinics for workers who wanted the treatment but could not afford it. Similarly inspired by the new atmosphere, Adolf Loos helped design massive public housing units. Robert Musil helped plan the restructuring of the military. Anton Webern organized workers' choirs and orchestras, which he guided through performances of avant-garde compositions. Hugo Bettauer founded *Er und Sie*, a weekly in which he promoted "erotic liberation" by debunking traditional values and institutions—especially marriage—while integrating the nascent science of sexology into the advice columns. Though short-lived and highly controversial, the newspaper was also a tremendous hit: *Er und Sie* quickly attracted around two hundred thousand readers, or about a tenth of the city's population. Thus when, for example, the novelist Stefan Zweig returned to Vienna not long after the war, he was astonished by the transformation of the cultural scene. With his loyalties to the more staid "world of yesterday," he was also appalled by it. Zweig conceded that expressionism, or as he bitterly dubbed it, "excessionism," had become all the rage.

Of course, the expressionists comprised a diverse group, which was far from being uniformly radical. The coterie of Gross, Werfel, and Kuh was far more revolutionary in its hopes and dithyrambic in its tone than, say, Hermann Bahr, who in 1919 packaged "Expressionismus" as a movement whose goal was overcoming the "passive" sensory habits of impressionism. Together the three writers planned a subversive journal of politicized expressionism: the *Blätter für die Bekämpfung des Machtwillens*.[12] With its over-the-top reference to the rather straitlaced *Blätter für dir Bekämpfung des Alkoholismus*, the title carried a wry note. But the magazine project was a serious undertaking, serious enough to elicit promises of support from Kafka. Having left such things to others, he declared himself ready to carry part of the editorial burden. He never got the chance to make good on his pledge. Because of growing disagreements between Werfel and Gross, the journal found its way into print, but the association with them shaped Kuh's thinking, and on his own Kuh pursued some of aims he had devised with his friends. In fact, it was in the spirit of their venture that he unveiled the term "Jewish self-hatred." According to Kuh, the Great War had really been a *Hakenkreuzzug*, or a "swastika crusade"; and by revealing the extent of German antisemitism, the war necessitated a new kind of discussion and, in turn, a new vocabulary.[13] The tag "Jewish antisemitism" would no longer do for another reason as well. That was the phrase "mockers," as Kuh puts it in *Juden und Deutsche* (1921), used to describe "aestheticized" Jewish self-criticism.[14] So what was also needed was a more respectful alternative. A proudly anti-systematic mind, Kuh omits to offer an immediately cogent definition of either the older Jewish self-flaying or the more radical one that, as we learn, he wants to see. But he does clearly place them far above both assimilationism, which now seemed utterly benighted, and Zionism, which he treats as a *Selbstbekennen* without *Selbsterkennen*[15] that deals in patriarchal norms and "imitation nationalism."[16]

Self-haters were at least trying to rebel against patriarchal authority, and Kuh may have chosen the uncommon term *Selbsthaß* in part because of how well it matches one of the leitmotifs of expressionist literature: father conflicts. After all, *Haß* and "hatred," more than "antisemitism," connote antipathy toward what is familiar. As the art critic Clement Greenberg would state—in acknowledging his "Jewish self-hatred"—"hatred is as intimate a thing as love." And Kuh would likely have agreed, because he frequently underscores the intimate dynamics of the phenomenon he wants to identify. For Jewish self-hatred to have come about, he theorizes, "a recalcitrant boy had to be born" to assimilated Jewish parents—the "knowing child" of "their curse" who counsels "rejection of the father."

Moreover, as in Kafka's famous letter to Max Brod of June 1921, in *Juden und Deutsche* a non-Freudian "father complex of Jewry" has a decisive impact on the culture German Jews generate.[17] In Kafka's missive, Jewish authors "stick with their hind legs to the Judaism of their fathers," while finding "no new ground" with their front ones. If the "despair" German Jewish writers feel over this serves as "their inspiration," it also limits them artistically. They can produce only a "paper language," according to Kafka. Similarly, Kuh maintains about Jewish *Selbsthaß* that it often makes for *Häßlichkeit*, or "ugliness," in both life and art.[18] That the German words for "hatred" and "ugly"—*Haß* and *häßlich*—are manifestly related may, then, have added to the appeal of the former one. Wouldn't the shared root of the terms have served to reinforce the causal link Kuh wanted to draw, especially in the ears of an audience eager to be dazzled by his verbal magic?

But according to Kuh, however, the really big problem with Jewish self-hatred is precisely that it is a big problem. In his reading Kraus's legalistic self-reproaches and constricting monomania ultimately derive from another preferred expressionist theme, self-alienation—from something, that is, that afflicts modern man in general. Indeed, like the Jews, the Germans suffer from a surfeit of reflexivity, from a life-diminishing *Überintellektualismus*. Hence Kuh's idea that the great German novel *Buddenbrooks* is overly cerebral in its approach to matters of emotion and, practically speaking, a "Jewish book."[19] Hence, as well, Kuh's juxtaposing of the terms *Juden* and *Deutsche* in his title.

But Jews are the most advanced self-haters, and if that is so for several reasons, a primary one has to do with sex. Are the Jews sexually satisfied?" Kuh asks.[20] "I would wager a no," reads his answer. To some degree, antisemitism is what made the Jews particularly self-aware—so self-aware that they cannot get the sensual satisfaction they need to feel at peace with themselves and at home in the world. Their ever-alert critical rationality is, Kuh muses, like a "light on in the bedroom."[21] Yet it was property even more than intellectuality that first disrupted the Jews' erotic and interpersonal experiences, sending them on the road to their Seinfeldian state—that is, a state of nervous hyper-self-awareness and erotic discontent.

Indeed, one key paradox in Kuh's book is that the blight of the Jews' hyper-self-awareness stems, above all, from a Jewish materialism—from the drive to own as an assertion of power. Drawing explicitly on Otto Gross's anti-patriarchal thought, Kuh proposes that it was the Jews who initiated the sexual slavery of marriage, and it is thus the Jews who feel guiltiest about it.[22] By extension, the Jews should be the ones to begin agitating seriously against the *Machtwille* [will to dominate] behind marriage. Much of their "mission," as Kuh puts it, is to show the world the way to real freedom and love, and especially to freedom in *love*.[23]

Indeed, a second heady paradox here is that the Jews' self-*hatred* will play *the* key role in enabling Jews to reach their calling. As in Jacques Derrida's analysis of the pharmakon, here the poisoning agent is simultaneously the cure. Thus Kuh writes, "The progress self-hatred brings about is no smaller than the harm it causes." And with their special guilt over marriage, and especially their long experience of being persecuted and unwanted, the Jews are in the best position to do what Kuh wants to see done, namely, "free the world from all those things that make national, social, and cultural violence possible."[24] Their full mission is nothing less than to "redeem" humanity, to become a "world brother," Kuh writes, modifying a line from his friend Werfel.[25] Unfortunately, most Jews have not yet recognized this. The only way they will is by bringing forth a ruthless *Selbsterkennen*. To do that, Jews must activate more fruitfully the "lawyerly self-judging Jewish perspective" and "creatively perfected" self-hatred, which stem from their uniquely ripened sexual guilt and their singular experience of being scattered and scorned.

Similarly, in *Jewish Self-Hate*, Lessing diagnoses a series of self-haters without once mentioning the antisemitic scurrilities with which they sometimes spiced their writings. He deems Kraus "the most revealing instance of Jewish self-hatred," because an excess of ethical severity got in the way of Kraus's "beautiful and pure natural talent."[26] Instead of composing great life-enhancing poetry, Kraus was forever berating corrupt reporters, with the result that all he had to show for his efforts was a "mountain" of splenetic meta-reportage. More or less the same can be said of psychoanalysis, which, as noted before, Lessing includes in his list of manifestations of Jewish self-hatred. Psychoanalysis makes what is beautiful seem ugly, according to Lessing. In his view, it emerges from and emblematizes the Jews' tragic distance from the pleasures of the material world. But even as he makes such claims, Lessing underscores the productive power of Jewish self-hatred. He refers to the Jews' "creative self-hatred" and their "self-hatred of genius,"

To be sure, internalized antisemitism has a role in Lessing's analysis, as it does in Kuh's. In one place, in fact, Lessing evokes Jewish self-hatred as a dramatic case "of the psychology of a suffering minority." He also declares that self-hatred arises from "loving the those who hate you"—that is, *Feindesliebe*.[27] Perhaps even more to the point, Lessing speaks of the Jews as being unique in trying to understand their persecution by looking inward, to their own defects. And he asserts, as well, that the Jews' proclivity for holding themselves responsible for their woes has left them vulnerable—vulnerable to accepting as true the counterfactual ideologies of their tormentors. As Lessing puts it, recycling an old adage of his, "You can only call a man a dog so many times before he starts to think of himself as a dog."[28] But in the self-hatred study the Jews capacity for self-blame turns out to be an epiphenomenon, a consequence of a deeper self-hatred. The ill at the root of Jewish "self-skewering" is the self-alienating "hyper-intellectualism" and "ethical severity" to which, according to Lessing, "the road of culture" always leads.

This is why, in his view, "self-hatred" can afflict not only "all humanity," but also "domesticated animals."[29] It is also why there is so much antisemitism in the world. Without acknowledging the Viennese philosopher and suicide Otto Weininger, whom he profiles in his book, Lessing follows him in stressing the projective mechanisms behind hatred of the Jews. People inveigh against, and try to localize in the Jews, the very things they abhor about themselves—namely, their unhappy abstraction, which has the consequence of making the Jews particularly abstract and superlatively unhappy. Being more embattled than others, the Jews, who were apparently once "beautiful darlings of life," have become more self-aware, more prone to self-judging, devitalizing intellectualism. And so their "psychology" best exemplifies the dynamics of self-hatred. And so it is, in turn, that Weininger's famous unease with female sensuality is for Lessing the truly telling symptom of his self-hatred, rather than all the bigoted things Weininger wrote about Jews ("the Jew can be anything because he is nothing," and so on).

Like Kuh, Lessing counsels his readers to embrace the paradox of a resolution-bringing awareness of undue self-awareness. He states that as the most evolved self-haters, Jews more than anyone else have been forced to work through their condition, and while still threatened by self-hatred, they have achieved a potential mastery over it.

By spreading insights they are uniquely prepared to attain, Jewish self-haters can become a source—or really, the source—of healing for the whole world. Among all those other things, Lessing was also a medical doctor who liked biological metaphors, and toward the end of his book he sees Jewish self-hatred as holding out the promise of a vaccine that could save humankind from the ravages of self-hatred. His concluding section reads: "The Jewish people are currently in the position of an organism that has survived an epidemic or an infection and become immune to a poisonous sickness, which is running wild among younger peoples, and whose overcoming is just now becoming the life or death question of all the peoples of the earth."[30]

Paul Reitter is Professor of Germanic Languages and Literatures at the Ohio State University and has been Director of the Humanities Institute at the same university. His scholarship focuses primarily on two areas: German-Jewish culture and the history of higher education. Of particular concern in both cases have been the links between intellectual and institutional history, the relationship of cultural crisis and cultural innovation, and the effects of technological change on humanistic culture. A practicing translator, he also is interested in the field of translation studies. He is the author of *The Anti-Journalist: Karl Kraus and Jewish Self-Fashioning in Fin-de-Siècle Europe* (University of Chicago

Press, 2008), *On the Origins of Jewish Self-Hatred* (Princeton University Press, 2012), and *Bambi's Jewish Roots: Essays on German-Jewish Culture* (Bloomsbury, 2015). His current project—coauthored with Chad Wellmon—considers how the factors and processes that allowed the modern humanities to flourish have at the same time made life difficult for the humanities. While the story the book tells is set mostly in nineteenth-century Germany, it engages vigorously with debates about the state of the humanities in our own day; it is titled *Permanent Crisis: The Humanities in a Disenchanted Age* (University of Chicago Press, 2021). His articles and essays have appeared in an array of venues, ranging from *Representations, American Imago,* and *Jewish Social Studies* to *Harper's Magazine,* the *TLS, The Nation,* the *LA Review of Books, Bookforum,* and *The Hedgehog Review*. His research has been supported by fellowships from the German Literature Archive (DLA) in Marbach, the Frankel Institute for Advanced Judaic Studies at the University of Michigan, the Simon Dubnow Institute for Jewish Studies in Leipzig, the Lion Feuchtwanger Archive at USC, and the American Academy in Berlin.

Notes

Sections of this afterword have been adapted and revised from Paul Reitter, *On the Origins of Jewish Self-Hatred* (Princeton, NJ: Princeton University Press, 2012).

1. Stadtarchiv Hanover, Theodor Lessing Nachlaß 1051; letter—or really, a postcard—of 10 April 1931 to Ada and Ruth Lessing—Ada was Lessing's wife, Ruth his daughter. Unless I indicate otherwise, all translations from German are mine.
2. Cited in Anatol Schenker, *Der jüdische Verlag, 1902–1938: Zwischen Aufbruch, Blüte und Vernichtung* (Niemeyer: Tübingen, 2003), 388.
3. Cited in Schenker, *Der jüdische Verlag,* 398.
4. Cited in Andrea Fabian-Boelke's dissertation "Das Selbst und die Anderen: Über das Dilemma der Ambilanz und die schwierige philosophische Selbstbestimmung von Deutschsein und Judesein, Theodor Lessings Essay Der jüdische Selbsthaß und seine Autobiographie Einmal und nie wieder" (Johann Wolfgang Goethe-Üniversität, Frankfurt am Main, 2003), 29.
5. Brod, it should be noted, wrote this statement some years after Lessing's book appeared, but in doing so he was recalling his initial response to *Jewish Self-Hatred*. See Max Brod, *Streibares Leben: Autobiographie* (Munich: Beck, 1987), 90.
6. Anonymous, *Die Stimme,* 11 February 1932, 5.
7. Anonymous, *Jüdische Rundschau,* 2 February 1931, 58.
8. Cited in *Das Selbst und die Anderen,* 28.
9. See Kurt Hiller's summary of a (lost) letter from Freud in Hiller, *Köpfe und Tröpfe: Profile aus einem Viertel Jahrhundert* (Hamburg: Rowohlt, 1950), 308.

10. Theodor Lessing, *Der jüdische Selbsthaß* (Berlin: Der jüdische Verlag, 1930), 25, hereafter cited as Lessing, *JSH*.
11. Dr. M.K., "Um die Seele des judischen Menschen," *C.V.-Zeitung*, 1 May 1931, 225.
12. This title can be translated as "Journal for Resisting Mentalities of Domination."
13. Anton Kuh, *Juden und Deutsche*, ed. Andreas Kilcher (Vienna: Böhlau Verlag, 2003), 121. Hereafter cited as *JD*.
14. *JD*, 76. Kuh seems to be at once calling for a new, less sullied terminology and suggesting that the old terminology is dated because the war has altered, or hopefully will alter, the old form of self-reproach. He writes that "the epoch of Jewish antisemitism" stretches exactly to the beginning of the war. It is worth noting that at the same time, Kuh was a programmatically, proudly unsystematic thinker who did not consistently hold to his own distinction—that is, he himself uses the term "Jewish antisemites," despite his criticisms of it.
15. "Confessing to be oneself," i.e., to be Jewish, without "understanding oneself." *JD*, 77.
16. *JD*, 92.
17. Franz Kafka, *Briefe 1902–1924*, ed. Max Brod (Frankfurt am Main: Fischer, 1966), 336f. As implied, like Kafka, Kuh was critical of the psychoanalytic approach to generational conflict. For a psychoanalytic interpretation of Jewish self-hatred that builds on Freud's remarks on the topic, see the Hermann Levi's chapter in Peter Gay, *Freud, Jews, and Other Germans: Masters and Victims in Modernist Culture* (Oxford and New York: Oxford University Press, 1978), 187–230.
18. *JD*, 79.
19. *JD*, 142–143.
20. *JD*, 80.
21. *JD*, 81.
22. *JD*, 84.
23. *JD*, 85, 127, 134.
24. *JD*, 107.
25. *JD*, 89.
26. Lessing, *JSH*, 43.
27. Lessing, *JSH*, 40.
28. Lessing, *JSH*, 17.
29. Lessing, *JSH*, 28.
30. Lessing, *JSH*, 217.

About the Translator

Peter C. Appelbaum is an Emeritus Professor of Pathology at Pennsylvania State University. His publications include *Loyalty Betrayed: Jewish Chaplains in the German Army During the First World War* (2014), *Loyal Sons: Jews in the German Army during the First World War* (2014), and, as translator and editor, *Hell on Earth* (2017) and *Carnage and Care on the Eastern Front: The War Diaries of Bernhard Bardach* (2018). He is the recipient of the TLS-Risa Domb/Porjes Prize for Hebrew-English Translation for 2019.

About the Editor

Benton Arnovitz is a long-time professional book acquisitions editor and executive with major publishing houses including Macmillan, Free Press, Collier Books, and Stein and Day. Among the many hundreds of works he has published are Isaiah Trunk's National Book Award–winning *Judenrat: The Jewish Councils in Eastern Europe Under Nazi Occupation*, the Raul Hilberg et al.-edited *The Warsaw Dairy of Adam Czerniakow: Prelude to Doom*, the Shah of Iran's *Answer to History*, Rabbi Meir Kahane's *Why Be Jewish? Intermarriage, Assimilation, and Alienation*, Solomon Perel's *Europa, Europa*, and H. G. Adler's *Theresienstadt 1941–1945*. His own articles have appeared in *Survey: A Journal of East and West Studies, Outpost, German Studies Association Newsletter, Washington Times,* and various Gannett newspapers. He served as Director of Academic Publications at the United States Holocaust Memorial Museum (1993–2018), and is a member of the editorial board of that museum's scholarly journal, *Holocaust and Genocide Studies*. A lieutenant colonel, US Army (Ret.), his degrees are from Cornell University and New York University, with additional graduations from the US Army Command and General Staff College and the National Defense University.

www.ingramcontent.com/pod-product-compliance
Lightning Source LLC
Chambersburg PA
CBHW070042120526
44589CB00035B/2251